# Dictionary of Cynical Quotations

Jonathon Green

NEW
ORCHARD

First published in the UK 1994
by Cassell
This edition has been produced
in 1995 by New Orchard Editions Ltd
(a Cassell company), Wellington House
125 Strand, London WC2R 0BB

ISBN 1-85079-277-1

Printed and bound in Finland by Werner Söderström Oy

# CONTENTS

# ACTING

Actresses will happen in the best regulated families.

**Addison Mizner and Oliver Herford, *The Entirely New Cynic's Calendar*, 1905**

Musical comedy is the Irish stew of drama. Anything may be put into it, with the certainty that it will improve the general effect.

**P.G. Wodehouse, *The Man with Two Left Feet*, 1917**

When actors begin to think, it's time for a change. They are not fitted for it.

**Stephen Leacock, *The Decline of Drama*, 1921**

If you have a message [in the theatre] call for Western Union.

**George S. Kaufman, quoted in *Wits End* by J.R. Gaines, 1977**

Satire is what closes Saturday night.

**George S. Kaufman**

Theatre director: a person engaged by the management to conceal the fact that the players cannot act.

**James Agate, *Ego*, 1935–48**

A character actor is one who cannot act and therefore makes an elaborate study of the disguise and stage tricks by which acting can be grotesquely simulated.

**George Bernard Shaw**

Acting is like roller skating – once you know how to do it, it is neither stimulating nor exciting.

**George Sanders**

For an actor, success is simply delayed failure.

**Graham Greene**

The art of acting consists in keeping people from coughing.

**Sir Ralph Richardson, in the *Observer*, 1947**

They shot too many pictures and not enough actors.

**Walter Winchell**

Some of the greatest love affairs I've known have involved one actor, unassisted.

**Wilson Mizner, quoted in *The Incredible Mizners*
by A. Johnson, 1953**

You can pick out the actors by the glazed look that comes into their eyes when the conversation wanders away from themselves.

**Michael Wilding**

Musicals: a series of catastrophes ending with a floorshow.

**Oscar Levant**

Glamour in the theatre is usually twenty chorus girls in a line all doing the same thing. It is assumed that twenty women are more glamorous than one.

**Peter Ustinov**

Acting is the expression of a neurotic impulse.

**Marlon Brando**

An actor is not quite a human being – but then, who is?

**George Sanders**

An actor's a guy who, if you ain't talkin' about him, ain't listening.

**Marlon Brando, quoted in the *Observer*, 1956**

A good many inconveniences attend play-going in any large city, but the greatest of them is usually the play itself.

**Kenneth Tynan, in the *New York Herald Tribune*, 1957**

Show me a congenital eavesdropper with the instincts of a Peeping Tom and I will show you the makings of a dramatist.

**Kenneth Tynan, *Pausing on the Stairs*, 1957**

Acting is all about honesty. If you can fake that, you've got it made.

**George Burns**

Modesty is the artifice of actors, similar to passion in call-girls.

**Jackie Gleason**

The relationship between the make-up man and the film actor is that of accomplices in crime.

**Marlene Dietrich**

The best audience is intelligent, well-educated and a little drunk.
  **Alben W. Barkley**

Galaxy: five or six actresses.
  **J.B. Morton ('Beachcomber'), in the *Daily Express*, passim**

The man was a major comedian, which is to say that he had the compassion of an icicle, the effrontery of a carnival shill and the generosity of a pawnbroker.
  **S.J. Perelman**

The question actors most often get asked is how can they bear saying the same things over and over again, night after night, but God knows what the answer to that is. Don't we all anyway; might as well get paid for it.
  **Elaine Dundy, *The Dud Avocado*, 1958**

That's a lot to see buggers jump.
  **Nigel Bruce, commenting on the cost of ballet tickets**

Generally speaking, the . . . theatre is the aspirin of the middle classes.
  **Wolcott Gibbs, *More in Sorrow*, 1958**

Fans are people who let an actor know he's not alone in the way he feels about himself.
  **Anonymous**

The whole motivation for any performer: 'Look at me, Ma!'
  **Lenny Bruce**

Acting is largely a matter of farting about in disguises.
  **Peter O'Toole**

A fan club is a group of people who tell an actor he is not alone in the way he feels about himself.
  **Jack Carson, quoted in *The Wit of the Theatre*, ed. R. May, 1969**

One begins with two people on a stage, and one of them had better say something pretty damn quick.
  **Moss Hart, on writing plays, quoted in *Contemporary Dramatists*, 1977**

The more you do for an actor the worse it hates you.

**Percy Hammond, quoted in *Selected Letters of James Thurber*, ed. H. Thurber and E. Weeks, 1981**

A starlet is any woman under thirty not actively employed in a brothel.

**Anonymous, quoted in *Halliwell's Filmgoer's Companion*, 1985**

Casting: deciding which of two faces the public is least tired of.

**Anonymous, quoted in *Halliwell's Filmgoer's Companion*, 1985**

There are two kind of directors in the theatre: those who think they are God and those who are certain of it.

**Rhetta Hughes**

*See also* HOLLYWOOD

# ADULTS

When childhood dies, its corpses are called adults and they enter society, one of the politer names of hell. That is why we dread children, even if we love them. They show us the state of our decay.

**Brian Aldiss, in the *Guardian*, 1971**

*See also* CHILDREN, FAMILIES, PARENTS

# ADVERTISING

Advertising is legalised lying.

**H.G. Wells**

Advertising may be described as the science of arresting the human intelligence long enough to get money from it.

**Stephen Leacock, *Garden of Folly*, 1924**

Advertising is the rattling of a stick inside a swill bucket.

**George Orwell**

Advertising is the whip which hustles humanity up the road to the Better Mousetrap. It is the vision which reproaches man for the paucity of his desires.

**E.S. Turner, *The Shocking History of Advertising*, 1952**

You can fool all the people all of the time if the advertising is right and the budget is big enough.

**Joseph E. Levine**

From any cross-section of ads, the general advertiser's attitude would seem to be: if you are a lousy, smelly, idle, underprivileged and over-sexed, status-seeking neurotic moron, give me your money.

**Kenneth Bromfield, in *Advertisers' Weekly* magazine, 1962**

If the package doesn't say 'New' these days, it had better say 'Seven Cents Off'.

**Spencer Klaw, in *Fortune* magazine, 1963**

It has been said that Public Relations is the art of winning friends and getting people under the influence.

**Jeremy Tunstall, *The Advertising Man*, 1964**

The essence of good advertising is not to inspire hope, but to create greed.

**Charles Adams, *Common Sense in Advertising*, 1966**

Advertising is the art of making whole lies out of half truths.

**Edgar A. Shoaff, quoted in *Peter's Quotations* by L. Peter, 1977**

When the client moans and sighs
Make his logo twice the size.
If he still should prove refractory,
Show a picture of his factory.
Only in the gravest cases
Should you show the clients' faces.

**Anonymous advertising agency jingle, quoted in *Ogilvy on Advertising* by David Ogilvy, 1983**

# ADVICE

The expert: an ordinary man, away from home, giving advice.

**Anonymous**

Old men are fond of giving good advice to console themselves for their inability to set a bad example.

**François, Duc de La Rochefoucauld, *Maxims*, 1665**

Few listen without a desire of conviction to those who advise them to spare their money.
**Samuel Johnson, *The Idler*, 1758–60**

To appear more warlike, you should ride with your sword drawn; but take care you do not cut your horse's ear off.
**Captain Francis Grose, *Advice to Officers of the British Army*, 1782**

The advice that is wanted is commonly unwelcome, and that which is not wanted is evidently impertinent.
**Samuel Johnson, in the letters to Hester Thrale, 1788**

Advice is seldom welcome, and those who want it most always like it least.
**Lord Chesterfield, *Letters to his Son*, 1774**

Advice is that which we ask for when we want approbation.
**Charles Caleb Colton, *Lacon*, 1820**

Good advice is one of those injuries which a good man ought, if possible, to forgive, but at all events to forget at once.
**'Horace' Smith, *Gaieties and Gravities*, 1826**

When we ask advice, we are usually looking for an accomplice.
**Marquis de La Grange, *Pensées*, 1872**

It is always a silly thing to give advice, but to give good advice is absolutely fatal.
**Oscar Wilde, *The Portrait of Mr W.H.*, 1889**

I always pass on good advice. It is the only thing to do with it. It is never any good to oneself.
**Oscar Wilde, *An Ideal Husband*, 1895**

The best careers advice to give to the young is 'Find out what you like doing best and get someone to pay you for doing it'.
**Katherine Whitehorn, in the *Observer*, 1975**

*See also* OPINIONS

# AFFAIRS

A painted face fills the husband with suspicion and the gallant with hope.

**Anonymous Swedish proverb**

Nobody knows how to manage a wife but a bachelor.

**George Colman the Elder, *The Jealous Wife*, 1761**

Love and a cottage, eh, Fanny! Ah, give me indifference and a coach and six!

**George Colman the Elder, *The Clandestine Marriage*, 1766**

The one charm of marriage is that it makes a life of deception absolutely necessary for both parties.

**Oscar Wilde, *The Picture of Dorian Gray*, 1891**

To our sweethearts and wives. May they never meet.

***Toasts for All Occasions*, 19th century**

Nothing looks so like innocence as indiscretion.

**Oscar Wilde, *Lady Windermere's Fan*, 1892**

There is nothing in the world like the devotion of a married woman. It's a thing no married man knows anything about.

**Oscar Wilde, *Lady Windermere's Fan*, 1892**

The happiness of a married man depends on the women he has not married.

**Oscar Wilde, *A Woman of No Importance*, 1893**

In married life, three is company and two is none.

**Oscar Wilde, *The Importance of Being Earnest*, 1895**

A husband should tell his wife everything that he is sure she will find out, and before anybody else does.

**Lord Thomas Dewar**

Fidelity, n. A virtue peculiar to those who are about to be betrayed.

**Ambrose Bierce, *The Devil's Dictionary*, 1911**

No modern woman with a grain of sense ever sends little notes to an unmarried man – not until she is married, anyway.

**Arthur Binstead, *Pitcher's Proverbs*, 1909**

A bachelor has to have inspiration for making love to a woman, a married man needs only an excuse.

**Helen Rowland**

One man's folly is another man's wife.

**Helen Rowland**

Every man wants a woman to appeal to his better side, his nobler instincts and his higher nature – and another woman to help him forget them.

**Helen Rowland, *A Guide to Men*, 1922**

The follies which a man regrets most in his life are those which he didn't commit when he had the opportunity.

**Helen Rowland, *A Guide to Men*, 1922**

There can only be one end to marriage without love, and that is love without marriage.

**John Churton Collins, in *The English Review*, 1914**

Husbands never become good. They merely become proficient.

**H.L. Mencken, *Sententiae*, 1916**

Jealousy is the theory that some other fellow has just as little taste.

**H.L. Mencken, *Sententiae*, 1916**

No matter how happily a woman may be married, it always pleases her to discover that there is a nice man who wishes she were not.

**H.L. Mencken, *A Mencken Chrestomathy*, 1949**

He would, wouldn't he.

**Mandy Rice-Davies, on being informed that Lord Astor had denied her allegations of 'impropriety' during the Profumo Affair, 1963**

Never tell. Not if you love your wife . . . In fact, if your old lady walks in on you, deny it. Yeah. Just flat out and she'll believe it: 'I'm tellin' ya. This chick came downstairs with a sign around her neck "Lay On Top Of Me Or I'll Die". I didn't know what I was gonna do . . .'

**Lenny Bruce, quoted in *The Essential Lenny Bruce*, ed J. Cohen, 1967**

There is little wife-swapping in suburbia . . . It is unnecessary, the females being all so similar.

**Richard Gordon**

Like Mariana of the Moated Grange, who hated late afternoon most of all, the unfaithful wife dreads the coming of 5.30, when the danger zone of her husband returning home has been entered and she knows now it's too late for the lover to telephone.

**Jilly Cooper, *The British in Love*, 1980**

*See also* DIVORCE, HUSBANDS, LOVE, LOVERS, MARRIAGE, SEX, WIVES

# AGE

All would live long, but none would be old.

**Benjamin Franklin**

Old men and comets have been reverenced for the same reason: their long beards and pretences to foretell events.

**Jonathan Swift, *Thoughts on Various Subjects*, 1706**

Tomorrow is an old deceiver, and his cheat never grows stale.

**Samuel Johnson, *The Idler*, 1758–60**

One of the pleasures of reading old letters is the knowledge that they need no answer.

**George Gordon, Lord Byron, quoted in *The Oxford Book of Aphorisms*, ed. J. Gross, 1983**

Grey hair is a sign of age, not of wisdom.

**Anonymous**

She may very well pass for forty-three
In the dusk, with a light behind her.

**W.S. Gilbert, *Trial by Jury*, 1875**

Many a man that couldn't direct you to the drugstore on the corner when he was thirty will get a respectful hearing when age has further impaired his mind.

**Finley Peter Dunne, *Mr Dooley On Making A Will*, 1919**

Age, n. That period of life in which we compound for the vices that we still cherish by reviling those that we have no longer the enterprise to commit.

**Ambrose Bierce,** *The Devil's Dictionary*, **1911**

No one thinks he looks as old as he is.

**Edgar Watson Howe,** *Country Town Sayings*, **1911**

She always believed in the old adage – leave them while you're looking good.

**Anita Loos,** *Gentlemen Prefer Blondes*, **1925**

The denunciation of the young is a necessary part of the hygiene of older people, and greatly assists the circulation of their blood.

**Logan Pearsall Smith,** *Afterthoughts*, **1931**

As I grow older and older
And totter towards the tomb
I find that I care less and less
Who goes to bed with whom.

**Dorothy L. Sayers**

There is only one cure for grey hair. It was invented by a Frenchman. It is called the guillotine.

**P.G. Wodehouse,** *The Old Reliable*, **1951**

If you live long enough, you'll see that every victory turns into a defeat.

**Simone de Beauvoir,** *All Men are Mortal*, **1955**

Maturity is behaviour determined by the plans other people have in mind.

**David Mercer,** *Let's Murder Vivaldi*, **1968**

Most men do not mature, they simply grow taller.

**Leo Rosten, in the** *Saturday Review*, **1970**

Remember that as a teenager you are in the last stage of your life when you will be happy to hear that the phone is for you.

**Fran Lebowitz,** *Social Studies*, **1981**

Anniversaries, those meaningless indicator boards in decimals which command us to exhume feeling.

**Neal Ascherson, in the** *Observer*, **1986**

*See also* DEATH

# AMBITION

What seems to be generosity is often only disguised ambition – which despises small interests to gain great ones.
**François, Duc de La Rochefoucauld, *Maxims*, 1665**

There are hardly two Creatures of a more differing Species than the same Man, when he is pretending to a Place, and when he is in possession of it.
**George Savile, Marquis of Halifax, *Political, Moral and Miscellaneous Thoughts and Reflexions*, c.1694**

Ambition often puts Men upon doing the meanest offices, so climbing is performed in the same position with creeping.
**Jonathan Swift, *Thoughts on Various Subjects*, 1706**

Ambition is but avarice on stilts, and masked.
**Walter Savage Landor**

Ambition is the last refuge of the failure.
**Oscar Wilde, *Phrases and Philosophies for the Use of the Young*, 1894**

Ambition, n. An overmastering desire to be vilified by enemies while living and made ridiculous by friends when dead.
**Ambrose Bierce, *The Devil's Dictionary*, 1911**

The higher a monkey climbs, the more you can see of his behind.
**General 'Vinegar Joe' Stilwell**

*See also* APPLAUSE, EGOTISM, FAME, SUCCESS

# APPLAUSE

I know mankind too well to think they are capable of receiving the truth, much less of applauding it.
**Lady Mary Wortley Montagu, letter to the Countess of Bute, 1763–7**

When the million applaud, you ask yourself what harm you have done; when they censure you, what good.
**Charles Caleb Colton, *Lacon*, 1820**

Applause, n. The echo of a platitude from the mouth of a fool.

**Ambrose Bierce,** *The Devil's Dictionary*, **1911**

When I hear a man applauded by the mob I always feel a pang of pity for him. All he has to do to be hissed is to live long enough.

**H.L. Mencken,** *Minority Report*, **1956**

Do not fear when your enemies criticise you. Beware when they applaud.

**Vo Dong Giang, in** *Time* **magazine, 1978**

*See also* AMBITION, EGOTISM, FAME, SUCCESS

# ARCHITECTURE

A doctor can bury his mistakes, but an architect can only advise his client to plant vines.

**Frank Lloyd Wright**

In my experience, if you have to keep the lavatory door shut by extending your left leg, it's modern architecture.

**Nancy Banks-Smith, in the** *Guardian*, **1969**

Post-war architecture is the accountant's revenge on the pre-war businessman's dreams.

**Rem Koolhaas,** *Delirious New York*, **1978**

What has happened to architecture since the Second World War that the only passers-by who can contemplate it without pain are those equipped with a white stick and a dog?

**Bernard Levin, in** *The Times*, **1983**

Architecture is very much like the oldest profession: it has only one aim, and that is to please for a fee.

**Philip Johnson, 1984**

Suburbia is where the developer bulldozes out the trees, then names the streets after them.

**Bill Vaughan**

The relationship between architects and the media is based on trust and understanding. The architects don't trust the media and the media don't understand the architects.

*Building Design Magazine*, **1986**

You have to give this much to the Luftwaffe – when it knocked down our buildings it did not replace them with anything more offensive than rubble. We did that.

**H.R.H. Charles, Prince of Wales, 1987**

# ARISTOCRACY

Nobility is nothing but ancient riches.

**John Ray, *A Collection of English Proverbs*, 1670**

Send your noble blood to market and see what it will bring.

**Thomas Fuller, M.D., *Gnomologia*, 1732**

The cure for admiring the House of Lords [is] to go and look at it.

**Walter Bagehot, *The English Constitution*, 1867**

We in the House of Lords are never in touch with public opinion. That makes us a civilised body.

**Oscar Wilde, *A Woman of No Importance*, 1893**

You should study the Peerage, Gerald . . . it is the best thing in fiction the English have ever done.

**Oscar Wilde, *A Woman of No Importance*, 1893**

Aristocracies, as a rule, all the world over, consist, and have always consisted, of barbaric conquerors or their descendants, who remain to the last, on the average of instances, at a lower grade of civilization and morals than the democracy they live among.

**Grant Allen, quoted in *The Westminster Gazette*, 1894**

Aristocracy is like the cheese: the older it is the higher it becomes.

**David Lloyd George, speech, 1910**

If there is any man today who believes that the object of the eternal struggle for existence will evolve a higher type, an aristocracy of class, nation or race, that man has failed to read the history of mankind. In other words, he is a hopeless optimist.

**Norman Lindsay, *Creative Effort*, 1924**

Democracy means government by the uneducated, while aristocracy means government by the badly educated.

**G.K. Chesterton, in the *New York Times*, 1931**

The House of Lords has a value – it is good evidence of life after death.
**Lord Soper**

*See also* CLASS, GENTLEMEN

# ART

The emperor loves art in the same way a butcher loves a fat ox.
**Napoleon Bonaparte**

Painting, n. The art of protecting flat surfaces from the weather and exposing them to the critic.
**Ambrose Bierce, *The Devil's Dictionary*, 1911**

It's easy to understand modern art: if it hangs on the wall it's a painting, if you can walk around it it's a sculpture.
**Anonymous**

If more than ten per cent of the public likes a painting, it should be burned.
**George Bernard Shaw**

Buy old masters. They fetch a better price than old mistresses.
**Lord Beaverbrook**

Sculptures are mud-pies which endure.
**Cyril Connolly**

Johnny, keep it out of focus. I want to win the foreign picture award.
**Billy Wilder, to his cameraman John Seitz, during the shooting of *Sunset Boulevard*, 1949**

Modern art is what happens when painters stop looking at girls and persuade themselves that they have had a better idea.
**John Ciardi**

Modern art is when you buy a picture to cover a hole in the wall and then decide that the hole looks much better.
**Anonymous**

If it sells, it's art.
**Frank Lloyd, in *The Legacy of Mark Rothko* by Lee Seldes, 1978**

Art for art's sake is a philosophy of the well-fed.

**Cao Yu, in the *Observer*, 1980**

The market is always converting works of art into passive fictions of eternity and immutability, of transcendent value for which no price may necessarily be too high. When the word 'priceless' crops up, the haggling has only just begun . . . A fair price is the highest one a collector can be induced to pay.

**Robert Hughes, in the *New York Review of Books*, 1984**

*See also* ARTISTS

# ARTISTS

Good painters imitate art, bad ones spew it up.

**Miguel de Cervantes**

He who anticipates his century is generally persecuted when living and is always pilfered when dead.

**Benjamin Disraeli**

The artistic temperament is a disease that afflicts amateurs.

**G.K. Chesterton, *Heretics*, 1905**

When we speak of the artistic temperament, we are usually referring to the sum of qualities which hinder the artist in producing.

**Arthur Schnitzler**

Most of those who call themselves artists are in reality picture dealers, only they make the pictures themselves.

**Samuel Butler, *Notebooks*, 1912**

Artists hate the enlightened amateur, unless he buys.

**Ernest Dimnett, *What We Live By*, 1932**

The moment you cheat for the sake of beauty, you know you are an artist.

**Max Jacob, *Art Poétique*, 1922**

I had a private income – the young artist's best friend.

**P.G. Wodehouse, *Quick Service*, 1940**

A primitive artist is an amateur whose work sells.
**Grandma Moses**

I always suspect an artist who is successful before he is dead.
**John Murray Fitzgibbon**

Remember I'm an artist. And you know what that means in a court of law: the next worst thing to an actress.
**Joyce Cary, *The Horse's Mouth*, 1944**

Artists can colour the sky red because they know it's blue. The rest of us, who aren't artists, must colour things the way they really are, or people might think we're stupid.
**Jules Feiffer**

Everyone wants an artist on the wall or on the shelf, but nobody wants him in the house.
**James Baldwin**

No poet or novelist wishes he was the only one who ever lived, but most of them wish they were the only one alive, and quite a number fondly believe their wish has been granted.
**W.H. Auden, *The Dyer's Hand*, 1963**

Immature artists imitate, mature artists steal.
**Lionel Trilling, in *Esquire* magazine, 1962**

Generation to generation . . . nothing changes in Bohemia.
**Nik Cohn, *Awopbopaloobopalopbamboom*, 1969**

He will lie even when it is inconvenient: the sign of a true artist.
**Gore Vidal, *Two Sisters*, 1970**

The key to building a superstar is to keep their mouth shut. To reveal an artist to the people can be to destroy him. It isn't to anyone's advantage to see the truth.
**Bob Ezrin**

Creators are the sacrificial objects of a bored society.
**David Williamson, *A Handful of Friends*, 1976**

It is very good advice to believe only what an artist does, rather than what he says about his work.
**David Hockney, *David Hockney*, 1976**

Photography is the 'art form' of the untalented.
   **Gore Vidal, in the *New Statesman* magazine, 1978**

Creativity is dead. The name of the game . . . is positioning.
   **Al Ries and Jack Trout, *Positioning*, 1981**

Aesthetic value is often the by-product of the artist striving to do
something else.
   **Evelyn Waugh, *The Letters of Evelyn Waugh*, ed. Mark
   Amory, 1980**

The fashionable drawing rooms of London have always been happy to
welcome outsiders – if only on their own, albeit undemanding terms.
That is to say, artists, so long as they are not too talented, men of humble birth, so long as they have since amassed several million pounds,
and socialists so long as they are Tories.
   **Christopher Booker, in *Now* magazine, 1981**

The artist is a member of the leisured classes who cannot pay for his
leisure.
   **Cyril Connolly, *Journal 1928–1937*, ed. D. Pryce-Jones, 1983**

The word 'masterpiece' . . . used to mean a work that proved an artist's
graduation into full professional skill, but now means an object whose
aura and accumulated myth strike people blind temporarily and render
their judgement timid.
   **Robert Hughes, quoted in the *New York Review of Books*,
   1984**

*See also* ART

# AUTHORS

The praise of ancient authors proceeds not from the reverence of the
dead, but from the competition and mutual envy of the living.
   **Thomas Hobbes, *Leviathan*, 1651**

Of all artificial relations formed between mankind, the most capricious
and variable is that between author and reader.
   **Earl of Shaftesbury, *Characteristics of Men, Manners, Opinions,
   Times*, 1711–13**

An author is a fool who, not content with having bored those who have lived with him, insists on boring future generations.

**Charles de Secondat, Baron de Montesquieu,** *Persian Letters,* **1721**

Novels are receipts to make a whore.

**Matthew Green,** *The Spleen,* **1737**

The reciprocal civility of authors is one of the most risible scenes in the farce of life.

**Samuel Johnson,** *Works* **vol. vi, 1787**

The promises of authors are like the vows of lovers.

**Samuel Johnson,** *Works* **vol. vii, 1787**

I consider an author's literary reputation to be alive only while his name will ensure a good price for his copy from the booksellers.

**Oliver Goldsmith, quoted in** *The Life of Samuel Johnson* **by J. Boswell, 1791**

Take away from Genesis the belief that Moses was the author, on which only the strange belief that it is the word of God has stood, and there remains nothing of Genesis but an anonymous book of stories, fables, and traditonary or invented absurdities, or of downright lies.

**Thomas Paine,** *The Age of Reason,* **1793**

Some books seem to have been written not to teach us anything, but to let us know that the author has known something.

**Johann Wolfgang von Goethe,** *Poetry and Truth,* **1811–31**

If an author writes better than his contemporaries, they will term him a plagiarist; if as well, a pretender, but if worse, he may stand some chance of commendation as a genius of some promise, from whom much may be expected by a due attention to their good counsel and advice.

**Charles Caleb Colton,** *Lacon,* **1820**

The hater of property and of government takes care to have his warranty deed recorded, and the book written against fame and learning has the author's name on the title page.

**Ralph Waldo Emerson,** *Journals,* **1909–14**

I never saw an author in my life . . . that did not purr as audibly as a full-grown cat on having his fur stroked the right way by a skilful hand.

**Oliver Wendell Holmes, *The Autocrat of the Breakfast-Table*, 1857–8**

One should not be too severe on English novelists. They are the only relaxation of the intellectually unemployed.

**Oscar Wilde**

There is no amount of praise which a man and an author cannot bear with equanimity. Some authors can even stand flattery.

**Maurice Baring, *Dead Letters*, 1910**

It is a mean thief, or a successful author that plunders the dead.

**Austin O'Malley**

An author, like any other so-called artist, is a man in whom the normal vanity of all men is so vastly exaggerated that he finds it a sheer impossibility to hold it in. His over-powering impulse is to gyrate before his fellow men, flapping his wings and emitting defiant yells. This being forbidden by the police of all civilized nations, he takes it out by putting his yells on paper. Such is the thing called self-expression.

**H.L. Mencken, *Prejudices*, 1919–27**

Every author really wants to have letters printed in the papers. Unable to make the grade, he drops down a rung on the ladder and writes novels.

**P.G. Wodehouse, *Louder and Funnier*, 1932**

It is part of prudence to thank an author for his book before reading it, so as to avoid the necessity of lying about it afterwards.

**George Santayana**

Authors are easy to get on with – if you're fond of children.

**Michael Joseph, in the *Observer*, 1949**

What an author likes to write most is his signature on the back of a cheque.

**Brendan Francis**

An author's first duty is to let down his country.

**Brendan Behan, in the *Guardian*, 1960**

It is usually a mistake to confuse the author's point of view with the form he has discovered for it. When the second is admirable, we give him the Nobel Prize for the first.

**Nigel Dennis, quoted in the New York Review of Books, 1971**

There can be no society of authors.

**Geoffrey Grigson, The Private Art, 1982**

*See also* BEST-SELLERS, BOOKS, WRITING

# BEAUTY

A beautiful woman should break her mirror early.

**Baltasar Gracian, The Art of Worldly Wisdom, 1647**

All heiresses are beautiful.

**John Dryden, King Arthur, 1691**

No woman can be a beauty without a fortune.

**George Farquhar, The Beaux Stratagem, 1707**

The blush is beautiful, but sometimes it is inconvenient.

**Carlo Goldoni**

If Jack's in love, he's no judge of Jill's beauty.

**Benjamin Franklin, Poor Richard's Almanack, 1733–58**

Women have, in general, but one object, which is their beauty; upon which, scarce any flattery is too gross for them to swallow. Nature has hardly formed a woman ugly enough to be insensible to flattery upon her person.

**Lord Chesterfield, Letters to his Son, 1774**

Women's beauty like men's wit, is generally fatal to the owners.

**Lord Chesterfield, Letters to his Son, 1774**

Rank is a great beautifier.

**Edward George Bulwer-Lytton, Baron Lytton, The Lady of Lyons, 1838**

When God provides a beautiful woman, the devil at once retorts with a fool to keep her.

**Jules-Amédée Barbey d'Aurevilly**

It is better to be beautiful than to be good, but . . . it is better to be good than to be ugly.
  **Oscar Wilde, *The Picture of Dorian Gray*, 1891**

He has nothing. He looks everything. What more can one desire?
  **Oscar Wilde, *The Importance of Being Earnest*, 1895**

I always say beauty is only sin deep.
  **Saki (H.H. Munro), *Reginald's Choir Treat*, 1904**

Somehow a bachelor never quite gets over the idea that he is a thing of beauty and a boy for ever.
  **Helen Rowland, *A Guide to Men*, 1922**

Beauty, n. The power by which a woman charms a lover and terrifies a husband.
  **Ambrose Bierce, *The Devil's Dictionary*, 1911**

Man admire devotion in their wives – and beauty in other women.
  **Mae West**

If a man hears much that a woman says, then she is not beautiful.
  **Henry Haskins, *Meditations in Wall Street*, 1940**

Beauty is still supposed to arouse desire. This is not the case. Beauty has nothing to do with the physical jerks underneath the coverlet. Ugliness is one of the most reliable stimulants.
  **Henry de Montherlant, *The Goddess Cypris*, 1944**

The average girl would rather have beauty than brains because she knows the average man can see much better than he can think.
  **Anonymous, quoted in *Ladies Home Journal*, 1947**

If beauty isn't genius it usually signals at least a high level of animal cunning.
  **Peter York, in *London Collection* magazine, 1978**

All God's children are not beautiful. Most of God's children are, in fact, barely presentable.
  **Fran Lebowitz, *Metropolitan Life*, 1978**

Most beautiful but dumb girls think they are smart and get away with it, because other people, on the whole, aren't much smarter.
  **Louise Brooks, quoted in *Show People* by Kenneth Tynan, 1980**

Distance is the soul of beauty.
**Simone Weil, quoted in the *New York Review of Books*, 1981**

# BELIEF

Everyone prefers belief to the exercise of judgement.
**Lucius Annaeus Seneca**

When men are in doubt, they always believe what is most agreeable.
**Flavius Arrianus, *The Anabasis of Alexander the Great*, c.AD150**

Nothing is so firmly believed as that which we least know.
**Michel de Montaigne, *Essays*, 1595**

It is gross ignorance that produces the dogmatic spirit. The man who knows next to nothing is always eager to teach what he has just learned.
**Jean de La Bruyère, *The Characters*, 1688**

We are inclined to believe those whom we do not know because they have never deceived us.
**Samuel Johnson, *The Idler*, 1758–60**

Our prejudices are our mistresses; reason is at best our wife, very often heard indeed, but seldom minded.
**Lord Chesterfield, *Letters to his Son*, 1774**

Prejudice is never easy unless it can pass itself off for reason.
**William Hazlitt, *Sketches and Essays*, 1839**

For those who do not think, it is best to rearrange their prejudices once in a while.
**Luther Burbank**

The whole history of civilization is strewn with creeds and institutions which were invaluable at first, and deadly afterward.
**Walter Bagehot, *Physics and Politics*, 1872**

Fanaticism consists in redoubling your effort when you have forgotten your aim.
**George Santayana, *The Life of Reason*, 1905–6**

Bigot, n. One who is obstinately and zealously attached to an opinion that you do not entertain.

**Ambrose Bierce, *The Devil's Dictionary*, 1911**

Doctrinaires are the vultures of principle. They feed upon principle after it is dead.

**David Lloyd George**

You can't learn too soon that the most useful thing about a principle is that it can always be sacrificed to expediency.

**W. Somerset Maugham, *The Circle*, 1921**

Every man thinks his own beliefs are the culmination of two and a half thousand years of Western philosophy.

**Alfred North Whitehead, quoted in the *Independent*, 1993**

Just as every conviction begins as a whim, so does every emancipator serve his apprenticeship as a crank. A fanatic is a great leader who is just entering the room.

**Heywood Broun, 1928**

The fact that an opinion has been widely held is no evidence whatsoever that it is not utterly absurd. Indeed, in view of the silliness of the majority of mankind, a widespread belief is more likely to be foolish than sensible.

**Bertrand Russell, *Marriage and Morals*, 1929**

That which has been believed by everyone, always and everywhere, has every chance of being false.

**Paul Valéry, *Tel quel*, 1943**

Only one more indispensable massacre of Capitalists or Communists or Fascists or Christians or Heretics and there we are – there we are in the Golden Future.

**Aldous Huxley, *Time Must Have a Stop*, 1945**

It is characteristic of all movements and crusades that the psychopathic elements rise to the top.

**Robert Linder, *Must You Conform*, 1956**

Human beings are perhaps never more frightening than when they are convinced beyond doubt that they are right,

**Laurens van der Post, *The Lost World of the Kalahari*, 1958**

When the need is strong there are those who will believe anything.
  **Arnold Lobel, *Fables*, 1980**

The more ridiculous a belief system, the higher the probability of its success.
  **Wayne R. Bartz, quoted in *Human Behaviour* magazine, 1975**

Not every problem someone has with his girlfriend is necessarily due to the capitalist mode of production.
  **Herbert Marcuse, in *The Listener* magazine, 1978**

An absurdity is anything advanced by our opponents, contrary to our own practice, or above our comprehension.
  **'Horace' Smith, quoted in *Definitive Quotations*,
  ed. J. Ferguson, 1981**

*See also* FAITH, IDEALS, IDEAS, MORALS, RELIGION, TRUE BELIEVERS, TRUTH

# BEST-SELLERS

The best-seller is the golden touch of mediocre talent.
  **Cyril Connolly, *Journal 1928–1937*, ed. D. Pryce-Jones, 1983**

Religion, aristocracy, sex and mystery: 'Christ,' said the Duchess, 'I'm pregnant. Whodunnit?'
  **W. Somerset Maugham, proposed recipe for a good story**

If we should ever inaugurate a hall of fame, it would be reserved exclusively and hopefully for authors who, having written four best-sellers, still refrained from starting out on a lecture tour.
  **E.B. White**

The principle of procrastinated rape is said to be the ruling one in all the great best-sellers.
  **V.S. Pritchett, *The Living Novel*, 1946**

The best-seller . . . gives an idea of what is read on the periphery of literacy, the reading matter of those who have graduated from the literature of the lavatory wall to the printed word.
  **Arthur Calder-Marshall, in the *Author* magazine, 1951**

A best-seller was a book which somehow sold well simply because it was selling well.
**Daniel J. Boorstin, *The Image*, 1962**

*See also* AUTHORS, BOOKS, WRITING

# BIOGRAPHY

Every great man nowadays has his disciples, and it is always Judas who writes the biography.
**Oscar Wilde, *The Critic as Artist*, 1891**

Biography, like big-game hunting, is one of the unrecognised forms of sport, and it is as unfair as only sport can be.
**Philip Guedalla, *Supers and Supermen*, 1920**

Autobiography is an unrivalled vehicle for telling the truth about other people.
**Philip Guedalla, *Supers and Supermen*, 1920**

I enjoy reading biographies because I want to know about the people who messed up the world.
**Marie Dressler, *Passing Show*, 1934**

To write one's memoirs is to speak ill of everyone but oneself.
**Henri-Philippe Pétain, 1946**

When you put down the good things you ought to have done, and leave out the bad ones you did do – that's Memoirs.
**Will Rogers, *The Autobiography of Will Rogers*, 1949**

Just how difficult it is to write biography can be reckoned by anybody who sits down and considers just how many people know the real truth about his or her love affairs.
**Rebecca West, in *Vogue* magazine, 1952**

Look out for yourself – or they'll pee on your grave.
**Louis B. Mayer**

Autobiography: a book of gossip about other people.
**J.B. Morton ('Beachcomber')**

The purpose of Presidential office is not power, or leadership of the Western world, but reminiscence, best-selling reminiscence.
  **Roger Jellinek, in *New York Times Book Review*, 1969**

Autobiography: probably the most respectable form of lying.
  **New York Times, 1982**

Biography: voyeurism embellished with footnotes.
  **Robert Skidelsky, 1987**

# BOOKS

Satire is a sort of glass, wherein beholders do generally discover everybody's face but their own.
  **Jonathan Swift, *The Battle of the Books*, 1697**

Weak men are the worse for the good sense they read in books because it furnisheth them only with more matter to mistake.
  **George Savile, Marquis of Halifax, *Political, Moral and Miscellaneous Thoughts and Reflexions*, c.1694**

Books . . . only teach people to talk about what they do not understand.
  **Jean-Jacques Rousseau, *Émile*, 1762**

The majority of books of our time give one the impression of having been manufactured in a day out of the books read the day before.
  **Nicolas de Chamfort, *Maximes et pensées*, 1805**

The success of many books is due to the affinity between the mediocrity of the author's ideas and those of the public.
  **Nicolas de Chamfort, *Maximes et pensées*, 1805**

There can hardly be a stranger commodity in the world than books. Printed by people who don't understand them; sold by people who don't understand them; bound, criticised and read by people who don't understand them, and now even written by people who don't understand them.
  **Georg Christoph Lichtenberg, *Aphorisms*, 1764–99**

When a new book is published, read an old one.
  **Samuel Rogers**

Many books require no thought from those that read them, and for a very simple reason – they made no such demand upon those who wrote them.

**Charles Caleb Colton, *Lacon*, 1820**

Books are made not like children but like pyramids . . . and they're just as useless! and they stay in the desert! . . . Jackals piss at their foot and the bourgeois climb up them.

**Gustave Flaubert, letter, 1857**

Books for general reading always smell badly; the odour of common people hangs about them.

**Friedrich Wilhelm Nietzsche, *Beyond Good and Evil*, 1886**

The good end happily, the bad unhappily. That is what fiction means.

**Oscar Wilde, *The Importance of Being Earnest*, 1895**

A classic is something that everyone wants to have read and nobody wants to read.

**Mark Twain, *The Disappearance of Literature*, 1900**

Publishers . . . like Methodists . . . love to keep the Sabbath and anything else they can lay their hands on.

**Anna Ross, 1910**

Novel, n. A species of composition bearing the same relation to literature that the panorama bears to art.

**Ambrose Bierce, *The Devil's Dictionary*, 1911**

The greatest masterpiece in literature is only a dictionary out of order.

**Jean Cocteau, *Le Potomak*, 1919**

Publisher: the patron saint of the mediocre.

**Elbert Hubbard, *The Roycroft Dictionary*, 1923**

The chief knowledge that a man gets from reading books is the knowledge that very few of them are worth reading.

**H.L. Mencken**

There are two motives for reading a book: one, that you enjoy it, the other that you can boast about it.

**Bertrand Russell, *The Conquest of Happiness*, 1930**

Literature: proclaiming in front of everyone what one is careful to conceal from one's immediate circle.

**Jean Rostand,** *Journal d'un caractère*, **1931**

Books – what they make a movie out of for television.

**Leonard L. Levinson**

The best part of the fiction in many novels is the notice that the characters are purely imaginary.

**Franklin P. Adams (F.P.A.)**

As repressed sadists are said to become policemen or butchers so those with an irrational fear of life become publishers.

**Cyril Connolly,** *Enemies of Promise*, **1938**

Literature is the orchestration of platitudes.

**Thornton Wilder, in** *Time* **magazine, 1953**

The possession of a book becomes a substitute for reading it.

**Anthony Burgess, in** *New York Times Book Review*, **1966**

Having been unpopular in high school is not just cause for book publication.

**Fran Lebowitz**

The ratio of literacy to illiteracy is constant, but nowadays the illiterates can read.

**Alberto Moravia, quoted in the** *Observer*, **1979**

An optimist is one who believes everything he reads on the jacket of a new book.

**Milwaukee Journal**

Great literature is like moral leadership: everyone deplores the lack of it, but there is a tendency to prefer it from the safely dead.

**Shirley Hazzard, 1982**

If pregnancy were a book they would cut the last two chapters.

**Nora Ephron,** *Heartburn*, **1983**

Fiction is licensed lie-telling

**William Amos,** *The Originals*, **1985**

*See also* AUTHORS, BEST-SELLERS, WRITING

# BORES

We often forgive those who bore us, but we cannot forgive those whom we bore.

**François, Duc de La Rochefoucauld,** *Maxims***, 1665**

Every hero becomes a bore at last.

**Ralph Waldo Emerson,** *Representative Men***, 1850**

All men are bores, except when we want them.

**Oliver Wendell Holmes**

Bore, n. A person who talks when you wish him to listen.

**Ambrose Bierce,** *The Devil's Dictionary***, 1911**

Virtuous people often revenge themselves for the constraints to which they submit by the boredom which they inspire.

**Gustave Le Bon,** *Aphorismes du temps présent***, 1913**

Make [the reader] laugh and he will think you a trivial fellow, but bore him in the right way and your reputation is assured.

**W. Somerset Maugham,** *The Gentleman in the Parlour***, 1930**

Perhaps the world's second worst crime is boredom. The first is being a bore.

**Cecil Beaton**

A gossip is one who talks to you about others, a bore is one who talks to you about himself; and a brilliant conversationalist is one who talks to you about yourself.

**Lisa Kirk, quoted in** *New York Journal American***, 1954**

Dear World, I am leaving you because I am bored. I am leaving you with your worries. Good luck.

**George Sanders, his suicide note, 1972**

In heaven they will bore you, in hell you will bore them.

**Katherine Whitehorn**

A bore is a fellow talking who can change the subject back to his topic of conversation faster than you can change it back to yours.

**Laurence J. Peter,** *Peter's Quotations***, 1977**

*See also* EGOTISM, TALK

# BOYS

A bachelor never quite gets over the idea that he is a thing of beauty and a boy for ever.

**Helen Rowland**

Boys will be boys, and so will a lot of middle-aged men.

**Kin Hubbard**

I never see any difference in boys. I only know two sorts of boys. Mealy boys and beef-faced boys.

**Charles Dickens,** *Oliver Twist*, **1838**

Teenage boys, goaded by their surging hormones, run in packs like the primal horde. They have only a brief season of exhilarating liberty between control by their mothers and control by their wives.

**Camille Paglia,** *Sex, Art and American Culture*, **1992**

*See also* CHILDREN

# BRAVERY

Courage is the fear of being thought a coward.

**'Horace' Smith**

People are only heroes when they can't do anything else.

**Paul Claudel**

Show me a hero, and I will write you a tragedy.

**F. Scott Fitzgerald,** *The Crack-Up*, **1936**

There is no such thing as bravery – only degrees of fear.

**John Wainwright, quoted in** *The Times*, **1980**

# BUREAUCRACY

Bureaucracy . . . the giant power wielded by pygmies.

**Honoré de Balzac,** *Les Employés*, **1838**

A memorandum is written not to inform the reader but to protect the writer.

**Dean Acheson**

The perfect bureaucrat everywhere is the man who manages to make no decisions and escape all responsibility.

**Brooks Atkinson,** *Once Around the Sun,* **1951**

The speed of exit of a civil servant is directly proportional to the quality of his service.

**Ralph Nader**

A basic rule of bureaucracies: the longer the title, the lower the rank.

**Hugh Rawson,** *A Dictionary of Euphemisms,* **1983**

*See also* COMMITTEES

# BUSINESS

Corruption is simply business without scruples.

**Anonymous**

A market is a place set apart for men to deceive and get the better of one another.

**Anacharsis, quoted in** *Lives and Opinions of Eminent Philosophers* **by Diogenes Laertius, c.225**

There is no kind of idleness by which we are so easily seduced as that which dignifies itself by the appearance of business.

**Samuel Johnson,** *The Idler,* **1758–60**

Here's the rule for bargains: 'Do other men, for they would do you'. That's the true business precept.

**Charles Dickens,** *Martin Chuzzlewit,* **1843–4**

It is well known what a middle man is: he is a man who bamboozles one party and plunders the other.

**Benjamin Disraeli, speech, 1845**

Everyone lives by selling something.

**Robert Louis Stevenson**

A financier is a pawnbroker with imagination.

**Arthur Pinero, 1893**

Look, we trade every day out there with hustlers, deal-makers, shysters, con-men. That's the way businesses get started. That's the way this country was built.

**Hubert Allen**

Financial sense is knowing that certain men will promise to do certain things and fail.

**Edgar Watson Howe, *Sinner Sermons*, 1926**

When two men in a business always agree, one of them is unnecessary.

**William Wrigley Jr**

Don't take a nickel, just hand them your business card.

**Richard M. Daley, advising on the safe enjoyment of graft**

The trouble with the profit system has always been that it was highly unprofitable to most people.

**E.B. White, *One Man's Meat*, 1944**

There is a good deal of solemn cant about the common interests of capital and labour. As matters stand, their only common interest is that of cutting each other's throat.

**Brooks Atkinson, *Once Around the Sun*, 1951**

There is little that can be said about most economic goods. A tooth-brush does little but clean teeth. Aspirin does little but dull pain. Alcohol is important mostly for making people more or less drunk . . . There being so little to be said, much is to be invented.

**John Kenneth Galbraith, *Economics, Peace and Laughter*, 1971**

Crime is a logical extension of the sort of behaviour that is often considered perfectly respectable in legitimate business.

**Robert Rice, *The Business of Crime*, 1956**

An actuary is someone who moved out of accountancy because he couldn't stand the excitement.

**Anonymous**

A hustler is a man who will talk you into giving him a free ride and make it seem as if he is doing you a great favour.

**Bill Veeck, 1965**

Commercialism is doing well that which should not be done at all.
  **Gore Vidal**

The only promotion rules I can think of are that a sense of shame is
to be avoided at all costs and there is never any reason for a hustler to
be less cunning than more virtuous men. Oh yes . . . whenever you
think you've got something really great, add ten per cent more.
  **Bill Veeck, 1965**

The value of anything is not what you get paid for it, nor what it cost
to produce, but what you can get for it at an auction.
  **William Lyon Phelps, quoted in the *National Observer*, 1969**

In a hierarchy every employee tends to rise to his level of incompetence . . . in time every post tends to be occupied by an employee who
is incompetent to carry out its duties . . . Work is accomplished by
those employees who have not yet reached their level of incompetence.
  **Laurence J. Peter, *The Peter Principle*, 1969**

An office party is not, as is sometimes supposed, the Managing Director's chance to kiss the tea-girl. It is the tea-girl's chance to kiss the
Managing Director (however bizarre an ambition this may seem to
anyone who has seen the Managing Director face on).
  **Katherine Whitehorn**

As long as people will accept crap, it will be financially profitable to
dispense it.
  **Dick Cavett, in *Playboy* magazine, 1971**

The first myth of management is that it exists. The second myth of
management is that success equals skill.
  **Robert Heller, *The Great Executive Dream*, 1972**

Nothing is illegal if one hundred businessmen decide to do it.
  **Andrew Young, 1976**

An accountant is a man hired to explain that you didn't make the
money you did.
  **Anonymous**

If you hype something and it succeeds, you're a genius – it wasn't a
hype. If you hype it and it fails, then it was just a hype.
  **Neil Bogart**

It comes down to that . . . business tactic: the guy that yells loudest is right.

**Irving Azoff, quoted in *Rolling Stone* magazine, 1976**

The business world worships mediocrity. Officially we revere free enterprise, initiative and individuality. Unofficially we fear it.

**George Lois, *The Art of Advertising*, 1977**

The arms business is founded on human folly. That is why its depths will never be plumbed and why it will go on forever. All weapons are defensive and all spare parts are non-lethal. The plainest print cannot be read through a solid gold sovereign, or a ruble or a golden eagle.

**Sam Cummings, 1978**

The salary of the chief executive of the large corporation is not a market award for achievement. It is frequently in the nature of a warm personal gesture by the individual to himself.

**John Kenneth Galbraith, *Annals of an Abiding Liberal*, 1980**

Management: an activity or art where those who have not yet succeeded and those who have proved unsuccessful are led by those who have not yet failed.

**Paulsson Frenckner, speech, 1984**

Contract: an agreement that is binding on the weaker party.

**Frederick Sawyer**

Supermarkets . . . symbols of man's inhumanity to women.

**Philip Adams, in *The Dictionary of Australian Quotations*, 1984**

*See also* MONEY, THE RICH

# CENSORSHIP

To forbid us anything is to make us have a mind for it.

**Michel de Montaigne, *Essays*, 1595**

Wherever they burn books, they will also, in the end, burn people.

**Heinrich Heine, *Almansor*, 1823**

A satire which the censor is able to understand deserves to be banned.

**Karl Kraus**

Assassination is the extreme form of censorship.

**George Bernard Shaw, *The Rejected Statement*, 1916**

I wouldn't tell the people anything until the war is over, and then I'd tell them who won.

**Anonymous American military censor, on the ideal use of the media in war, 1943**

Obscenity is what happens to shock some elderly and ignorant magistrate.

**Bertrand Russell, in *Look* magazine, 1954**

When there is official censorship it is a sign that speech is serious. When there is none, it is pretty certain that the official spokesmen have all the loudspeakers.

**Paul Goodman, *Growing Up Absurd*, 1960**

The First Amendment forbids any law 'abridging the freedom of speech'. It doesn't say, 'except for commercials on children's television' or 'unless somebody says "cunt" in a rap song or "chick" on a college campus'.

**P.J. O'Rourke, *Parliament of Whores*, 1991**

Obscenity is whatever gives a judge an erection.

**Anonymous American lawyer**

*See also* TALK, WRITING

# CHARITY

An open hand makes a blind eye.

**Francis Quarles, *Enchyridion*, 1641**

All are apt to shrink from those that lean upon them.

**George Savile, Marquis of Halifax, *Political, Moral and Miscellaneous Thoughts and Reflexions*, c.1694**

He that feeds upon charity has a cold dinner and no supper.

**Thomas Fuller, M.D., *Gnomologia*, 1732**

Everyone in this world has as much as they can do in caring for themselves, and few have leisure really to think of their neighbour's distresses, however they may delight their tongues with talking of them.

**Samuel Johnson**

The most genuine and efficacious charity is that which greases the paws of the priests; such charity covers a multitude of sins.

**Voltaire, *Philosophical Dictionary*, 1764**

Charity, like nature, abhors a vaccuum. Next to putting it into the bank, men like to squander their superfluous wealth on those to whom it is sure of doing the least possible good.

**William Hazlitt, *Butts of Different Sorts*, 1829**

We do not quite forgive a giver. The hand that feeds us is in some danger of being bitten.

**Ralph Waldo Emerson, *Journals*, 1909–14**

Take egotism out, and you would castrate the benefactors.

**Ralph Waldo Emerson, *Journals* 1909–14**

The worst of charity is, that the lives you are asked to preserve are not worth preserving.

**Ralph Waldo Emerson**

One can always be kind to people about whom one cares nothing.

**Oscar Wilde, *The Picture of Dorian Gray*, 1891**

Altruism: the art of doing unselfish things for selfish reasons.

**Anonymous**

Charity is the sterilised milk of human kindness.

**Oliver Herford**

People who mean well – always a poisonous class.

**E.V. Lucas**

Philanthropy seems to me to have become simply the refuge of people who want to annoy their fellow creatures.

**Oscar Wilde, *An Ideal Husband*, 1895**

Man is the only animal which esteems itself rich in proportion to the number and voracity of its parasites.

**George Bernard Shaw, *Man and Superman*, 1903**

Self-sacrifice enables us to sacrifice other people without blushing.
**George Bernard Shaw, *Man and Superman*, 1903**

The Princess had always defended a friend's complexion if it was really bad. With her . . . charity began at homeliness and did not generally progress much further.
**Saki (H.H. Munro), *Reginald in Russia*, 1910**

Dependent, adj. Reliant upon another's generosity for the support which you are not in a position to exact from his fears.
**Ambrose Bierce, *The Devil's Dictionary*, 1911**

When a benefactor has no other confidant than the beneficiary, his secret, as a rule, is only too safe.
**Alexandre Vinet, quoted in *A Cynic's Breviary* by J.R. Solly, 1925**

You can only help one of your luckless brothers
By trampling down a dozen others.
**Bertolt Brecht, *The Good Person of Szechuan*, 1943**

We'd all like a reputation for generosity, and we'd all like to buy it cheap.
**Mignon McLaughlin, *The Neurotic's Notebook*, 1963**

There is only one word for aid that is genuinely without strings and that word is blackmail.
**Colm Brogan**

Without the skeleton at the feast, it is questionable whether the feast tastes good.
**George Buchanan**

Compassion is a luxury of the affluent.
**Tony Randall, quoted in *Playboy* magazine, 1974**

*See also* LIBERALS, MONEY, RELIGION

# CHILDREN

The reason why parents love the younger children best is because they now have so little hope that the elder will do well.
**Japanese proverb**

You are to have as strict a Guard upon yourself among your Children as if you were among your Enemies.

**George Savile, Marquis of Halifax,** *Political, Moral and Miscellaneous Thoughts and Reflexions,* *c.*1694

As fathers commonly go, it is seldom a misfortune to be fatherless; and considering the general run of sons, as seldom a misfortune to be childless.

**Lord Chesterfield,** *Letters to his Son,* 1774

Bachelors' wives and old maids' children are always perfect.

**Nicolas de Chamfort,** *Maximes et pensées,* 1805

When I consider how little of a rarity children are . . . I cannot for the life of me tell what cause for pride there can possibly be in having them.

**Charles Lamb,** *Essays of Elia,* 1823

Children are never too tender to be whipped: like tough beefsteaks, the more you beat them the more tender they become.

**Edgar Allen Poe, in** *Graham's Magazine,* 1850

If you desire to drain to the dregs the fullest cup of scorn and hatred that a human fellow creature can pour out for you, let a young mother hear you call her baby 'it'.

**Jerome K. Jerome,** *Idle Thoughts of an Idle Fellow,* 1886

Children begin by loving their parents. After a time they judge them . . . rarely, if ever, do they forgive them.

**Oscar Wilde,** *A Woman of No Importance,* 1893

It must have been some unmarried fool that said 'A child can ask questions that a wise man cannot answer'; because, in any decent house, a brat that starts asking questions is promptly packed off to bed.

**Arthur Binstead,** *Pitcher's Proverbs,* 1909

The parent who could see his boy as he really is would shake his head and say, 'Willie is no good. I'll sell him.'

**Stephen Leacock,** *Literary Lapses,* 1910

Childhood, n. The period of human life intermediate between the idiocy of infancy and the folly of youth – two removes from the sin of manhood and three from the remorse of age.

**Ambrose Bierce,** *The Devil's Dictionary,* 1911

The best way to keep children at home is to make the home atmosphere pleasant – and to let the air out of the tyres.
**Dorothy Parker**

Nature makes boys and girls lovely to look upon so they can be tolerated until they acquire some sense.
**William Lyon Phelps**

Beat your son every day; you may not know why, but he will.
**Anonymous**

The effects of infantile instruction, like those of syphilis, are never completely cured.
**Robert Briffault, *Sin and Sex*, 1931**

Anyone who hates children and dogs can't be all bad.
**W.C. Fields**

Destroy him as you will, the bourgeois always bounces up. Execute him, expropriate him, starve him out *en masse*, and he reappears in your children.
**Cyril Connolly, 1937**

There is no more sombre enemy of good art than the pram in the hall.
**Cyril Connolly, *Enemies of Promise*, 1938**

Adolescence: a stage between infancy and adultery.
**Anonymous, quoted in *H.L. Mencken's Dictionary of Quotations*, 1942**

The state of innocence contains the germs of all future sin.
**Alexandre Arnoux**

What is an adult? A child blown up by age.
**Simone de Beauvoir, *The Woman Destroyed*, 1969**

I love children. Especially when they cry – for then someone takes them away.
**Nancy Mitford**

Children have never been very good at listening to their elders, but they have never failed to imitate them.
**James Baldwin, in *Esquire* magazine, 1960**

The easiest way for your children to learn about money is for you not to have any.

**Katherine Whitehorn, *How To Survive Children*, 1975**

It is no wonder people are so horrible when they start life as children.

**Kingsley Amis, *One Fat Englishman*, 1963**

Children are cruel, ruthless, cunning and almost incredibly self-centred. Far from cementing a marriage, children more frequently disrupt it. Child-rearing is on the whole an expensive and unrewarding bore, in which more has to be invested, both materially and spiritually, than ever comes out in dividends.

**Nigel Balchin, quoted in the *Sunday Express*, 1965**

Society highly values its normal men. It educates children to lose themselves and to become absurd, and thus be normal. Normal men have killed perhaps 100,000,000 of their fellow normal men in the last fifty years.

**R.D. Laing, *The Politics of Experience*, 1967**

I know what 'custody' [of the children] means. 'Get even'. That's all custody means. Get even with your old lady.

**Lenny Bruce, quoted in *The Essential Lenny Bruce*,
ed. J. Cohen, 1967**

Children's talent to endure stems from their ignorance of alternatives.

**Maya Angelou, *I Know Why the Caged Bird Sings*, 1969**

The Jewish man with parents alive is a fifteen-year-old boy and will remain a fifteen-year-old boy until they die.

**Philip Roth, *Portnoy's Complaint*, 1967**

Cleaning your house while your kids are still growing
Is like shovelling the walk before it stops snowing.

**Phyllis Diller**

Boys will be boys. And even that wouldn't matter if we could prevent girls from being girls.

**Anthony Hope (Sir Anthony Hope Hawkins), *The Dolly Dialogues*, 1894**

*See also* ADULTS, BOYS, FAMILIES, GIRLS, PARENTS

# CHRISTIANS

Men of simple understanding, little inquisitive and little instructed, make good Christians.
**Michel de Montaigne, *Essays*, 1595**

Christ: a parish demagogue.
**Percy Bysshe Shelley**

What is more harmful than any vice? Practical sympathy for the botched and weak – Christianity.
**Friedrich Wilhelm Nietzsche, *The Antichrist*, 1888**

Christianity has done love a great service by making it a sin.
**Anatole France, *The Garden of Epicurus*, 1894**

People may say what they like about the decay of Christianity; the religious system that produced green Chartreuse can never really die.
**Saki (H.H. Munro), *Reginald on Christmas Presents*, 1904**

Popular Christianity has for its emblem a gibbet, for its chief sensation a sanguinary execution after torture, for its central mystery an insane vengeance brought off by a trumpery expiation.
**George Bernard Shaw, *Major Barbara*, 1907**

Christian, n. One who believes that the New Testament is a divinely inspired book admirably suited to the spiritual need of his neighbour.
**Ambrose Bierce, *The Devil's Dictionary*, 1911**

Heaven: the Coney Island of the Christian imagination.
**Elbert Hubbard, *The Notebook*, 1927**

Christ died for our sins. Dare we make his martyrdom meaningless by not committing them?
**Jules Feiffer, quoted in *Peter's Quotations*, ed. L. Peter, 1977**

*See also* BELIEF, THE CLERGY, FAITH, GOD, HYPOCRISY, MORALS, RELIGION

# CIVILISATION

Our civilisation is founded on the shambles, and every individual existence goes out in a lonely spasm of helpless agony.

**William James, *Varieties of Religious Experience*, 1902**

Civilisation is the lamb's skin in which barbarism masquerades.

**Thomas B. Aldrich, *Ponkapog Papers*, 1903**

There is a vast difference between the savage and civilised man, but it is never apparent to their wives until after breakfast.

**Helen Rowland, *A Guide to Men*, 1922**

The major advances in civilisation are processes that all but wreck the societies in which they occur.

**Alfred North Whitehead**

Civilisation is nothing else but the attempt to reduce force to being the last resort.

**José Ortega y Gasset, *The Revolt of the Masses*, 1930**

It is so stupid of modern civilisation to have given up believing in the devil when he is the only explanation of it.

**Ronald Knox, *Let Dons Delight*, 1939**

The civilised are those who get more out of life than the uncivilised, and for this the uncivilised have not forgiven them.

**Cyril Connolly (Palinurus), *The Unquiet Grave*, 1944**

The civilisation of one epoch becomes the manure of the next.

**Cyril Connolly (Palinurus), *The Unquiet Grave*, 1944**

You can't say civilisation don't advance . . . for in every war they kill you a new way.

**Will Rogers, *The Autobiography of Will Rogers*, 1949**

We are born princes and the civilising process makes us frogs.

**Eric Berne, *The Games People Play*, 1964**

All that is left for the civilised man is to laugh at the absurdity of the human condition.

**Auberon Waugh, in *Esquire* magazine, 1968**

We are all born charming, fresh and spontaneous and must be civilised before we are fit to participate in society.

**Judith Martin, *Miss Manners' Guide to Excruciatingly Correct Behaviour*, 1983**

*See also* HUMANITY, LIFE

# CLASS

The difference between what is commonly called ordinary company and good company is only hearing the same things said in a little room or in a large salon, at small tables or at great tables, before two candles or twenty sconces.

**Alexander Pope**

Barbarians, Philistines, Populace . . . the three great classes into which our society is divided.

**Matthew Arnold, *Culture and Anarchy*, 1869**

The danger is not that a particular class is unfit to govern. Every class is unfit to govern.

**Sir J.E.E. Dalberg, first Baron Acton, letter to Mary Gladstone, 1881**

It is only by not paying one's bills that one can hope to live in the memory of the commercial classes.

**Oscar Wilde, *Phrases and Philosophies for the Use of the Young*, 1894**

Never speak disrespectfully of society – only people who can't get into it do that.

**Oscar Wilde, *The Importance of Being Earnest*, 1895**

I think she must have been very strictly brought up, she's so desperately anxious to do the wrong thing correctly.

**Saki (H.H.Munro), *Reginald on Worries*, 1904**

I don't think you want too much sincerity in society. It would be like an iron girder in a house of cards.

**W. Somerset Maugham, *The Circle*, 1921**

Society is like the air: neccessary to breathe, but insufficient to live on.

**George Santayana**

Broadly speaking, human beings may be divided into three classes: those who are billed to death, those who are worried to death and those who are bored to death.

**Sir Winston Churchill**

A broad definition of crime in England is that it is any lower-class activity that is displeasing to the upper class.

**David Frost and Antony Jay**

The genius of our ruling class is that it has kept a majority of the people from ever questioning the inequity of a system where most people drudge along paying heavy taxes for which they get nothing in return.

**Gore Vidal**

Class: when they're running you out of town, to look like you're leading the parade.

**Bill Battie, in *Sports Illustrated* magazine, 1976**

The working classes have a reputation for potency and being good in bed – a myth probably started by middle-class novelists and by graphologists who claim that anyone with loopy writing must be highly sexed.

**Jilly Cooper, *Class*, 1979**

*See also* ARISTOCRACY, GENTLEMEN, THE MASSES

# THE CLERGY

A priest is a man who is called Father by everyone except his own children, who are obliged to call him Uncle.

**Anonymous Italian saying**

The Clergy would have us believe them against our own reason, as the woman would have had her husband against his own eyes, when he took her with another man, which she yet stoutly denied: 'What, will you believe your own eyes before your own sweet wife?'

**John Selden, *Table Talk*, 1689**

A clergyman is one who feels himself called upon to live without working at the expense of the rascals who work to live.

**Voltaire**

To the philosophical eye the vices of the clergy are far less dangerous than their virtues.

**Edward Gibbon, *Decline and Fall of the Roman Empire*, 1776–88**

Priests and conjurors are of the same trade.

**Thomas Paine, *The Age of Reason*, 1793**

And priests dare babble of a God of peace,
Even whilst their hands are red with guiltless blood,
Murdering the while, uprooting every germ
Of truth, exterminating, spoiling all,
Making the earth a slaughter-house!

**Percy Bysshe Shelley, *Queen Mab*, 1813**

In every country and in every age the priest has been hostile to liberty. He is always in alliance with the despot, abetting his abuses in return for protection of his own.

**Thomas Jefferson, letter, 1814**

Mothers, wives and maids,
These be the tools with which priests manage men.

**Robert Browning, *The Ring and the Book*, 1868–9**

How large a share of vanity must spur the piety of the missionary. There is something melodramatic in landing on some Fiji island, in baptising, debauching and ultimately murdering the unsuspecting savage; then in taking his land in the name of the Most High.

**Richard Birnie, *Essays*, 1879**

In all ages hypocrites, called priests, have put crowns on the heads of thieves, called kings.

**Robert G. Ingersoll, 1884**

'Sins' are indispensable to every society organized on an ecclesiastical basis; they are the only reliable weapons of power; the priest lives upon sins; it is necessary to him that there be 'sinning'.

**Friedrich Wilhelm Nietzsche, *The Antichrist*, 1888**

Priests . . . these turkey-cocks of God.

**Friedrich Wilhelm Nietzsche, *The Antichrist*, 1888**

Clergyman, n. A man who undertakes the management of our spiritual affairs as a method of bettering his temporal ones.

**Ambrose Bierce, *The Devil's Dictionary*, 1911**

Parsons always seem to be specially horrified about things like sun-bathing and naked bodies. They don't mind poverty and misery and cruelty to animals nearly as much.

**Susan Ertz**

Of learned men, the clergy show the lowest development of professional ethics. Any pastor is free to cadge customers from the divines of rival sects, and to denounce the divines themselves as theological quacks.

**H.L. Mencken, *Minority Report*, 1956**

*See also* BELIEF, FAITH, GOD, HYPOCRISY, MORALS, RELIGION

# COMMITTEES

A committee should consist of three men, two of whom are absent.

**Sir Herbert Beerbohm Tree**

A committee is a group that keeps the minutes and loses hours.

**Milton Berle, 1954**

A conference is a gathering of important people who singly can do nothing but together can decide that nothing can be done.

**Fred Allen**

What is a committee? A group of the unwilling, picked from the unfit, to do the unnecessary.

**Richard Harkness, quoted in the *New York Herald Tribune*, 1960**

Meetings are indispensable when you don't want to do anything.

**John Kenneth Galbraith, *Ambassador's Journal*, 1969**

A committee is a cul-de-sac down which ideas are lured and then quietly strangled.

**Sir Barnett Cocks, in *New Scientist* magazine, 1973**

*See also* BUREAUCRACY

# COMPUTERS

If you put tomfoolery into a computer, nothing comes out but tomfoolery. But this tomfoolery, having passed through a very expensive machine, is somehow ennobled and no-one dares criticise it.

**Pierre Gallois**

Machines from the Maxim gun to the computer are for the most part means by which a minority can keep free men in subjection.
**Kenneth Clark,** *Civilisation,* **1969**

To err is human, but to really foul things up requires a computer.
**Farmers' Almanac, 1978**

# CONFORMITY

          . . . and obedience,
Bane of all genius, virtue, freedom, truth,
Makes slaves of men, and, of the human frame,
A mechanised automaton.
**Percy Bysshe Shelley,** *Queen Mab,* **1813**

Conformity, humility, acceptance – with these coins we are to pay our fares to paradise.
**Robert Lindner,** *Must You Conform?,* **1956**

*See also* CONSERVATIVES, CONSISTENCY

# CONSCIENCE

Conscience is, in most men, an anticipation of the opinions of others.
**Sir Henry Taylor,** *The Statesman,* **1836**

Conscience and cowardice are really the same things. Conscience is the trade-name of the firm.
**Oscar Wilde,** *The Picture of Dorian Gray,* **1891**

So long as there are earnest believers in the world, they will always wish to punish opinions, even if their judgement tells them that it is unwise and their conscience that it is wrong.
**Walter Bagehot,** *Literary Studies,* **1879–95**

The conscience is a watch that everyone sets by the time of his own country.
**Aurelien Scholl, quoted in** *Reflections on the Art of Life*
**by J.R. Solly, 1902**

A guilty conscience is the mother of invention.
**Carolyn Wells**

Pangs of conscience are the sadistic stirrings of Christianity.
  **Karl Kraus, *Half Truths and One and a Half Truths*, 1986**

Conscience is a cur that does not stop us from passing but that we cannot prevent from barking.
  **Nicolas de Chamfort, quoted in *A Cynic's Breviary***
  **by J.R. Solly, 1925**

Most people sell their souls, and live with a good conscience on the proceeds.
  **Logan Pearsall Smith, *Afterthoughts*, 1933**

If you really want to do something new, the good won't help you with it. Let me have men about me that are arrant knaves. The wicked, who have something on their conscience, are obliging, quick to hear threats, because they know how it's done, and for booty. You can offer them things because they will take them. Because they have no hesitations. You can hang them if they get out of step. Let me have men about me that are utter villains – provided that I have the power, the absolute power, over life and death.
  **Hermann Göring**

One lives with so many bad deeds on one's conscience and some good intentions in one's heart.
  **Pierre Reverdy, *Le livre de mon bord*, 1948**

Living with a conscience is like driving a car with the brakes on.
  **Budd Schulberg, *What Makes Sammy Run?*, 1941**

Conscience is what your mother told you before you were six years old.
  **Dr Brock Chisholm, quoted in *Ladies Home Journal*, 1949**

Conscience is the inner voice that warns us that someone might be looking.
  **H.L. Mencken, *A Mecken Chrestomathy*, 1949**

The Anglo-Saxon conscience does not prevent the Anglo-Saxon from sinning, it merely prevents him from enjoying his sin.
  **Salvador de Madariaga**

A conscience which has been bought once will be bought twice.
  **Norbert Wiener, *The Human Use of Human Beings*, 1954**

*See also* HONESTY, HYPOCRISY

# CONSERVATIVES

Tory: a cant term, derived, I suppose, from an Irish word, signifying savage.

**Samuel Johnson, *A Dictionary of the English Language*, 1755**

There are only two great currents in the history of mankind: the baseness which makes conservatives and the envy which makes revolutionaries.

**Edmond and Jules de Goncourt, *Diary*, 12, July 1867**

Conservatism . . . is mainly due to want of imagination . . . Conservatism, in the lump, is a euphemism for selfishness . . . Stupid people can only see their own side of a question; they cannot even imagine any other side possible. So, as a rule stupid people are Conservative.

**Grant Allen, quoted in *The Westminster Gazette*, 1894**

Radicalism, n. The conservatism of tomorrow injected into the affairs of today.

**Ambrose Bierce, *The Devil's Dictionary*, 1911**

Conservative, n. A statesman who is enamoured of existing evils, as distinguished from the Liberal who wishes to replace them with others.

**Ambrose Bierce, *The Devil's Dictionary*, 1911**

A conservative is a man who is too cowardly to fight and too fat to run.

**Elbert Hubbard, *The Notebook*, 1927**

The radical invents the views. When he has worn them out, the conservative adopts them.

**Mark Twain, *Notebook*, 1935**

How can wealth persuade poverty to use its political freedom to keep wealth in power? Here lies the whole art of Conservative politics in the 20th century.

**Aneurin Bevan, *In Place of Fear*, 1952**

There is nothing more disgusting in British political life than a Conservative who thinks he has public opinion behind him.

**Auberon Waugh, in the *Spectator* magazine, 1986**

*See also* CONFORMITY, CONSISTENCY, GOVERNMENT, PARTIES, POLITICIANS, POLITICS

# CONSISTENCY

There is nothing in this world constant but inconstancy.

**Jonathan Swift, *A Critical Essay upon the Faculties of Mind*, 1707**

No perverseness equals that which is supported by system, no errors are as difficult to root out as those which the understanding has pledged its credit to uphold.

**William Wordsworth, *Poems*, 1815**

Consistency is the hobgoblin of little minds, adored by little statesmen and philosophers and divines.

**Ralph Waldo Emerson, *Essays*, 1841**

Consistency requires you to be as ignorant today as you were a year ago.

**Bernard Berenson, *Notebook*, 1892**

One is often kept in the right road by a rut.

**Gustave Droz, quoted in *Reflections on the Art of Life* by J.R. Solly, 1902**

*See also* CONFORMITY, CONSERVATIVES

# COWARDICE

Most of the time the word *realism* is a polite translation of the word *cowardice*.

**Jean Dutourd, *Taxis of the Marne*, 1957**

# CRIME

All criminals turn preachers under the gallows.

**Italian proverb**

Successful and fortunate crime is called virtue.

**Lucius Annaeus Seneca, *Hercules Furens*, c.AD50**

Society . . . prepares crimes; criminals are only the instruments necessary for executing them.

**L.A.J. Quételet**

The state calls its own violence law, but that of the individual crime.

**Max Stirner,** *The Ego and His Own*, **1845**

Thieves respect property; they merely wish the property to become their property that they may more perfectly respect it.

**G.K. Chesterton,** *The Man Who Was Thursday*, **1908**

Organised crime is just the dirty side of the sharp dollar.

**Raymond Chandler,** *The Long Goodbye*, **1953**

My fellow-prisoners seemed to me in no way morally inferior to the rest of the population though they were on the whole slightly below the usual level of intelligence, as was shown by their having been caught.

**Bertrand Russell,** *Autobiography*, **1967**

What's the difference between a guy in the bighouse and the average guy you pass in the street? The guy in the bighouse is a Loser who tried.

**Charles Bukowski,** *Notes of a Dirty Old Man*, **1969**

*See also* LAW

# CRITICS & CRITICISM

Critics are the stupid who discuss the wise.

**Anonymous**

Critics are like brushers of nobleman's clothes.

**Sir Henry Wotton**

They who write ill and they who durst not write,
Turn critics out of mere revenge and spite.

**John Dryden,** *The Conquest of Granada*, **1670**

Though by whim, envy or resentment led,
They damn those authors whom they never read.

**Charles Churchill,** *The Candidate*, **1764**

The great contention of criticism is to to find the faults of the moderns and the beauties of the ancients. While an author is yet living we estimate his powers by his worst performance, and when he is dead we rate them by his best.

**Samuel Johnson, *The Plays of Shakespeare*, 1765**

I never read a book before reviewing it – it prejudices a man so.

**Sydney Smith, quoted in *The Smith of Smiths* by Hesketh Pearson, 1934**

As a bankrupt thief turns thief-taker, so an unsuccessful author turns critic.

**Percy Bysshe Shelley, *Adonais*, 1821**

Taking to pieces is the trade of those who cannot construct.

**Ralph Waldo Emerson**

Nature fits all her children with something to do,
He who would write and can't write, would surely review,
Can set up a small booth as a critic, and sell us his
Petty conceit and his pettier jealousies.

**James Lowell, *A Fable for Critics*, 1848**

You know who critics are? – the men who have failed in literature and art.

**Benjamin Disraeli, *Lothair*, 1870**

A man is a critic when he cannot be an artist, just as a man becomes a stool pigeon when he cannot be a soldier.

**Gustave Flaubert**

It is only an auctioneer who can equally and impartially admire all schools of art.

**Oscar Wilde, *The Critic as Artist*, 1891**

Caviler, n. A critic of our own work.

**Ambrose Bierce, *The Devil's Dictionary*, 1911**

Reviewing has one advantage over suicide: in suicide you take it out on yourself; in reviewing you take it out on other people.

**George Bernard Shaw**

Criticism is prejudice made plausible.
  **H.L. Mencken**

Reviewers . . . seemed to fall into two classes: those who had little to
say, and those that had nothing.
  **Max Beerbohm, *Seven Men*, 1919**

Critics . . . are of two sorts: those who merely relieve themselves
against the flower of beauty, and those, less continent, who afterwards
scratch it up.
  **William Empson, *Seven Types of Ambiguity*, 1930**

A critic is a gong at a railroad crossing clanging loudly and vainly as
the train goes by.
  **Christopher Morley**

Time is the only critic without ambition.
  **John Steinbeck**

A critic is a legless man who teaches running.
  **Channing Pollock**

A critic is a man who writes about things he doesn't like.
  **Anonymous, quoted in *H.L. Mencken's Dictionary of Quotations*,
  1942**

Any fool can criticise – and many of them do.
  **Cyril Garbett**

A musicologist is a man who can read music but can't hear it.
  **Sir Thomas Beecham, quoted in *Beecham Remembered*
  by H. Proctor-Gregg, 1976**

A critic is a man created to praise greater men than himself, but he is
never able to find them.
  **Richard Le Gallienne**

My native habitat is the theatre, I toil not, neither do I spin. I am a
critic and a commentator. I am essential to the theatre – as ants to a
picnic, as the boll weevil to a cotton field.
  **Joseph Mankiewicz, screenplay for *All About Eve*, 1950**

A drama critic is a man who leaves no turn unstoned.
  **George Bernard Shaw, quoted in the *New York Times*, 1950**

Be fairly ruthless, I think, with opponents of 'modern' painting. If you are lucky enough to find a man who still says 'I don't know about pictures but I know what I like' point out to him that because he does not know about pictures he does not know what he likes and repeat this in a thundering voice . . . If your man says of some picture 'Yes, but what does it mean?' ask him, and keep on asking him, what his carpet means, or the circular patterns on his rubber overshoes. Make him lift up his foot to look at them.

**Stephen Potter, *One-Upmanship*, 1952**

What critics call 'dirty' in our films they call 'lusty' in foreign films.

**Billy Wilder**

Critics are like eunuchs in a harem: they know how it's done, they've seen it done every day, but they're unable to do it themselves.

**Brendan Behan**

Reviewmanship . . . 'how to be one up on the author without actually tampering with the text'. In other words how, as a critic, to show that it is really yourself who should have written the book, if you had had the time, and since you hadn't are glad that someone else has, although obviously it might have been done better.

**Stephen Potter, *Supermanship*, 1958**

The avocation of assessing the failures of better men can be turned into a comfortable livelihood, providing you back it up with a Ph.D.

**Nelson Algren, *Writers at Work* 1st series, 1958**

Critics are eunuchs at a gang-bang.

**George Burns**

A critic is a bundle of biases held loosely together by a sense of taste.

**Whitney Balliett, *Dinosaurs in the Morning*, 1962**

Asking a working writer what he feels about critics is like asking a lamp-post what it feels about dogs.

**John Osborne**

A critic is a man who knows the way but can't drive the car.

**Kenneth Tynan, in the *New York Times*, 1966**

Friendly attacks should begin with faint praise, but be careful not to use adjectives or phrases of which the publisher can make use in advertisements.

**John Betjeman**

It is wrong to read the books one reviews – it creates a prejudice.
**George Croly**

A good review from the critics is just another stay of execution.
**Dustin Hoffman, quoted in *Playboy* magazine, 1975**

A drama critic is a person who surprises a playwright by informing him what he meant.
**Wilson Mizner, quoted in *The People's Almanac*, 1976**

Criticism of the arts . . . taken by and large, ends in a display of suburban omniscience which sees no further than into the next-door garden.
**Sir Thomas Beecham, quoted in *Beecham Stories* by Harold Atkins and Archie Newman, 1978**

I read a good deal of criticism, but only as a vice: not so good as reading science fiction, rather better than reading mystery stories.
**Gore Vidal**

Pop music is the kind played so fast that you can't work out which classical composer it was pinched from.
**Anonymous**

*See also* ACTING, WRITING

# CULTURE

Mass culture: a contradiction in terms.
**Anonymous**

Culture is an instrument wielded by professors to manufacture professors, who when their turn comes, will manufacture professors.
**Simone Weil, *The Need for Roots*, 1952**

Great cultural changes begin in affectation and end in routine.
**Jacques Barzun, *The House of Intellect*, 1959**

It is only the middle-class people who, quite mistakenly, imagine that a lively pursuit of the latest in reading or painting will advance their status in the world.
**Mary McCarthy, *On the Contrary*, 1962**

The old complaint that mass culture is designed for eleven-year-olds is of course a shameful canard. The key age has traditionally been more like fourteen.

**Robert Christgau, in *Esquire* magazine, 1969**

It strikes me as gruesome and comical that in our culture we have an expectation that a man can always solve his problems. This is so untrue that it makes me want to cry – or laugh.

**Kurt Vonnegut Jr, in *Playboy* magazine, 1973**

Culture . . . television programmes so boring that they cannot be classified as entertainment.

**Quentin Crisp, *How To Become a Virgin*, 1981**

Mass culture is a machine for showing desire. Here is what must interest you, it says, as if it guessed that men are incapable of finding out what to desire by themselves.

**Roland Barthes, quoted in the *New York Review of Books*, 1982**

# CYNICISM

Cynic, n. A blackguard whose faulty vision sees things as they are, not as they ought to be.

**Ambrose Bierce, *The Devil's Dictionary*, 1911**

A cynic is not merely one who reads bitter lessons from the past, he is one who is prematurely disappointed in the future.

**Sydney J. Harris, *On the Contrary*, 1962**

Cynicism: an extension of ennui maintaining that not only are you bored, you are in a state of disbelief as well. And you cannot be convinced otherwise . . . more than a pose; it's also a handy time saver. By deflating your companion's enthusiasm, you can cut conversations in half.

**Lisa Bernbach, *The Official Preppy Handbook*, 1981**

*See also* TRUTH

# DEATH

Death is life's answer to the question 'Why?'

**Graffito**

I desire to go hell, not heaven. In hell I shall enjoy the company of popes, kings and princes, but in heaven are only beggars, monks, hermits and apostles.

**Niccolò Machiavelli, on his deathbed, 1527**

Six feet of earth make all men equal.

**James Howell, *Proverbs*, 1659**

O Death, all-eloquent! you only prove
What dust we dote on, when 'tis man we love.

**Alexander Pope, *Eloisa to Abelard*, 1717**

The first breath is the beginning of death.

**Thomas Fuller, M.D., *Gnomologia*, 1732**

I know of nobody that has a mind to die this year.

**Thomas Fuller, M.D., *Gnomologia*, 1732**

In this world, nothing can be said to be certain but death and taxes.

**Benjamin Franklin, letter, 1789**

I have no relish for the country: it is a kind of grave.

**Sydney Smith, letter, 1838**

The play is the tragedy 'Man'
And its hero the conqueror, Worm.

**Edgar Allen Poe, *The Raven and Other Poems*, 1845**

To beings constituted as we are the monotony of singing psalms would be as great an affliction as the pains of hell, and might even be pleasantly interrupted by them.

**Benjamin Jowett, from his introduction to Plato's *Phaedo*, 1871**

It is not true that the dying man is generally more honest than the living. On the contrary, by the solemn attitude of the by-standers and the flowing or repressed streams of tears, everyone present is now inveigled into a comedy of vanity, now conscious, now unconscious.

**Friedrich Wilhelm Nietzsche, *Human, All Too Human*, 1878**

Nowhere probably is there more true feeling, and nowhere worse taste, than in a churchyard.

**Benjamin Jowett, *Letters*, 1899**

Razors pain you;
Rivers are damp;
Acids stain you;
And drugs cause cramp.
Guns aren't lawful;
Nooses give;
Gas smells awful;
You might as well live.

**Dorothy Parker,** *Résumé*, **1926**

De mortuis nil nisi bunkum.

**Harold Laski**

A single death is a tragedy, a million deaths is a statistic.

**Joseph Stalin**

The living are the dead on holiday.

**Maurice Maeterlinck**

All our knowledge merely helps us to die a more painful death than
the animals that know nothing.

**Maurice Maeterlinck**

I have no need of your God-damned sympathy. I only wish to be entertained by some of your grosser reminiscences.

**Alexander Woollcott, to a visitor during his last illness, 1943**

Millions long for immortality who do not know what to do with
themselves on a rainy Sunday afternoon.

**Susan Ertz,** *Anger in the Sky*, **1943**

One wants to stay alive, of course, but one only stays alive by virtue
of the fear of death.

**George Orwell,** *Shooting an Elephant*, **1950**

Many a man has decided to stay alive not because of the will to live,
but because of the determination not to give assorted surviving bastards
the satisfaction of his death.

**Brendan Francis**

Dying is a very dull, dreary affair. My advice to you is to have nothing
whatever to do with it.

**W. Somerset Maugham, attributed as his last words, 1965**

Don't look forward to the day when you stop suffering. Because when it comes you'll know that you're dead.

**Tennessee Williams, in the *Observer*, 1958**

Many men on the point of an edifying death would be furious if they were suddenly restored to health.

**Cesare Pavese, quoted in *The Faber Book of Aphorisms*, ed. W.H. Auden and L. Kronenberger, 1964**

For the unhappy man death is the commutation of a sentence of life imprisonment.

**Alexander Chase, *Perspectives*, 1966**

The destruction of this planet would have no significance on a cosmic scale. To an observer in the Andromeda nebula, the sign of our extinction would be no more than a match flaring for a second in the heavens.

**Stanley Kubrick**

Death is nature's way of telling you to slow down.

**Severn Darden**

Every suicide is a solution to a problem.

**Jean Baechler, *Suicides*, 1980**

We all end up as packaged goods.

**Westbrook Pegler, quoted in the *New York Review of Books*, 1981**

The past is the only dead thing that smells sweet.

**Cyril Connolly, *Journal 1928–1937*, ed. D. Pryce-Jones, 1983**

*See also* AGE

# DECENCY

The only way for a woman to provide for herself decently is for her to be good to some man that can afford to be good to her.

**George Bernard Shaw, *Mrs Warren's Profession*, 1898**

Decency is indecency's conspiracy of silence.

**George Bernard Shaw, *Maxims for Revolutionists*, 1903**

All decent people live beyond their incomes nowadays, and those who aren't respectable live beyond other people's. A few gifted individuals manage to do both.

**Saki (H.H. Munro),** *The Match-maker,* **1911**

When you have told anyone you have left them a legacy the only decent thing to do is to die at once.

**Samuel Butler,** *Notebooks,* **1912**

Decency . . . must be an even more exhausting state to maintain than its opposite. Those who succeed seem to need a stupefying amount of sleep.

**Quentin Crisp,** *The Naked Civil Servant,* **1968**

*See also* HONESTY

# DEMOCRACY

A democracy is a government in the hands of men of low birth, no property and vulgar employments.

**Aristotle,** *Politics,* **c.322BC**

Democracy is an aristocracy of blackguards.

**George Gordon, Lord Byron**

Democracy gives every man the right to be his own oppressor.

**James Russell Lowell**

Democracy becomes a government of bullies, tempered by editors.

**Ralph Waldo Emerson,** *Journals,* **1909–14**

Universal suffrage is the government of a house by its nursery.

**Otto von Bismarck**

High hopes were once formed of democracy, but democracy means simply the bludgeoning of the people, by the people, for the people.

**Oscar Wilde,** *The Soul of Man under Socialism,* **1891**

Parliaments are the great lie of our time.

**Konstantin Pobedonostsev, 1896**

Democracy substitutes election by the incompetent many for appointment by the corrupt few.

**George Bernard Shaw, *Man and Superman*, 1903**

Democracy is the name we give to the people each time we need them.

**Robert, Marquis de Flers and Arman de Cavaillet, *L'habit vert*, 1912**

Democracy is the art of running the circus from the monkey cage.

**H.L. Mencken, *Sententiae*, 1916**

Democracy is a form of religion. It is the worship of jackals by jackasses.

**H.L. Mencken, *Sententiae*, 1916**

That a peasant may become king does not render the kingdom democratic.

**Woodrow Wilson, 1917**

A democracy is a state which recognises the subjection of the minority to the majority, that is, an organisation for the systematic use of violence by one class against another, by one part of the population against another.

**V.I. Lenin, *The State and Revolution*, 1917**

Democracy is the theory that the common people know what they want, and deserve to get it good and hard.

**H.L. Mencken, *A Book of Burlesques*, 1920**

The most popular man under a democracy is not the most democratic man, but the most despotic man. The common folk delight in the exactions of such a man. They like him to boss them. Their natural gait is the goosestep.

**H.L. Mencken**

Democracy is a device which ensures that we shall be governed no better than we deserve.

**George Bernard Shaw**

Democracy is grounded upon so childish a complex of fallacies that they must be protected by a rigid system of taboos, else even halfwits would argue it to pieces. Its first concern must thus be to penalise the free play of ideas.

**H.L. Mencken, *In Defence of Women*, 1923**

An honest politician will not be tolerated by a democracy unless he is very stupid . . . because only a very stupid man can honestly share the prejudices of more than half the nation.

**Bertrand Russell, Presidential Address to LSE students, 1923**

Democracy . . . a form of government by popular ignorance.

**Kin Hubbard, 1923**

A man may have strong humanitarian and democratic principles, but if he happens to have been brought up as a bath-taking, shirt-changing lover of fresh air, he will have to overcome certain physical repugnances before he can bring himself to put these principles into practice.

**Aldous Huxley, *Jesting Pilate*, 1926**

The democratic disease which expresses its tyranny by reducing everything to the level of the herd.

**Henry Miller, *The Wisdom of the Heart*, 1941**

In Switzerland they had brotherly love, five hundred years of democracy and peace and what did they produce? The cuckoo clock!

**Orson Welles and Graham Greene, screenplay for *The Third Man*, 1949**

Democracy: in which you say what you like and do what you're told.

**Gerald Barry**

Our great democracies still tend to think that a stupid man is more likely to become honest than a clever man and our politicians take advantage of this by pretending to be even more stupid than nature made them.

**Bertrand Russell, *New Hopes for a Changing World*, 1951**

The blind lead the blind. It's the democratic way.

**Henry Miller, *The Air-conditioned Nightmare*, 1945**

Under democracy, one party always devotes its chief energies to trying to prove that the other party is unfit to rule – and both commonly succeed, and are right.

**H.L. Mencken, *Minority Report*, 1956**

Democracy: a festival of mediocrity.

**E.M. Cioran**

Democracy is the art of saying 'Nice doggie' until you can find a rock.
**Wynn Catlin**

Those who set out nobly to be their brother's keeper sometimes end up by becoming his jailer. Every emancipation has in it the seeds of a new slavery, and every truth easily becomes a lie.
**I.F. Stone, 1969**

The House of Commons: the longest running farce in the West End.
**Cyril Smith, 1973**

Democracy consists of choosing your dictators, after they've told you what it is you think you want to hear.
**Alan Coren, in the *Daily Mail*, 1975**

Democracy is a process by which the people are free to choose the man who will get the blame.
**Laurence J. Peter, *Peter's Quotations*, 1977**

Democracy is an abuse of statistics.
**Jorge Luis Borges, quoted in *Prisoner Without a Name, Cell Without a Number* by Jacobo Timerman, 1981**

Democracy is supposed to give you the feeling of choice, like Painkiller X and Painkiller Y. But they're both just aspirin.
**Gore Vidal, quoted in the *Observer*, 1982**

Democrats are the party of government activism, the party that says government can make you richer, smarter, taller and get the chickweed out of your lawn. Republicans are the party that says government doesn't work, and then they get elected and prove it.
**P.J. O'Rourke, *Parliament of Whores*, 1991**

Now majority rule is a precious, sacred thing worth dying for. But – like other precious, sacred things . . . it's not only worth dying for; it can make you wish you were dead. Imagine if all life were determined by majority rule. Every meal would be a pizza.
**P.J. O'Rourke, *Parliament of Whores*, 1991**

*See also* ARISTOCRACY, EQUALITY, GOVERNMENT, LEADERS, POLITICS, POWER, VOTING

# DIPLOMACY

An ambassador is an honest man sent abroad to lie for the good of his country.

**Sir Henry Wotton, written in the autograph album of Christopher Fleckamore, 1604**

I have discovered the art of deceiving diplomats: I speak the truth and they never believe me.

**Camillo di Cavour**

How is the world ruled and how do wars start? Diplomats tell lies to journalists, and they believe what they read.

**Karl Kraus, *Aphorisms and More Aphorisms*, 1909**

Diplomats: babies in silk hats playing with dynamite.

**Alexander Woollcott**

He seemed such a nice old gentleman I thought I would give him my autograph as a souvenir.

**Adolf Hitler, on signing the Munich Pact; 'he' is Neville Chamberlain, 1938**

Sincere diplomacy is no more possible than dry water or wooden iron.

**Joseph Stalin**

Power politics is the diplomatic name for the law of the jungle.

**Ely Culbertson, *Must We Fight Russia?*, 1946**

An appeaser is one who feeds a crocodile – hoping that it will eat him last.

**Sir Winston Churchill, 1954**

All diplomacy is a continuation of war by other means.

**Chou En-lai, 1954**

British education is probably the best in the world, if you can survive it. If you can't there is nothing left for you but the diplomatic corps.

**Peter Ustinov**

A diplomat is a person who can tell you to go to hell in such a way that you actually look forward to the trip.

**Caskie Stinnett, *Out of the Red*, 1960**

One function of diplomacy is to dress realism in morality.
   **Will and Ariel Durant**

Treaties are like roses and young girls – they last while they last.
   **Charles de Gaulle, 1963**

Diplomacy is letting someone else have your way.
   **Lester Pearson, 1965**

A real diplomat is one who can cut his neighbour's throat without having his neighbour notice it.
   **Trygve Lie**

Personal diplomacy has caused a lot of mischief and harm . . . It leads to a very great fallacy, the almost pathetic belief of some Foreign Ministers, that if they had lunch with someone and called him by his Christian name, they have changed the fundamental facts of relationships between nations.
   **Sir Paul Hasluck, 1982**

Diplomacy is about surviving until the next century. Politics is about surviving until Friday afternon.
   **Antony Jay and Jonathan Lynn,** *Yes, Prime Minister,* **1986**

Foreign aid is taxing poor people in rich countries for the benefit of rich people in poor countries.
   **Bernard Rosenberg**

*See also* PATRIOTISM

# DIVORCE

Divorce is probably of nearly the same date as marriage. I believe, however, that marriage is some weeks the more ancient.
   **Voltaire,** *Philosophical Dictionary,* **1764**

Alimony: the fine for speeding in the joy-ride of matrimony.
   **Oliver Herford and John Clay,** *Cupid's Cyclopedia,* **1910**

Wedding: a necessary formality before securing a divorce.
   **Oliver Herford and John Clay,** *Cupid's Cyclopedia,* **1910**

Love, the quest, marriage, the conquest; divorce, the inquest.
  **Helen Rowland**

Alimony – the ransom that the happy pay to the devil.
  **H.L. Mencken, *A Book of Burlesques*, 1920**

Judges, as a class, display, in the matter of arranging alimony, that reckless generosity which is found only in men who are giving away someone else's cash.
  **P.G. Wodehouse, *Louder and Funnier*, 1932**

Alimony is like buying oats for a dead horse.
  **Arthur Baer**

They say that in America marriage counts as reasonable grounds for divorce.
  **William Douglas-Home, *The Manor of Northstead*, 1954**

You don't know a woman until you've met her in court.
  **Norman Mailer**

The *vie de bohème* is a way of life that has two formidable enemies – time and marriage. Even hooligans marry, though they know that marriage is but for a little while. It is alimony that is for ever.
  **Quentin Crisp, *The Naked Civil Servant*, 1968**

There are four stages to a marriage. First there's the affair, then there's the marriage, then children and finally the fourth stage, without which you cannot know a woman, the divorce.
  **Norman Mailer, in *Nova* magazine, 1969**

Insanity is considered a ground for divorce, though by the very same token it is the shortest detour to marriage.
  **Wilson Mizner, quoted in *The People's Almanac*, 1976**

Alimony is the curse of the writing classes.
  **Norman Mailer, 1980**

*See also* AFFAIRS, HUSBANDS, LOVE, LOVERS, MARRIAGE, WIVES

# DRINK

The wages of Gin is Debt.

**Addison Mizner and Oliver Herford, *The Entirely New Cynic's Calendar*, 1905**

Alcohol is a very necessary article . . . It enables Parliament to do things at eleven at night that no sane person would do at eleven in the morning.

**George Bernard Shaw, *Major Barbara*, 1907**

Abstainer, n. A weak person who yields to the temptation of denying himself a pleasure.

**Ambrose Bierce, *The Devil's Dictionary*, 1911**

Drinking makes such fools of people, and people are such fools to begin with, that it's compounding a felony.

**Robert Benchley**

Drink and dance and laugh and lie,
Love, the reeling midnight through
For tomorrow we shall die!
(But, alas, we never do.)

**Dorothy Parker, *The Flaw in Paganism*, 1931**

An alcoholic is someone you don't like who drinks as much as you do.

**Dylan Thomas, quoted in *Life of Dylan Thomas* by Constantine Fitzgibbon, 1965**

Work is the curse of the drinking classes.

**Mike Romanoff**

Ladies and Gentlemen, I give you a toast. It is: Absinthe makes the tart grow fonder!

**Hugh Drummond, quoted in *The Vintage Years* by Seymour Hicks, 1943**

Alcohol is like love: the first kiss is magic, the second is intimate, the third is routine. After that you just take the girl's clothes off.

**Raymond Chandler, *The Long Goodbye*, 1953**

Fishing, with me, has always been an excuse to drink in the daytime.

**Jimmy Cannon, quoted in *No Cheering in the Pressbox*
by J. Holtzman, 1973**

Drunks are rarely amusing unless they know some good songs and lose a lot at poker.

**Karl Roosevelt, in the *New York Times*, 1975**

Most . . . drugs are self-limiting. If you drink you act like hell. But if you keep drinking you pass out. Then your battered wife sets fire to your bed and Farrah Fawcett stars in the TV movie about your brief, sorry life.

**P.J. O'Rourke, *Parliament of Whores*, 1991**

# DULLNESS

Anger makes dull men witty – but it keeps them poor.

**Francis Bacon**

What age was not dull? When were not the majority wicked? or what progress was ever made by society? Society is always flat and foolish.

**Ralph Waldo Emerson, 1850**

Dullness is the coming of age of seriousness.

**Oscar Wilde, *Phrases and Philosophies for the Use of the Young*, 1894**

Dullness is the first requisite of a good husband.

**W. Somerset Maugham, *Lady Frederick*, 1907**

It is the dull man who is always sure and the sure man who is always dull.

**H.L. Mencken, *Prejudices* 2nd series, 1922**

The trouble with telling a good story is that it invariably reminds the other fellow of a dull one.

**Sid Caesar**

The first requirement of a statesman is that he be dull. This is not always easy to achieve.

**Dean Acheson, 1970**

# DUTY

Whenever one person is found adequate to the discharge of a duty by close application thereto, it is worse executed by two persons and scarcely done at all if three or more are employed therein.

**George Washington**

The absurd duty, so often inculcated, of obeying a parent only on account of his being a parent, shackles the mind, and prepares it for a slavish submission to any power but reason.

**Mary Wollstonecraft, *A Vindication of the Rights of Woman*, 1792**

Duty is what one expects from others.

**Oscar Wilde, *A Woman of No Importance*, 1893**

When a stupid man is doing something he is ashamed of, he always declares that it is his duty.

**George Bernard Shaw, *Caesar and Cleopatra*, 1901**

Most affections are habits or duties we lack the courage to end.

**Henry de Montherlant, *Queen After Death*, 1942**

# EDUCATION

Classical education in the English public schools consists of casting sham pearls in front of real swine.

**Anonymous**

The Vanity of teaching often tempteth a Man to forget he is a Blockhead.

**George Savile, Marquis of Halifax, *Political, Moral and Miscellaneous Thoughts and Reflexions*, c.1694**

Education is what remains when we have forgotten all that we have been taught.

**George Savile, Marquis of Halifax, *Political, Moral and Miscellaneous Thoughts and Reflexions*, c.1694**

An English university is a sanctuary in which exploded systems and obsolete prejudices find shelter and protection after they have been hunted out of every corner of the world.

**Adam Smith, *The Wealth of Nations*, 1776**

Anyone who has passed through the regular gradations of a classical education, and is not made a fool by it, may consider himself as having had a very narrow escape.

**William Hazlitt, *The Ignorance of the Learned*, 1821**

A scholar is a man with this inconvenience, that, when you ask him his opinion of any matter, he must go home and look up his manuscripts to know.

**Ralph Waldo Emerson**

In large states public education will always be mediocre, for the same reason that in large kitchens the cooking is usually bad.

**Friedrich Wilhelm Nietzsche, *Human, All Too Human*, 1878**

The universities are a sort of lunatic asylum for keeping young men out of mischief.

**Bishop Mandell Creighton**

Education is fatal to anyone with a spark of artistic feeling. Education should be confined to clerks, and even them it drives to drink.

**George Moore, *Confessions of a Young Man*, 1888**

A college is a place where pebbles are polished and diamonds dimmed.

**Robert G. Ingersoll**

What is the task of higher education? To make man into a machine. What are the means employed? He is taught how to suffer being bored.

**Friedrich Wilhelm Nietzsche, *The Twilight of the Idols*, 1889**

Education is an admirable thing, but it is well to remember from time to time that nothing that is worth knowing can be taught.

**Oscar Wilde, *The Critic as Artist*, 1891**

Education is what you must acquire without any interference from your schooling.

**Mark Twain**

It is only the learned who care to learn, the ignorant who prefer to teach.

**Edouard Le Berquier**

In an examination those who do not wish to know ask questions of those who cannot tell.

**Sir Walter Raleigh**

A musical education is necessary for musical judgement. What most people relish is hardly music; it is rather a drowsy reverie relieved by nervous thrills.

**George Santayana, *The Life of Reason*, 1905–6**

It doesn't make much difference what you study so long as you hate it.

**Finley Peter Dunne, *Mr Dooley Remembers*, 1910**

You can't expect a boy to be vicious until he's been to a good school.

**Saki (H.H.Munro), *The Baker's Dozen*, 1910**

Education is a state-controlled manufactory of echoes.

**Norman Douglas**

University: . . . a place where rich men send their sons who have no aptitude for business.

**Kin Hubbard, 1923**

Education is the inculcation of the incomprehensible into the indifferent by the incompetent.

**John Maynard Keynes**

I have been in the scholastic profession long enough to know that nobody enters it unless he has some very good reason that he is anxious to conceal.

**Evelyn Waugh, *Decline and Fall*, 1928**

The difference between intelligence and education is this: intelligence will make you a good living.

**Charles F. Kettering**

Teaching is the last refuge of feeble minds with a classical education.

**Aldous Huxley**

A professor is a man whose job is to tell students how to solve the problems of life which he himself has tried to avoid by becoming a professor.

**Anonymous**

The first star a child gets in school for the mere performance of a needful task is its first lesson in graft.

**Philip Wylie, *Generation of Vipers*, 1942**

The average Ph.D. thesis is nothing but the transference of bones from one graveyard to another.

**J. Frank Dobie, *A Texan in England*, 1945**

I am inclined to think that one's education has been in vain if one fails to learn that most schoolmasters are idiots.

**Hesketh Pearson**

Education is what survives when what has been learnt has been forgotten.

**B.F. Skinner, quoted in the *New Scientist* magazine, 1964**

Education, the great mumbo-jumbo and fraud of the age, purports to equip us to live and is prescribed as a universal remedy for everything from juvenile delinquency to premature senility. For the most part it only serves to enlarge stupidity, inflate conceit, enchance credulity and put those subjected to it at the mercy of brain-washers with printing, presses, radio and TV at their disposal.

**Malcolm Muggeridge, in the *Observer*, 1966**

An education enables you to earn more than an educator.

**Anonymous, quoted in *Resistance to Knowledge*
by Hans Gaffron, 1970**

That's the trouble with these people who went to state schools. They don't know how to confuse the public.

**Alexander Buzo, *Martello Towers*, 1976**

Education is a method whereby one acquires a higher grade of prejudices.

**Laurence J. Peter, *Peter's Quotations*, 1977**

Fourteen years in the professor dodge has taught me that one can argue ingeniously on behalf of any theory, applied to any piece of literature. This is rarely harmful, because normally no-one reads such essays.

**Robert B. Parker, quoted in *Murder Ink*, ed. D. Wynn, 1977**

Education is a progressive discovery of our own ignorance.

**Will Durant, quoted in the *National Enquirer*, 1980**

Do know the difference between education and experience? Education is when you read the fine print; experience is what you get when you don't.

**Pete Seeger, quoted in *Loose Talk*, ed. L. Botts, 1980**

Educational television should be absolutely forbidden. It can only lead to unreasonable disappointment when your child discovers that the letters of the alphabet do not leap up out of books and dance around with royal-blue chickens.

**Fran Lebowitz, *Social Studies*, 1981**

Of all human activities, education is the one most likely to give rise to cant, pomposity and fraudulent expertise.

**John Rae, in the *Observer*, 1983**

Education is what most people receive, many pass on and few have.

**Karl Kraus, *Half Truths and One and a Half Truths*, 1986**

# EGOTISM

A cock has great influence on his own dunghill.

**Publilius Syrus, *Moral Sayings*, c.50BC**

What makes other people's vanity intolerable is that it wounds our own.

**François, Duc de La Rochefoucauld, *Maxims*, 1665**

The reason why so few people are agreeable in conversation is that each is thinking more about what he intends to say than about what others are saying, and we never listen when we are eager to speak.

**François, Duc de La Rochefoucauld, *Maxims*, 1665**

We would rather speak of ourselves than not talk at all.

**François, Duc de La Rochefoucauld, *Maxims*, 1665**

It is as easy to deceive oneself without perceiving it as it is difficult to deceive others without their perceiving it.

**François, Duc de La Rochefoucauld, *Maxims*, 1665**

If the commending others did not recommend ourselves, there would be few panegyrics.

**George Savile, Marquis of Halifax, *Political Moral and Miscellaneous Thoughts and Reflexions*, c.1694**

The greatest magnifying glasses in the world are a man's own eyes when they look upon his own person.

**Alexander Pope, letter, 1705**

I must complain the cards are ill-shuffled, until I have a good hand.
  **Jonathan Swift**

There are many things we despise in order that we may not have to despise ourselves.
  **Luc de Clapiers, Marquis Vauvenargues, *Reflections and Maxims*, 1746**

No cause more frequently produces bashfulness than too high an opinion of our own importance.
  **Samuel Johnson, *The Rambler*, 1749–52**

Pride is a vice which pride itself inclines every man to find in others and to overlook in himself.
  **Samuel Johnson, *Works* vol. vi, 1787**

He who is in love with himself has at least this advantage – he won't encounter many rivals.
  **Georg Christoph Lichtenberg, *Aphorisms*, 1764–99**

There is nothing more likely to betray a man into absurdity than condecension when he seems to suppose his understanding too powerful for his company.
  **Samuel Johnson, *The Life of Samuel Johnson* by J. Boswell, 1791**

We grow tired of everything but turning others into ridicule and congratulating ourselves on their defects.
  **William Hazlitt, *The Plain Speaker*, 1826**

We are not satisfied to be right, unless we can prove others to be quite wrong.
  **William Hazlitt, *Conversations*, 1830**

We go on fancying that each man is thinking of us, but he is not; he is like us: he is thinking of himself.
  **Charles Reade**

Apology is only egotism wrong side out.
  **Oliver Wendell Holmes**

We do what we must, and call it by the best names.
  **Ralph Waldo Emerson**

It is in the ability to deceive oneself that one shows the greatest talent.
   **Anatole France**

'I have done that', says my memory. 'I cannot have done that', says my pride, and remains silent. At last – memory yields.
   **Friedrich Wilhelm Nietzsche, *Beyond Good and Evil*, 1886**

He who despises himself nevertheless esteems himself as a self-despiser.
   **Friedrich Wilhelm Nietzsche**

The only thing that consoles man for the stupid things he does is the praise he always gives himself for doing them.
   **Oscar Wilde**

Modesty: the gentle art of enhancing your charm by pretending not to be aware of it.
   **Oliver Herford**

The least pain in our little finger gives us more concern and uneasiness than the destruction of millions of our fellow-beings.
   **William Hazlitt, *Collected Works*, 1904**

Caution is the confidential agent of selfishness.
   **Woodrow Wilson, speech, 1909**

Admiration, n. Our polite recognition of another's resemblance to ourselves.
   **Ambrose Bierce, *The Devil's Dictionary*, 1911**

Egotist, n. A person of low taste, more interested in himself than in me.
   **Ambrose Bierce, *The Devil's Dictionary*, 1911**

If one hides one's talent under a bushel, one must be careful to point out the exact bushel under which it is hidden.
   **Saki (H.H. Munro), *The Unbearable Bassington*, 1912**

The craving to be understood may in the end be the merest egoism.
   **F.H. Bradley, *Essay on Truth and Reality*, 1914**

Self-respect – the secure feeling that no-one, as yet, is suspicious.
   **H.L. Mencken, *Sententiae*, 1916**

Vanity is other people's pride.

**Sacha Guitry**

We don't ask others to be faultless, we only ask that their faults should not incommode our own.

**Gyp, quoted in *A Cynic's Breviary* by J.R. Solly, 1925**

One is vain by nature, modest by necessity.

**Pierre Reverdy, *En vrac*, 1956**

Most people have a furious itch to talk about themselves and are restrained only by the disinclination of others to listen. Reserve is an artificial quality that is developed in most of us as the result of inumerable rebuffs.

**W. Somerset Maugham, *The Summing Up*, 1938**

Sentimentality – that's what we call the sentiment we don't share.

**Graham Greene**

The most difficult secret for a man to keep is his own opinion of himself.

**Marcel Pagnol, 1954**

Egotism is the anaesthetic that dulls the pain of stupidity.

**Frank Leary, in *Look* magazine, 1955**

Men are not against you; they are merely for themselves.

**Gene Fowler, *Skyline*, 1961**

Innocence ends when one is stripped of the delusion that one likes oneself.

**Joan Didion, *On Self Respect*, 1961**

Every stink that fights the ventilator thinks it is Don Quixote.

**Stanislaw J. Lec, *Unkempt Thoughts*, 1962**

If you do not raise your eyes, you will think that you are the highest point.

**Antonio Porchia, *Voces*, 1968**

Confidence is simply that quiet, assured feeling you have before you fall flat on your face.

**Dr L. Binder, quoted in *Quote and Unquote*, 1970**

The only time to believe any kind of rating is when it shows you at the top.

**Bob Hope, quoted in *Playboy* magazine, 1973**

Words of delight, praise and enthusiasm are like visiting-cards. The bigger the card, the less important the man; the bigger the word, the less important the emotion.

**Francis King, in *The Listener* magazine, 1978**

What matters isn't just that I should win, it's that you should lose.

**Anonymous**

*See also* BORES

# ELECTIONS

People never lie so much as after a hunt, during a war or before an election.

**Otto von Bismarck**

Bad officials are elected by good citizens who do not vote.

**George Jean Nathan**

In general, we elect men of the type that subscribes to only one principle – to get re-elected.

**Terry M. Townshend, speech 1940**

Whatever politicians, activists and manipulators propose, it is the phlegmatic, indifferent, ingrained electorate which disposes.

**Don Aitkin, quoted, 1969**

Lansdale seized on the idea of using Nixon to build support for the [Vietnamese] elections . . . really honest elections, this time. 'Oh, sure, honest, yes, that's right,' Nixon said, 'so long as you win!' With that he winked, drove his elbow into Lansdale's arm and slapped his own knee.

**Richard M. Nixon, quoted in *Sideshow* by William Shawcross, 1979**

*See also* AMBITION, APPLAUSE, FAME, SUCCESS

# ENEMIES

The pleasantest laughter is at the expense of our enemies.
  **Sophocles, *Ajax*, c.450BC**

Our years, our debts, and our enemies are always more numerous than
we imagine.
  **Charles Nodier**

One should forgive one's enemies, but not before they are hanged.
  **Heinrich Heine**

Contempt, n. The feeling of a prudent man for an enemy who is too
formidable safely to be opposed.
  **Ambrose Bierce, *The Devil's Dictionary*, 1911**

What is important is food, money and opportunities for scoring off
one's enemies. Give a man these three things and you won't hear much
squawking out of him.
  **Brian O'Nolan, *The Best of Myles*, 1968**

An enemy is someone you haven't seen for a while.
  **Bob Ellis, 1977**

*See also* HATRED

# ENGLAND

The people of England are never so happy as when you tell them they
are ruined.
  **Arthur Murray, *The Upholsterer*, 1758**

The English people fancy they are free; it is only during the election
of Members of Parliament that they are so. As soon as these are elected
the people are slaves . . . In the brief moments of their liberation the
abuse made of it fully deserves that it should be lost.
  **Jean-Jacques Rousseau, *The Social Contract*, 1761**

It is only necessary to raise a bugbear before the English imagination
in order to govern it at will. Whatever they hate or fear, they implicitly
believe in, merely from the scope it gives to these passions.
  **William Hazlitt, *The Life of Napoleon Buonaparte*, 1828–30**

Silence can be defined as a conversation with an Englishman.
  **Heinrich Heine**

We know of no spectacle so ridiculous as the British public in one of its periodical fits of morality.
  **Thomas Babington Macaulay, Baron Macaulay, in the**
  **Edinburgh Review, 1831**

One has often wondered whether upon the whole earth there is anything so unintelligent, so unapt to perceive how the world is really going as an ordinary young Englishman of our upper class.
  **Matthew Arnold, Culture and Anarchy, 1869**

In our English popular religion the common conception of a future state of bliss is that of . . . a kind of perfected middle-class home, with labour ended, the table spread, goodness all around, the lost ones restored, hymnody incessant.
  **Matthew Arnold, Literature and Dogma, 1873**

The Englishman has all the qualities of a poker, except its occasional warmth.
  **Daniel O'Connell**

In England it is enough for a man to try and produce any serious, beautiful work to lose all his rights as a citizen.
  **Oscar Wilde, lecture, 1882**

To disagree with three-fourths of the British public on all points is one of the first elements of sanity, one of the deepest consolations in all moments of spiritual doubt.
  **Oscar Wilde, lecture, 1882**

Freedom of discussion is in England little else than the right to write or say anything which a jury of twelve shopkeepers think it expedient should be said or written.
  **A.V. Dicey, Introduction to the Study of the Law of the**
  **Constitution, 1885**

Thinking is the most unhealthy thing in the world, and people die of it just as they die of any other disease. Fortunately, in England at any rate, thought is not catching.
  **Oscar Wilde, The Decay of Lying, 1891**

An Englishman does everything on principle: he fights you on patriotic principles; he robs you on business principles; he enslaves you on imperial principles.

**George Bernard Shaw, *The Man of Destiny*, 1898**

Englishmen never will be slaves; they are free to do whatever the government and public opinion allow them.

**George Bernard Shaw, *Man and Superman*, 1903**

'English fair play' is a fine expression. It justifies the bashing of the puny draper's assistant by the big hairy blacksmith, and this to the perfect satisfaction of both parties, if they are worthy the name of Englishman.

**Joseph Furphy, *Such Is Life*, 1903**

In England we have come to rely upon a comfortable time-lag or a century intervening between the perception that something ought to be done and a serious attempt to do it.

**H.G. Wells, *The Work, Wealth and Happiness of Mankind*, 1934**

The English instinctively admire any man who has no talent and is modest about it.

**James Agate, *Ego*, 1935–48**

It pays in England to be a revolutionary and a bible-smacker most of one's life, and then come round.

**Lord Alfred Douglas, 1938**

Continental people have a sex life; the English have hot-water bottles.

**George Mikes, *How To Be an Alien*, 1946**

In Germany democracy died by the headsman's axe. In Britain it can be by pernicious anaemia.

**Aneurin Bevan**

The attitude of the English towards English history reminds one a good deal of the attitude of a Hollywood director towards love.

**Margaret Halsey, *With Malice Toward Some*, 1938**

The English never smash in a face. They merely refrain from asking it to dinner.

**Margaret Halsey, *With Malice Toward Some*, 1938**

A ready means of being cherished by the English is to adopt the simple expedient of living a long time.

**Malcolm Muggeridge, in *Esquire* magazine, 1961**

Fay: The British police force used to be run by men of integrity. Truscott: That is a mistake which has been rectified.

**Joe Orton, *Loot*, 1966**

The English think that incompetence is the same thing as sincerity.

**Quentin Crisp, in the *New York Times*, 1977**

About one thing the Englishman has a particularly strict code. If a bird says 'Cluk bik bik bik bik' and 'caw' you may kill it, eat it or ask Fortnums to pickle it in Napoleon brandy with wild strawberries. If it says 'tweet' it is a dear and precious friend and you'd better lay off it if you want to remain a member of Boodles.

**Clement Freud, *Freud on Food*, 1978**

The depressing thing about an Englishman's traditional love of animals is the dishonesty thereof . . . Get a barbed hook into the upper lip of a salmon, drag him endlessly around the water until he loses his strength, pull him to the bank, hit him on the head with a stone, and you may well become fisherman of the year. Shoot the salmon and you'll never be asked again.

**Clement Freud, *Freud on Food*, 1978**

I know why the sun never sets on the British Empire – God wouldn't trust an Englishman in the dark.

**Duncan Spaeth, quoted in *The Book of Insults* by N. McPhee, 1978**

English Law: where there are two alternatives: one intelligent, one stupid; one attractive, one vulgar; one noble, one ape-like; one serious and sincere, one undignified and false; one far-sighted, one short; EVERYBODY will INVARIABLY choose the latter.

**Cyril Connolly, *Journal 1928–1937*, ed. D. Pryce-Jones, 1983**

The two sides of industry have traditionally always regarded each other in Britain with the greatest possible loathing, mistrust and contempt. They are both absolutely right.

**Auberon Waugh, in *Private Eye* magazine, 1983**

England: the only country in the world where the food is more dangerous than the sex.

**Jackie Mason, 1990**

# ENVY

The praise we give newcomers into the world arises from the envy we bear to those who are established.
  **François, Duc de La Rochefoucauld, *Maxims*, 1665**

Few envy the consideration enjoyed by the oldest inhabitant.
  **Ralph Waldo Emerson**

Envy is the most stupid of vices, for there is no single advantage to be gained from it.
  **Honoré de Balzac, quoted in *Reflections on the Art of Life* by J.R. Solly, 1902**

Envy is the sincerest form of flattery.
  **John Churton Collins, in *The English Review*, 1914**

# EQUALITY

When security and equality are in conflict, it will not do to hesitate a moment – equality must yield.
  **Jeremy Bentham, *Introduction to Principles of Morals and Legislation*, 1789**

The defect of equality is that we desire it only with our superiors.
  **Henri Becque, *Querelles littéraires*, 1890**

All animals are created equal, but some animals are more equal than others.
  **George Orwell, *Animal Farm*, 1945**

We clamour for equality chiefly in matters in which we ourselves cannot hope to gain excellence.
  **Eric Hoffer, *The Passionate State of Mind*, 1954**

The social process requires the standardisation of man and this standardisation is called equality.
  **Erich Fromm, *The Art of Loving*, 1956**

There is no snobbishness like that of professional equalitarians.
  **Malcolm Muggeridge, *Chronicles of Wasted Time* vol.i, 1978**

*See also* DEMOCRACY

# EXCUSE

Any excuse will serve a tyrant.
**Aesop, *Fables*, 550BC**

Whores and priests will never want excuse.
**Daniel Defoe, *The True-born Englishman*, 1701**

Destiny, n. A tyrant's authority for crime and a fool's excuse for failure.
**Ambrose Bierce, *The Devil's Dictionary*, 1911**

Tyrants are always assassinated too late. That is their great excuse.
**E.M. Cioran**

Usually, terrible things that are done with the excuse that progress requires them are not really progress at all, but just terrible things.
**Russell Baker, *The Sayings of Poor Russell*, 1972**

Two wrongs don't make a right, but they make a good excuse.
**Thomas Szasz, *The Second Sin*, 1974**

# EXPERIENCE

Experience is the name everyone gives to their mistakes.
**Oscar Wilde, *Lady Windermere's Fan*, 1892**

Experience: an expensive tutor.
**Oliver Herford and John Clay, *Cupid's Cyclopedia*, 1910**

The only thing experience teaches us is that experience teaches us nothing.
**André Maurois**

Experience enables you to recognise a mistake when you make it again.
**Franklin P. Jones**

You cannot create experience, you must undergo it.
**Albert Camus, *Notebooks*, 1962**

Yesterday's avant-garde experience is today's chic and tomorrow's cliché.
**Richard Hofstadter, *Anti-Intellectualism in American Life*, 1963**

Experience – a comb life gives you after you lose your hair.
   **Judith Stern**

*See also* LIFE, TIME

# EXPERTS

A professional is a person who tells you what you know already, but in a way you cannot understand.
   **Anonymous**

No man can be a pure specialist without being in the strict sense an idiot.
   **George Bernard Shaw, *Maxims for Revolutionists*, 1903**

An expert is a man who has made all the mistakes which can be made, in a very narrow field.
   **Niels Bohr**

The mere eminence of a specialist makes him the more dangerous.
   **Alexis Carrel, *L'Homme cet inconnu*, 1935**

An expert is a mechanic away from home.
   **Charles E. Wilson**

Sooner or later an expert will say, 'But I'm talking too much' – always a prelude to talking some more.
   **Stephen Potter, *Some Notes on Lifemanship*, 1950**

An expert is a man who has stopped thinking. Why should he think? He is an expert.
   **Frank Lloyd Wright, quoted in the *Daily Express*, 1959**

The function of the expert is not to be more right than other people, but to be wrong for more sophisticated reasons.
   **Dr David Butler, in the *Observer*, 1969**

To spot the expert, pick the one who predicts the job will take the longest and cost the most.
   **Warren's Rule, quoted in *Murphy's Law Book Two* by A. Bloch, 1980**

Specialists are people who always repeat the same mistakes.

**Walter Gropius, quoted in *Contemporary Architects*, 1980**

# FAILURE

Every failure teaches a man something; to wit, that he will probably fail again the next time.

**H.L. Mencken, *Sententiae*, 1916**

Calamity, n. A more than commonly plain and unmistakable reminder that the affairs of this life are not of our own ordering. Calamities are of two types: misfortune to ourselves, and good fortune to others.

**Ambrose Bierce, *The Devil's Dictionary*, 1911**

# FAITH

Faith is a necessary fraud at best.

**Charles Churchill, *Gotham*, 1764**

The beast faith lives on its own dung.

**A.C. Swinburne, *Dirae*, 1875**

A casual stroll through a lunatic asylum shows that faith does not prove anything.

**Friedrich Wilhelm Nietzsche**

A miracle is an event described by those to whom it was told by people who did not see it.

**Elbert Hubbard, *The Philistine*, 1909**

Delusion, n. The father of a most respectable family, comprising Enthusiasm, Affection, Self-Denial, Faith, Hope, Charity and many other goodly sons and daughters.

**Ambrose Bierce, *The Devil's Dictionary*, 1911**

Faith, n. Belief without evidence in what is told by one who speaks without knowledge, of things without parallel.

**Ambrose Bierce, *The Devil's Dictionary*, 1911**

Faith is an illogical belief in the occurrence of the improbable.

**H.L. Mencken**

Orthodoxy is a corpse that doesn't know it's dead.

**Elbert Hubbard, *Epigrams*, 1923**

A creed is an ossified metaphor.

**Elbert Hubbard, *The Notebook*, 1927**

I respect faith, but doubt is what gives you an education.

**Wilson Mizner, quoted in *H.L. Mencken's Dictionary of Quotations*, 1942**

Man is a credulous animal and must believe something. In the absence of good grounds for belief, he will be satisfied with bad ones.

**Bertrand Russell, *Unpopular Essays*, 1950**

There is no nonsense so arrant that it cannot be made the creed of the vast majority by adequate governmental action.

**Bertrand Russell, *Unpopular Essays*, 1950**

There lies at the back of every creed something terrible and hard for which the worshipper may one day be required to suffer.

**E.M. Forster, *Two Cheers for Democracy*, 1951**

I confused things with their names: that is belief.

**Jean-Paul Sartre, *The Words*, 1964**

Faith is much better than belief. Belief is when someone else does the thinking.

**Buckminster Fuller, in *Playboy* magazine, 1972**

In the name of religion, one tortures, persecutes, builds pyres. In the guise of ideologies, one massacres, tortures and kills. In the name of justice one punishes . . . in the name of love of one's country or of one's race one hates other countries, despises them, massacres them. In the name of equality and brotherhood there is suppression and torture. There is nothing in common between the means and the end, the means go far beyond the end . . . ideologies and religions . . . are the alibis of the means.

**Eugène Ionesco, in *Esquire* magazine, 1974**

Faith is that quality which enables us to believe what we know to be untrue.

**Anonymous, quoted in *Definitive Quotations*, ed. J. Ferguson, 1981**

*See also* BELIEF, CHRISTIANS, IDEALS, IDEAS, MORALS, RELIGION, TRUE BELIEVERS, TRUTH

# FAME

The renown of great men should always be measured by the means which they have used to acquire it.
**François, Duc de La Rochefoucauld,** *Maxims,* **1665**

Fame is but the breath of the people, and that is often unwholesome.
**Thomas Fuller, M.D.,** *Gnomologia,* **1732**

Fame is the advantage of being known by people of whom you yourself know nothing, and for whom you care as little.
**Stanislaus Leszcynski,** *Oeuvres du philosophe bien-faisant,* **1763**

Many men and women enjoy popular esteem, not because they are known, but because they are unknown.
**Nicolas de Chamfort**

A good part of the fame of most celebrated men is due to the short-sightedness of their admirers.
**Georg Christoph Lichtenberg,** *Aphorisms,* **1764–99**

He who comes up to his own idea of greatness must always have had a very low standard of it in his mind.
**William Hazlitt**

Fame is an undertaker that pays but little attention to the living, but bedizens the dead, furnishes out their funerals and follows them to the grave.
**Charles Caleb Colton,** *Lacon,* **1820**

If a man was great while living, he becomes tenfold greater when dead.
**Thomas Carlyle,** *On Heroes, Hero-Worship and the Heroic in History,* **1840**

Fame is proof that the people are gullible.
**Ralph Waldo Emerson**

Most celebrated men live in a condition of prostitution.
**Charles-Augustin Sainte-Beuve,** *Notebooks,* **1876**

Martyrdom is the only way in which a man can become famous without ability.
  **George Bernard Shaw**, *The Devil's Disciple*, 1901

If you would be accounted great by your contemporaries, be not too much greater than they.
  **Ambrose Bierce**, *Collected Works*, 1909–12

Acquaintance, n. A person whom we know well enough to borrow from but not well enough to lend to. A degree of friendship called slight when the object is poor or obscure, and intimate when he is rich or famous.
  **Ambrose Bierce**, *The Devil's Dictionary*, 1911

A celebrity is one who is known to many persons he is glad he doesn't know.
  **H.L. Mencken**, *Sententiae*, 1916

What is glory? It is to have a lot of nonsense talked about you.
  **Gustave Flaubert, quoted in *A Cynic's Breviary* by J.R. Solly, 1925**

Fame is the aggregate of all the misunderstanding that collects around a new name.
  **Rainer Maria Rilke**

Fame is the beauty-parlour of the dead.
  **Benjamin DeCasseres**, *Fantasia Impromptu*, 1933

No one can make us hate ourselves like an admirer.
  **Cyril Connolly**, *Enemies of Promise*, 1938

A sign of a celebrity is that his name is often worth more than his services.
  **Daniel J. Boorstin**, *The Image*, 1961

A celebrity is a person who works hard all his life to become well-known, then wears dark glasses to avoid being recognised.
  **Fred Allen**

Every society honours its live conformists and its dead troublemakers.
  **Mignon McLaughlin**, *The Neurotic's Notebook*, 1963

*See also:* AMBITION, APPLAUSE, EGOTISM, SUCCESS

# FAMILIES

A family is but too often a commonwealth of malignants.

**Jonathan Swift, *Thoughts on Various Subjects*, 1706**

He that has no fools, knaves nor beggars in his family was begot by a flash of lightning.

**Thomas Fuller, M.D., *Gnomologia*, 1732**

The Family! Home of all social evils, a charitable institution for indolent women, a prison workshop for the slaving breadwinner and a hell for children.

**August Strindberg, *The Son of a Servant*, 1886**

Sacred family! . . . The supposed home of all the virtues, where innocent children are tortured into their first falsehoods, where wills are broken by parental tyranny, and self-respect smothered by crowded, jostling egos.

**August Strindberg, *The Son of a Servant*, 1886**

Relations are simply a tedious pack of people who haven't got the remotest knowledge of how to live, nor the smallest instinct about when to die.

**Oscar Wilde, *The Picture of Dorian Gray*, 1891**

Fathers should neither be seen nor heard. That is the only proper basis for family life.

**Oscar Wilde, *An Ideal Husband*, 1895**

Home is the girl's prison and the woman's workhouse.

**George Bernard Shaw, *Maxims for Revolutionists*, 1903**

Home life is no more natural to us than a cage is natural to a cockatoo.

**George Bernard Shaw, *Getting Married*, 1908**

'Home Sweet Home' must surely have been written by a bachelor.

**Samuel Butler, *Notebooks*, 1912**

Near relations are those that have a brilliant career. The others are only distant ones.

**Charles Nairey, quoted in *A Cynic's Breviary* by J.R. Solly, 1925**

Whenever a guy starts boasting to me about his family tree, I seem to smell a strong sniff of sap rising.

**Mae West**

The family is a court of justice which never shuts down for night or day.

**Malcolm de Chazal, *Sens plastique*, 1949**

Home is the place where, when you have to go there, they have to take you in.

**Robert Frost**

A 'good' family is one that used to be better.

**Cleveland Amory, *Who Killed Society*, 1960**

Far from being the basis of good society, the family, with its narrow privacy and tawdry secrets, is the source of all our discontents.

**Edmund Leach, Reith lecture, 1967**

Mother is the dead heart of the family, spending father's earnings on consumer goods to enhance the environment in which he eats, sleeps and watches the television.

**Germaine Greer, *The Female Eunuch*, 1970**

*See also* ADULTS, CHILDREN, PARENTS

# FASHION

Fashion condems us to many follies; the greatest is to make oneself its slave.

**Napoleon Bonaparte**

Change in fashion is the tax which the industry of the poor levies on the vanity of the rich.

**Nicolas de Chamfort, *Maximes et pensées*, 1805**

Fashion is what one wears oneself. What is unfashionable is what other people wear.

**Oscar Wilde, *An Ideal Husband*, 1895**

Fashion is a form of ugliness so intolerable that we have to alter it every six months,

**Oscar Wilde**

Fashions, after all, are only induced epidemics.

**George Bernard Shaw, *The Doctor's Dilemma*, 1906**

Where's the man could ease a heart
Like a satin gown?

**Dorothy Parker, *The Satin Dress*, 1927**

Fashion: a barricade behind which men hide their nothingness.

**Kin Hubbard, 1923**

Fashion exists for women with no taste, etiquette for people with no breeding.

**Marie, Queen of Romania**

To call a fashion wearable is the kiss of death. No new fashion worth its salt is ever wearable.

**Eugenia Sheppard, quoted in the *New York Herald Tribune*, 1960**

# FOOD

A man seldom thinks with more earnestness of anything than he does of his dinner.

**Samuel Johnson, attrib. in *Anecdotes of the late Samuel Johnson* by Hester Thrale, 1786**

There is no love sincerer than the love of food.

**George Bernard Shaw, *Man and Superman*, 1903**

A gourmet is just a glutton with brains.

**Philip Haberman Jr, in *Vogue* magazine, 1961**

# FOOLS

Is there anything so assured, resolved, disdainful, contemplative, solemn and serious as an ass?

**Michel de Montaigne, *Essays*, 1595**

He who pleads his own cause has a fool for a client.

**Anonymous proverb**

If you wish to avoid seeing a fool you must first break your mirror.

**François Rabelais**

Promises are the pitfalls of fools.
  **Baltasar Gracian, *The Art of Worldly Wisdom*, 1647**

There are more Fools than Knaves in the world, else the Knaves would not have enough to live on.
  **Samuel Butler, *Prose Observations 1660–1680*, ed. Hugh de Quehen, 1980**

Men would not live long in society were they not the dupes of one another.
  **François, Duc de La Rochefoucauld, *Maxims*, 1665**

Zeal is fit only for wise men, but is found mostly in fools.
  **Thomas Fuller, M.D., *Gnomologia*, 1732**

Most fools think they are only ignorant.
  **Benjamin Franklin, *Poor Richard's Almanack*, 1733–58**

A generous man is merely a fool in the eyes of a thief.
  **Henry Fielding, *The History of Tom Jones*, 1749**

That the vulgar express their thoughts clearly is far from true; and what perspicuity can be found among them proceeds not from the easiness of their language, but the shallowness of their thoughts.
  **Samuel Johnson, *The Idler*, 1758–60**

The number of wise men will always be small. It is true that it has increased; but that is nothing compared with the fools, and unfortunately it is said that God is always on the side of the big battalions.
  **Voltaire, letter, 1770**

He that teaches himself has a fool for a master.
  **Benjamin Franklin**

Ever since Adam fools have been in the majority.
  **Casimir Delavigne**

The greater the fool the better the dancer.
  **Theodore Hook, *Sayings and Doings*, 1824–8**

There is nothing too monstrous for human credibility.
  **Thomas Love Peacock, *Gryll Grange*, 1860–1**

I prefer rogues to imbeciles, because they sometimes take a rest.
  **Alexander Dumas fils**

You can generally make people ridiculous by taking them at their word.
  **Jerome K. Jerome, *Three Men on the Bummel*, 1900**

Whenever a man feels like publicly making a fool of himself, he can always find someone to egg him on by giving him a cheer.
  **Arthur Binstead, *Pitcher's Proverbs*, 1909**

Before a man speaks it is always safe to assume that he is a fool. After he speaks, it is seldom necessary to assume it.
  **H.L. Mencken, *Sententiae*, 1916**

What good are brains to a man? They only unsettle him.
  **P.G. Wodehouse, *The Adventures of Sally*, 1920**

As a rule men are foolish, ungrateful, jealous, covetous of others' goods, abusing their superiority when they are strong and rascals when they are weak.
  **Voltaire, quoted in *A Cynic's Breviary* by J.R. Solly, 1925**

The average man's opinions are much less foolish than they would be if he thought for himself.
  **Bertrand Russell**

Many a man is praised for his reserve and so-called shyness when he is simply too proud to risk making a fool of himself.
  **J.B. Priestley, *All About Ourselves*, 1956**

It's innocence when it charms us, ignorance when it doesn't.
  **Mignon McLaughlin, *The Neurotic's Notebook*, 1963**

A fellow who's always declaring that he's no fool usually has his suspicions.
  **Wilson Mizner, quoted in *The People's Almanac*, 1976**

Never argue with a fool – people might not know the difference.
  **First Law of Debate, quoted in *Murphy's Law* by A. Bloch, 1979**

Build a system that even a fool can use, and only a fool will want to use it.
  **Shaw's System, quoted in *Murphy's Law* by A. Bloch, 1979**

Earnestness is just stupidity sent to college.

**P.J. O'Rourke, *Holidays in Hell*, 1988**

# FREEDOM

When the People contend for their Liberty they seldom get anything for their Victory but new Masters.

**George Savile, Marquis of Halifax, *Political, Moral and Miscellaneous Thoughts and Reflexions*, c.1694**

Corruption . . . the most infallible symptom of constitutional liberty.

**Edward Gibbon, *The Decline and Fall of the Roman Empire*, 1776–88**

If any ask me what a free government is, I answer that for any practical purposes, it is what the people think so.

**Edmund Burke, letter to the sheriffs of Bristol, 1777**

It has been observed, that they who most loudly clamour for liberty do not most liberally grant it.

**Samuel Johnson, *Works*, 1787**

The great half-truth, liberty.

**William Blake, *The Marriage of Heaven and Hell*, 1790**

Despotism sits nowhere so secure as under the effigy and ensigns of Freedom.

**Walter Savage Landor**

Freedom is the recognition of necessity.

**Friedrich Engels**

The most essential mental quality for a free people, whose liberty is to be progressive, permanent and on a large scale, is much stupidity.

**Walter Bagehot**

Give a Frenchman twenty-five lashes, and if you only make a fine speech to him about the freedom and dignity of man he will persuade himself that he is not lashed at all.

**Otto von Bismarck, 1875**

In our country we have three unspeakably precious things: freedom of speech, freedom of conscience and the prudence never to practise either.

**Mark Twain, *Pudd'nhead Wilson's New Calendar*, 1894**

Liberal institutions straightway cease from being liberal the moment they are soundly established: once this is attained, no more grievous and more thorough enemies of freedom exist than liberal institutions.
    **Friedrich Wilhelm Nietzsche, 1888**

Liberty means responsibility, that is why most men dread it.
    **George Bernard Shaw, *Man and Superman*, 1903**

Liberty, n. One of imagination's most precious possessions.
    **Ambrose Bierce, *The Devil's Dictionary*, 1911**

It is true that liberty is precious: so precious that it must be rationed.
    **V.I. Lenin, *The State and Revolution*, 1917**

Free speech is about as good a cause as the world has ever known. But it . . . gets shoved aside in favour of things which seem at a given moment more vital . . . everybody favours free speech in the slack moments when no axes are being ground.
    **Heywood Broun, 1926**

It is often safer to be in chains than to be free.
    **Franz Kafka, *The Castle*, 1926**

Liberty don't work as good in practice as it does in speech.
    **Will Rogers, 1927**

Advocates of capitalism are very apt to appeal to the sacred principles of liberty, which are embodied in one maxim: The fortunate must not be restrained in the exercise of tyranny over the unfortunate.
    **Bertrand Russell, *Sceptical Essays*, 1928**

Liberty is so much latitude as the powerful choose to accord to the weak.
    **Judge Learned Hand, 1930**

Freedom – a drunken whore
Sprawling in a power maddened soldier's arms.
    **Marina Tsvetayeva**

Freedom is the right to tell people what they do not want to hear.
    **George Orwell, *The Road to Wigan Pier*, 1937**

Man is condemned to be free.

**Jean-Paul Sartre, *Existentialism and Humanism*, 1947**

When people are free to do as they please, they usually imitate each other.

**Eric Hoffer, *The Passionate State of Mind*, 1955**

If people have to choose between freedom and sandwiches, they will take sandwiches.

**Lord Boyd-Orr, 1955**

Most people want security in this world, not liberty.

**H.L. Mencken, *Minority Report*, 1956**

What good is freedom if you've not got the money for it? It's all very fine to go on about Nora's escape at the end of *A Doll's House*, but just how was she planning to eat that night?

**Lillian Hellman**

If society fits you comfortably enough, you call it freedom.

**Robert Frost, in *Esquire* magazine, 1965**

The brotherhood of man is evoked by particular men according to their circumstances. But it seldom extends to all men. In the name of our freedom and our brotherhood we are prepared to blow up the other half of the world and to be blown up in our turn.

**R.D. Laing, *The Politics of Experience*, 1967**

There's no such thing as a free lunch.

**Milton Friedman**

Freedom's just another word for nothing else to lose.

**Kris Kristofferson, *Me and Bobby McGee*, 1969**

The more a regime claims to be the embodiment of liberty the more tyrannical it is likely to be.

**Ian Gilmour, *Inside Right*, 1977**

Man persuades himself he is emancipated every time he decorates a new servitude with the name of liberty.

**Achille Tournier, quoted in *The Oxford Book of Aphorisms*, ed. J. Gross, 1983**

*See also* DEMOCRACY, REVOLUTION

# FRIENDS

No-one ever really minds seeing a friend fall off a roof.

**Confucius**

In the misfortune of our friends we find something that is not displeasing to us.

**François, Duc de La Rochefoucauld,** *Maxims*, **1665**

It is to receive a rare favour from a friend if, after he has achieved a high position in the world, he remembers you as an acquaintance.

**Jean de La Bruyère,** *The Characters*, **1688**

I am no married man, and thou canst not lie with my wife. I am very poor, and thou canst not borrow money from me. Then what use am I as a friend?

**William Congreve,** *The Double Dealer*, **1694**

I advise thee to visit Relations and friends, but I advise thee not to live too near them.

**Thomas Fuller, M.D.,** *Introductio ad Sapientiam, or, The Art of Right Thinking*, **1731**

Distrust all those who love you extremely upon a very slight acquaintance and without any visible reason.

**Lord Chesterfield,** *Letters to his Son*, **1774**

Friendship is a disinterested commerce between equals; love, an abject intercourse between tyrants and slaves.

**Oliver Goldsmith,** *The Good-Natured Man*, **1768**

Distance either of time or place is sufficient to reconcile weak minds to wonderful relations.

**Samuel Johnson,** *Works* vol. v, **1787**

Friendship among women is only a suspension of hostilities.

**Antoine Rivaroli, Comte de Rivarol**

Never speak ill of yourself, your friends will always say enough on that subject.

**Charles-Maurice de Talleyrand, quoted in** *A Cynic's Breviary* **by J.R. Solly, 1925**

Most of our misfortunes are more supportable than the comments of our friends upon them.

**Charles Caleb Colton,** *Lacon*, **1820**

It is always safe to learn, even from our enemies – seldom safe to venture to instruct, even our friends.

**Charles Caleb Colton,** *Lacon*, **1820**

Never join with your friend when he abuses his horse or his wife, unless the one is about to be sold, the other to be buried.

**Charles Caleb Colton,** *Lacon*, **1820**

If you want enemies, excel others; if you want friends, let others excel you.

**Charles Caleb Colton,** *Lacon*, **1820**

Discussing the characters and foibles of common friends is a great sweetener and cement of friendship.

**William Hazlitt,** *Table Talk*, **1821–2**

Give me the avowed, the erect, amd manly foe,
Firm I can meet – perhaps may turn his blow!
But of all plagues, good Heaven, thy wrath can send,
Save me, oh, save me from the candid friend.

**George Canning,** *New Morality*, **1823**

I like a friend better for having faults that one can talk about.

**William Hazlitt,** *The Plain Speaker*, **1826**

Friendships last when each friend thinks he has a slight superiority over the other.

**Honoré de Balzac**

It is difficult to say who do you the worst mischief, enemies with the worst intentions or friends with the best.

**Edward George Bulwer-Lytton, Baron Lytton**

What is commonly called friendship is only a little more honour among rogues.

**Henry David Thoreau**

What men call social virtues, good fellowship, is commonly but the virtue of pigs in a litter, which lie close together to keep each other warm.

**Henry David Thoreau,** *Journal*, **1851**

Nobody ever forgets where he buried the hatchet.

**Kin Hubbard,** *Abe Martin's Broadcast,* **1926**

The best way to keep your friends is not to give them away.

**Wilson Mizner, quoted in** *The Incredible Mizners*
**by A. Johnson, 1953**

God gives us our relatives; thank God, we can choose our friends.

**Addison Mizner and Oliver Herford,** *The Cynic's Calendar,*
**1901**

People say you mustn't love your friend's wife, but how are you to love
your enemy's wife?

**George Moore**

Distress, n. A disease incurred by exposure to the prosperity of a
friend.

**Ambrose Bierce,** *The Devil's Dictionary,* **1911**

Friendless, adj. Having no favours to bestow. Destitute of fortune.
Addicted to utterance of truth and common sense.

**Ambrose Bierce,** *The Devil's Dictionary,* **1911**

Beggar, n. One who has relied on the assistance of his friends.

**Ambrose Bierce,** *The Devil's Dictionary,* **1911**

Acquaintance, n. A person whom we know well enough to borrow
from but not well enough to lend to. A degree of friendship called
slight when its object is poor or obscure, and intimate when he is rich
or famous.

**Ambrose Bierce,** *The Devil's Dictionary,* **1911**

In prosperity our friends know us; in adversity we know our friends.

**John Churton Collins, in** *The English Review,* **1914**

Friendship is a common belief in the same fallacies, mountebanks and
hobgoblins.

**H.L. Mencken,** *Sententiae,* **1916**

When a man laughs at his troubles he loses a great many friends. They
never forgive the loss of their prerogative.

**H.L. Mencken,** *Sententiae,* **1916**

The full potentialities of human fury cannot be reached until a friend of both parties tactfully interferes.
**G.K. Chesterton**

To find a friend one must close one eye; to keep him – two.
**Norman Douglas, *An Almanac*, 1941**

Friendship will not stand the strain of very much good advice for very long.
**Robert Lynd**

A girl's best friend is her mutter.
**Dorothy Parker, quoted in *Wits End*, ed. R.E. Drennan, 1968**

One of the most mawkish of human delusions is the notion that friendship should be lifelong. The fact is that a man of resilient mind outwears his friendships as certainly as he outwears his love affairs and his politics.
**H.L. Mencken, *Prejudices*, 1919–27**

The most disagreeable thing that your worst enemy says to your face does not approach what your best friends say behind your back.
**Alfred de Musset, quoted in *A Cynic's Breviary* by J.R. Solly, 1925**

Lord, defend me from my friends; I can account for my enemies.
**Charles d'Héricault, quoted in *A Cynic's Breviary* by J.R. Solly, 1925**

It's amazing how nice people are to you when they know you're going away.
**Michael Arlen**

I always choose my friends for their good looks and my enemies for their good intellects. Man cannot be too careful in his choice of enemies.
**Albert Lewin, screenplay for *The Picture of Dorian Gray*, 1945**

It's what the guests say as they swing out of the drive that counts.
**Anonymous, quoted in the *New York Times*, 1947**

No one is completely unhappy at the failure of his best friend.
**Groucho Marx**

When you are down and out something always turns up – and it is usually the noses of your friends.

**Orson Welles, in the *New York Times*, 1962**

A stranger loses half his charm the day he is no longer a stranger.

**Genevieve Antoine-Dariaux, *The Men in Your Life*, 1968**

A Code of Honour: never approach a friend's girlfriend or wife with mischief as your goal. There are too many women in the world to justify that sort of dishonourable behaviour. Unless she's really attractive.

**Bruce J. Friedman, *Sex and the Lonely Guy*, 1977**

Rough diamonds are a girl's best friend.

**Jilly Cooper, *Class*, 1979**

# GENIUS

When a true genius appears in the world you may know him by this sign: that all the dunces are in confederacy against him.

**Jonathan Swift, *Thoughts on Various Subjects*, 1706**

I have always thought geniuses much inferior to the plain sense of a cookmaid, who can make a good pudding and keep the kitchen in order.

**Lady Mary Wortley Montagu, letter to the Countess of Pomfret, 1739**

Sometimes men come by the name of genius in the same way that certain insects come by the name of centipede: not because they have a hundred feet, but because most people can't count above fourteen.

**Georg Christoph Lichtenberg, *Reflections*, 1799**

Genius, in one respect, is like gold; numbers of persons are constantly writing about both, who have neither.

**Charles Caleb Colton, *Lacon*, 1820**

Genius is the talent of a man who is dead.

**Edmond de Goncourt**

The dull pray, the geniuses are light mockers.

**Ralph Waldo Emerson**

Unless one is a genius, it is best to aim at being intelligible.

**Anthony Hope (Sir Anthony Hope Hawkins), *The Dolly Dialogues*, 1894**

Genius . . . has been defined as a supreme capacity for taking trouble . . . It might be more fitly described as a supreme capacity for getting its possessors into trouble of all kinds.

**Samuel Butler, *Notebooks*, 1912**

We define genius as the capacity for productive reaction against one's training.

**Bernard Berenson**

Skill is fine, and genius is splendid, but the right contacts are more valuable than either.

**Sir Archibald McIndoe, quoted in *The Wit of Medicine*, ed. L. and M. Cowan, 1972**

*See also* INTELLECTUALS

# GENTLEMEN

A thief passes for a gentleman when stealing has made him rich.

**Thomas Fuller, M.D., *Gnomologia*, 1732**

The only infallible rule we know is, that the man who is always talking about being a gentleman never is one.

**Robert Surtees, *Ask Mamma*, 1858**

There is no such thing as a democratic gentleman. The adjective and the noun are hyphenated by a drawn sword.

**Joseph Furphy, *Such Is Life*, 1903**

I am a gentleman: I live by robbing the poor.

**George Bernard Shaw, *Man and Superman*, 1903**

A true gentleman is one who knows how to play the bagpipes – but doesn't.

**Anonymous**

A gentleman is one who never strikes a woman without provocation.

**H.L. Mencken, *Sententiae*, 1916**

The concept of the gentleman was invented by the aristocrats to keep the middle classes in order.

**Bertrand Russell**

The criterion of a gentleman is that however poor he may be, he still refuses to do useful work.

**George Mikes, *How To Be An Alien*, 1946**

A gentleman is a man who wouldn't hit a lady with his hat on.

**Evan Esar**

A gentleman is a patient wolf.

**Henrietta Tiarks, 1957**

My experience of gentlemen's agreements is that, when it comes to the pinch, there are rarely enough bloody gentlemen around.

**Ben Chifley, quoted in *Ben Chifley* by L.F. Crisp, 1961**

*See also* ARISTOCRACY, CLASS

# GIRLS

The girl who can't dance says the band can't play.

**Yiddish proverb**

After a girl gets too big for Santa Claus, she begins to cast around for an easy mark.

**Kin Hubbard, *Abe Martin's Primer*, 1892**

The hardest task in a girl's life is to prove to a man that his intentions are serious.

**Helen Rowland, *Reflections of a Bachelor Girl*, 1909**

I like the girls who do,
I like the girls who don't;
I hate the girl who says she will
And then she says she won't.
But the girl that I like best of all
And I think you'll say I'm right –
Is the girl who says she never has
But looks as if she . . .
'Ere, listen . . . !

**Max Miller**

There was a little girl
Who had a little curl
When she was good, she was very, very good
And when she was bad, she was very, very popular.

**Max Miller**

Any girl can be glamorous: all you have to do is stand still and look stupid.

**Hedy Lamarr**

One girl can be pretty – but a dozen are only a chorus.

**F. Scott Fitzgerald, *The Last Tycoon*, 1941**

From birth to age eighteen a girl needs good parents, from eighteen to thirty-five she needs good looks, from thirty-five she needs a good personality. From fifty-five on, she needs good cash.

**Sophie Tucker, 1953**

The girl with a future avoids the man with a past.

**Evan Esar, *The Humour of Humour*, 1954**

The first girl you go to bed with is always pretty.

**Walter Matthau, in *Esquire* magazine, 1968**

Girls who put out are tramps. Girls who don't are ladies. This is, however, a rather archaic use of the word. Should one of you boys happen upon a girl who doesn't put out, do not jump to the conclusion that you have found a lady. What you have probably found is a lesbian.

**Fran Lebowitz, *Metropolitan Life*, 1978**

When you meet a pretty teenage girl, make a beeline for the mother. I've found it to be usually very rewarding.

**Jeffrey Barnard, in *The Spectator* magazine**

*See also* BOYS, CHILDREN

# GOD

God is alive, he just doesn't want to get involved.

**Graffito**

If God lived on earth, people would break his windows.

**Yiddish proverb**

If God did not exist, it would be necessary to invent him.
**Voltaire, *Letters* vol. xcvi, 1769**

The only excuse for God is that he doesn't exist.
**Stendhal**

God will forgive me, it is his trade.
**Heinrich Heine, last words, 1856**

We are always making God our accomplice so that we may legalise our own iniquities. Every successful massacre is consecrated by a *Te Deum*, and the clergy have never been wanting in benedictions for any victorious enormity.
**Henri-Frédéric Amiel, *Journal intime*, 1885**

Priests, kings, statesmen, soldiers, bankers and public functionaries of all sorts; policemen, jailers and hangmen; capitalists, usurers, businessmen and property-owners; lawyers, economists and politicians – all of them, down to the meanest grocer, repeat in chorus the words of Voltaire, that if there were no God it would be necessary to invent Him.
**Mikhail Bakunin, *Dieu et l'état*, 1871**

Which is it: is man one of God's blunders, or is God one of man's blunders?
**Friedrich Wilhelm Nietzsche, *Twilight of the Idols*, 1889**

It must be remembered that we have heard only one side of the case. God has written all the books.
**Samuel Butler, *Notebooks*, 1912**

God is a thought that makes crooked all that is straight.
**Friedrich Wilhelm Nietzsche**

The soul must have its chosen sewers to carry away its ordure. This function is performed by persons, relationships, professions, the fatherland, the world, or finally, for the really arrogant – I mean our modern pessimists – by the Good God himself.
**Friedrich Wilhelm Nietzsche**

The Creator is a comedian whose audience is afraid to laugh.
**H.L. Mencken**

God – the John Doe of philosophy and religion.
  **Elbert Hubbard, *The Notebook*, 1927**

Those who set out to serve both God and Mammon soon discover that there is no God.
  **Logan Pearsall Smith**

God, that dumping ground of our dreams.
  **Jean Rostand**

Every man thinks God is on his side. The rich and powerful know that he is.
  **Jean Anouilh, *The Lark*, 1953**

Kill one man and you are a murderer. Kill millions and you are a conqueror. Kill all and you are a God.
  **Jean Rostand, *Thoughts of a Biologist*, 1955**

God is the immemorial refuge of the incompetent, the helpless, the miserable. They find not only sanctuary in His arms, but also a kind of superiority, soothing to their macerated egos; He will set them above their betters.
  **H.L. Mencken, *Minority Report*, 1956**

It takes a long while for a naturally trustful person to reconcile himself to the idea that after all God will not help him.
  **H.L. Mencken, *Minority Report*, 1956**

What men usually ask of God when they pray is that two and two not make four.
  **Anonymous, quoted in *The Faber Book of Aphorisms*,**
  **ed. W.H. Auden and L. Kronenberger, 1964**

Respectable people believed in God in order to avoid having to speak about him.
  **Jean-Paul Sartre, *The Words*, 1964**

If you talk to God, you are praying; if God talks to you, you have schizophrenia.
  **Thomas Szasz, *The Second Sin*, 1973**

God is dead, but fifty thousand social workers have risen to take his place.
  **Dr J.D. McCoughey, in *The Bulletin* magazine, 1974**

God is not dead. He is alive and working on a much less ambitious project.
  **Graffito 1975**

God is love, but get it in writing.
  **Gypsy Rose Lee, 1975**

*See also* BELIEF, THE CLERGY, FAITH, HYPOCRISY, MORALS, RELIGION

# GOVERNMENT

The punishment which the wise suffer, who refuse to take part in the government, is, to live under the government of worse men.
  **Plato, 370BC**

Whoever desires to found a state and give it laws, must start with assuming that all men are bad and ever ready to display their vicious natures, whenever they may find occasion for it.
  **Niccolò Machiavelli, *Discourse upon the First Ten Books of Livy*, 1518**

No government has ever been, or can ever be, wherein time-servers and blockheads will not be uppermost.
  **John Dryden**

Let the people think they govern and they will be governed.
  **William Penn, *Some Fruits of Solitude*, 1693**

Nothing appears more surprising to those who consider human affairs with a philosophical eye, than the ease with which the many are governed by the few and the implicit submission with which men resign their own sentiments and passions to those of their rulers.
  **David Hume, *The First Principles of Government*, 1742**

To govern mankind one must not over-rate them.
  **Lord Chesterfield, *Letters to his Son*, 1774**

In general, the art of government consists in taking as much money as possible from one party of the citizens to give to the other.
  **Voltaire**

The pleasure of governing must certainly be exquisite, if we may judge from the vast numbers who are eager to be concerned with it.

**Voltaire, *Philosophical Dictionary*, 1764**

I would not give half a guinea to live under one form of government rather than another. It is of no moment to the happiness of an individual.

**Samuel Johnson, 1772**

Kings govern by means of popular assemblies only when they cannot do without them.

**Charles James Fox, 1776**

Society is produced by our wants and government by our wickedness.

**Thomas Paine, *Common Sense*, 1776**

Every country has the government it deserves.

**Joseph de Maistre, letter, 1811**

That government is best which governs least.

**Henry David Thoreau, *Civil Disobedience*, 1849**

The best form of government (setting aside questions of morality) is one where the masses have little power, and seem to have a great deal.

**Marquess of Salisbury, *Oxford Essays*, 1858**

To be governed is to be watched, inspected, spied upon, directed, law-ridden, regulated, penned up, indoctrinated, preached at, checked, appraised, seized, censured, commanded by beings who have neither title, knowledge nor virtue.

**Pierre-Joseph Proudhon**

Order means obedience. A government is said to preserve order if it succeeds in getting itself obeyed.

**John Stuart Mill, *Representative Government*, 1861**

Government is the great fiction, through which everybody endeavours to live at the expense of everybody else.

**Frédéric Bastiat, *Essays on Political Economy*, 1872**

Government is an association of men who do violence to the rest of us.

**Leo Tolstoy, *The Kingdom of God Is Within You*, 1893**

Our laws make law impossible, our liberties destroy all freedom, our property is organised robbery, our morality is an impudent hypocrisy, our wisdom is administered by inexperienced or mal-experienced dupes, our power wielded by cowards and weaklings and our honour false in all its points. I am an enemy of the existing order for good reasons.
   **George Bernard Shaw,** *Major Barbara*, **1907**

Opposition, n. In politics the party that prevents the government from running amuck by hamstringing it.
   **Ambrose Bierce,** *The Devil's Dictionary*, **1911**

It is perfectly true that that government is best which governs least. It is equally true that that government is best which provides most.
   **Walter Lippmann,** *A Preface to Politics*, **1914**

All government, in its essence, is a conspiracy against the superior man.
   **H.L. Mencken, in** *The Smart Set* **magazine, 1919**

A well governed people are generally a people who do not think much.
   **André Siegfried**

Government: a kind of legalised pillage.
   **Kin Hubbard, 1923**

The selfish wish to govern is often mistaken for a holy zeal in the cause of humanity.
   **Elbert Hubbard,** *The Notebook*, **1927**

To prevent resentment, governments attribute misfortunes to natural causes; to create resentment, oppositions attribute them to human causes.
   **Bertrand Russell,** *Sceptical Essays*, **1928**

It would be desirable if every government, when it comes to power, should have its old speeches burned.
   **Philip Snowden**

The worst government is the most moral. One composed of cynics is often very tolerant and humane. But when the fanatics are on top there is no limit to oppression.
   **H.L. Mencken**

Universal suffrage almost inevitably leads to government by mass bribery, an auction of the wordly goods of the unrepresented minority.

**William R. Inge**

The working of great institutions is mainly the result of a vast mass of routine, petty malice, self interest, carelessness and sheer mistake. Only a residual fraction is thought.

**George Santayana**

Public office is the last refuge of a scoundrel.

**Boies Penrose, 1931**

Governments last as long as the under-taxed can defend themselves against the over-taxed.

**Bernard Berenson**

The only good government is a bad one in a hell of a fright.

**Joyce Cary, *The Horse's Mouth*, 1944**

I will undoubtedly have to seek what is happily known as gainful employment, which I am glad to say does not describe holding public office.

**Dean Acheson, on leaving his post as Secretary of State, 1952**

Too bad all the people who know how to run the country are busy driving cabs and cutting hair.

**George Burns**

A politician is a man who understands government and it takes a politician to run a government. A statesman is a politician who's been dead ten or fifteen years.

**Harry S. Truman, 1958**

Every government is a device by which a few control the actions of many . . . on both sides at the moment complex human societies depend for the final decisions of war and peace on a group of elderly men any sensible plant personnel manager, whether under capitalism or Communism, would hesitate to hire.

**I.F. Stone, 1959**

The taxpayer, that's someone who works for the federal government, but doesn't have to take a civil service examination.

**Ronald Reagan**

A government is the only known vessel that leaks from the top.
**James Reston**

Governments, like individuals, should beware when all men speak well of them.
**R.H. Tawney, in the *Guardian*, 1963**

It is a function of government to invent philosophies to explain the demands of its own convenience.
**Murray Kempton, *America Comes of Middle Age*, 1963**

A government that is big enough to give you all you want is big enough to take it all away.
**Barry Goldwater, speech, 1964**

Government is like a baby. An alimentary canal with a big appetite at one end and no sense of responsibility at the other.
**Ronald Reagan, in the *Saturday Evening Post*, 1965**

One should be suspicious of 'love' as a political slogan. A government which purports to 'love' its citizens invariably desires all the prerogatives of a lover: to share the loved one's thoughts and to keep him in bondage.
**Eric Julber, in *Esquire* magazine, 1969**

Any official denial is de facto a confirmation.
**John Kifner, in the *New York Times*, 1969**

Every government is run by liars and nothing they say should be believed.
**I.F. Stone**

Governments never learn. Only people learn.
**Milton Friedman, 1980**

Feeling good about government is like looking on the bright side of any catastrophe. When you quit looking on the bright side, the catastrophe is still there.
**P.J. O'Rourke, *Parliament of Whores*, 1991**

*See also* CONSERVATIVES, DEMOCRACY, LEADERS, PARTIES, POLITICIANS, POLITICS, POWER, VOTING

# HAPPINESS

Happiness is the perpetual possession of being well deceived.
**Jonathan Swift**

Amusement is the happiness of those who cannot think.
**Alexander Pope**

Illusion is the first of the pleasures.
**Voltaire**

Nothing is more conducive to peace of mind than not having any opinion at all.
**Georg Christoph Lichtenberg,** *Aphorisms*, **1764–99**

Happiness, n: An agreeable sensation arising from contemplating the misery of another.
**Ambrose Bierce,** *The Devil's Dictionary*, **1911**

We must select the illusion which appeals to our temperament and embrace it with passion, if we want to be happy.
**Cyril Connolly (Palinurus),** *The Unquiet Grave*, **1944**

When you jump for joy, beware that no one moves the ground from beneath your feet.
**Stanislaw J. Lec,** *Unkempt Thoughts*, **1962**

Happiness is an imaginary condition, formerly attributed by the living to the dead, now usually attributed by adults to children, and by children to adults.
**Thomas Szasz,** *The Second Sin*, **1973**

Never . . . was any generation of men intent upon the pursuit of happiness more advantageously placed to attain it who yet, with seeming deliberation, took the opposite course – towards chaos, not order, towards breakdown, not stability, towards death, destruction and darkness, not life, creativity and light.
**Malcolm Muggeridge, in** *Esquire* **magazine, 1970**

*See also* LAUGHTER, OPTIMISM

# HATRED

Now hatred is by far the longest pleasure;
Men love in haste, but they detest at leisure.
**George Gordon, Lord Byron, *Don Juan*, 1819–24**

Organised hatred, that is unity.
**John Jay Chapman, *Lines on the Death of Bismarck*, 1898**

Abhorrence, n. One of the degrees of disapproval due to what is imperfectly understood.
**Ambrose Bierce, *The Devil's Dictionary*, 1911**

Hate must make one productive. Otherwise one might as well love.
**Karl Kraus, *Half Truths and One and a Half Truths*, 1986**

It does not matter much what a man hates, provided he hates something.
**Samuel Butler, *Notebooks*, 1912**

To know all is not to forgive all. It is to despise everybody.
**Quentin Crisp, *The Naked Civil Servant*, 1968**

*See also* ENEMIES

# HISTORY

Very few things happen at the right time, and the rest do not happen at all. The conscientious historian will correct these defects.
**Herodotus, 450BC**

The more corrupt the state, the more numerous the laws.
**Tacitus, *History*, AD 68–96**

If a historian were to relate truthfully all the crimes, weaknesses and disorders of mankind, his readers would take his work for satire rather than for history.
**Pierre Bayle, *Dictionary*, 1695–7**

All our history . . . is no more than accepted fiction.
**Voltaire, *Jeannot et Colin*, 1764**

History is just the portrayal of crimes and misfortunes.
**Voltaire, *L'Ingénu*, 1767**

The history of mankind is little else than a narrative of designs which have failed, and hopes that have been disappointed.

**Samuel Johnson, Works vol. ix, 1787**

History is little more than the register of the crimes, follies and misfortunes of mankind.

**Edward Gibbon, The Decline and Fall of the Roman Empire, 1776–88**

If a man could say nothing against a character but what he can prove, history could not be written.

**Samuel Johnson, quoted in The Life of Samuel Johnson by J. Boswell, 1791**

We learn from history that we do not learn from history.

**George Wilhelm Friedrich Hegel**

History is the version of past events that people have decided to agree on.

**Napoleon Bonaparte, Maxims, 1804–15**

History in general only informs us what bad government is.

**Thomas Jefferson, letter to John Narvell, 1807**

For what is history but a kind of Newgate Calendar, a register of the crimes and miseries that man has inflicted on his fellow men? It is a huge libel on human nature.

**Washington Irving, A History of New York, 1809**

The more we know of history, the less shall we esteem the subjects of it, and to despise our species, is the price we must too often pay for our knowledge of it.

**Charles Caleb Colton, Lacon, 1820**

Man is fed with fables through life and leaves it in the belief he knows something of what has been passing, when in truth he has known nothing but what has passed under his own eye.

**Thomas Jefferson, letter to Thomas Cooper, 1823**

History is nothing but a collection of fables and useless trifles, cluttered up with a mass of unnecessary figures and proper names.

**Leo Tolstoy, 1846**

Historical phenomena always happen twice – the first time as tragedy, the second as farce.
  **Karl Marx**

History is all party pamphlets.
  **Ralph Waldo Emerson** *Journals*, **1909–14**

History is the autobiography of a madman.
  **Alexander Herzen**

Happy are the people whose annals are blank in the history books.
  **Thomas Carlyle,** *Frederick the Great*, **1858–65**

There are only two great currents in the history of mankind: the baseness which makes conservatives and the envy which makes revolutionaries.
  **Edmond and Jules de Goncourt,** *Diary*, **1867**

History is simply a piece of paper covered with print.
  **Otto von Bismarck**

When a history book contains no lies it is always tedious.
  **Anatole France,** *Le crime de Sylvestre Bonnard*, **1881**

The only duty we owe history is to rewrite it.
  **Oscar Wilde,** *The Critic as Artist*, **1891**

The past always looks better than it was; it's only pleasant because it isn't here.
  **Finley Peter Dunne**

Those who do not remember the past are condemned to repeat it.
  **George Santayana,** *The Life of Reason*, **1905–6**

History, n. An account mostly false, of events mostly unimportant, which are brought about by rulers, mostly knaves, and soldiers mostly fools.
  **Ambrose Bierce,** *The Devil's Dictionary*, **1911**

Mythology, n. The body of a primitive people's beliefs, concerning its origin, early history, heroes, deities and so forth, as distinguished from the the true accounts which it invents later.
  **Ambrose Bierce,** *The Devil's Dictionary*, **1911**

God cannot alter the past, that is why he is obliged to connive at the existence of historians.
  **Samuel Butler**

Human history becomes more and more a race between education and catastrophe.
  **H.G. Wells, *The Outline of History*, 1920**

History . . . is a nightmare from which I am trying to awake.
  **James Joyce, *Ulysses*, 1922**

History is largely concerned with arranging good entrances for people and later exits not always quite so good.
  **Heywood Broun, *Pieces of Hate*, 1922**

History – that little sewer where man loves to wallow.
  **François Ponge**

History repeats itself. Historians repeat each other.
  **Philip Guedalla, *Supers and Supermen*, 1920**

History is attractive to the more timid of us . . . we can recover self-confidence by snubbing the dead.
  **E.M. Forster, *Abinger Harvest*, 1936**

History is full of ignominious getaways by the great and famous.
  **George Orwell, *Who Are the War Criminals*, 1942**

It is sometimes very hard to tell the difference between history and the smell of skunk.
  **Rebecca West, *Black Lamb and Grey Falcon*, 1941**

You don't change the course of history by turning the faces of portraits to the wall.
  **Jawaharlal Nehru**

History is mostly guessing, the rest is prejudice.
  **Will and Ariel Durant**

History is the study of man's unhappiness
  **Raymond Queneau, *A Model History*, 1966**

The history of ideas is the history of the grudges of solitary men.
   **E.M. Cioran, *Syllogismes de l'amertume*, 1952**

What is history after all? History is facts which become legend in the end; legends are lies which become history in the end.
   **Jean Cocteau, 1957**

That men do not learn very much from history is the most important of all the lessons that history has to teach.
   **Aldous Huxley, *Collected Essays*, 1959**

History is littered with wars which everybody knew would never happen.
   **J. Enoch Powell, 1967**

The horror of the twentieth century is the size of each event and the paucity of its reverberation.
   **Norman Mailer, *Of A Fire on the Moon*, 1970**

Crimes of which a people is ashamed constitute its real history. The same is true of man.
   **Jean Genet, notes for *The Screens*, 1973**

Those who don't study the past will repeat its errors; those who do study it will find other ways to err.
   **Charles Wolf Jr, quoted in the *Wall Street Journal*, 1976**

History is an endless repetition of the wrong way of living.
   **Lawrence Durrell, in *The Listener*, 1978**

History repeats itself – the first time as tragi-comedy, the second time as bedroom farce.
   **Private Eye magazine, 1978**

Those who lie on the rails of history must expect to have their legs chopped off.
   **Rudé Právo, Czech party newspaper, quoted in *The Listener* magazine, 1979**

On the whole history tends to be rather poor fiction – except at its best.
   **Gore Vidal, *Writers at Work* 4th series, 1981**

A historian is often only a journalist facing backwards.
  **Karl Kraus,** *Half Truths and One and a Half Truths*, **1986**

Once you've made your mark on history those who can't will be so grateful they'll turn it into a cage for you.
  **Lester Bangs,** *Psychotic Reactions and Carburetor Dung*, **1988**

That perfect confusion known as history (a.k.a. the survivors' revenge).
  **Gore Vidal,** *A View from the Diner's Club*, **1991**

Tradition is just nostalgia walking about fully dressed in public.
  **Andrew Marr, in the** *Independent*, **1993**

May you live in interesting times.
  **Chinese curse**

# HOLLYWOOD

Hollywood: the place where girls go to look for husbands and husbands go to look for girls.
  **Anonymous**

Hollywood is a carnival where there are no concessions . . . a sewer, with service from the Ritz Carlton.
  **Wilson Mizner**

A leader of public thought in Hollywood wouldn't have sufficient mental acumen anywhere else to hold down a place in the bread line.
  **Anita Loos**

Hollywood impresses me as being ten million dollars worth of intricate and highly ingenious machinery functioning elaborately to put the skin on baloney.
  **George Jean Nathan**

I've spent several years in Hollywood, and I still think the movie heroes are in the audience.
  **Wilson Mizner**

The only 'ism' Hollywood believes in is plagiarism.
  **Dorothy Parker**

In Hollywood the eternal triangle consists of the actor, his wife and himself.

**Anonymous**

Strip the phoney tinsel off Hollywood and you'll find the real tinsel underneath.

**Oscar Levant**

The title 'Little Napoleon' in Hollywood is equivalent to the title 'Mister' in any other community.

**Alva Johnston**

Hollywood is a great place if you're an orange. *(Also cited as* California is a fine place to live in – if you're an orange.)

**Fred Allen**

Every day, to earn my daily bread
I go to the market where lies are bought
Hopefully
I take up my place among the sellers.

**Bertolt Brecht, 'Hollywood' in *Collected Poems 1913–1956*, 1976**

In a novel the hero can lay ten girls and marry a virgin for the finish. In a movie that is not allowed. The villain can lay anybody he wants, have as much fun as he wants cheating and stealing, getting rich and whipping the servants. But you have to shoot him in the end. When he falls with a bullet in the forehead it is advisable that he clutch at the Gobelin tapestry on the wall and bring it down over his head like a symbolic shroud. Also, covered by such a tapestry, the actor does not have to hold his breath while being photographed as a dead man.

**Herman Mankiewicz, 1940**

Hollywood . . . the most beautiful slave quarters in the world.

**Moss Hart**

Hollywood buys a good story about a bad girl and changes it to a bad story about a good girl.

**Anonymous**

There's only one thing that can kill the movies – and that is education.

**Will Rogers, *The Autobiography of Will Rogers*, 1949**

Hollywood is a place where people from Iowa mistake each other for a star.

**Fred Allen**

God felt sorry for actors, so he created Hollywood to give them a place in the sun and a swimming pool. The price they had to pay was to surrender their talent.

**Sir Cedric Hardwicke**

Hollywood must never permit censorship to collapse – it's far too good for the box office.

**Claude Binyon**

In Hollywood all marriages are happy. It's trying to live together afterwards that causes the problems.

**Shelley Winters**

A Hollywood aristocrat is anyone who can trace his ancestry back to his father.

**Anonymous**

American motion pictures are written by the half-educated for the half-witted.

**Sir John Irving, in the *New York Mirror*, 1963**

In Hollywood, if you don't have happiness, you send out for it.

**Rex Reed**

It proves what they say, give the public what they want to see and they'll come out for it.

**Red Skelton, surveying the crowded funeral of loathed
Hollywood mogul, Harry Cohn, 1957; also attributed to Samuel
Goldwyn, attending his rival Louis B. Mayer's obsequies, 1958**

That's what show business is – sincere insincerity.

**Benny Hill, in the *Observer*, 1977**

Popcorn is the last area of the movie business where good taste is still a concern.

**Mike Barfield, in *The Oldie* magazine, 1992**

Film directors are people too short to become actors.

**Josh Greenfield**

A Hollywood marriage is one in which the couple vow to be faithful to each other until after the honeymoon.

**Anonymous**

*See also* ACTING

# HONESTY

Men keep their agreements when it is to the advantage of neither to break them.

**Solon**

In this Age, when it is said of a Man, he knows *how to live*, it may be implied that he is not very honest.

**George Savile, Marquis of Halifax, *Political, Moral and Miscellaneous Thoughts and Reflexions*, c.1694**

To be honest is nothing: the reputation of it is all.

**William Congreve, *The Old Bachelor*, 1693**

He is only honest who is not discovered.

**Susannah Centlivre, *The Artifice*, 1710**

He that resolves to deal with none but honest men, must leave off dealing.

**Thomas Fuller, M.D., *Gnomologia*, 1732**

Honesty is not greater where elegance is less.

**Samuel Johnson, *Works* vol. ix, 1787**

The surest way to remain poor is to be an honest man.

**Napoleon Bonaparte, *Maxims*, 1804–15**

Put a rogue in the limelight and he will act like an honest man.

**Napoleon Bonaparte, *Maxims*, 1804–15**

A moderately honest man with a moderately faithful wife, moderate drinkers both in a moderately healthy house: that is the true middle-class unit.

**George Bernard Shaw, *Maxims for Revolutionists*, 1903**

Confessions may be good for the soul, but they are bad for the reputation.

**Lord Thomas Dewar**

Honesty consists not in never stealing, but in knowing when to stop in stealing, and how to make good use of what one does steal.
   **Samuel Butler, *Notebooks*, 1912**

We have to distrust each other. It's our only defence against betrayal.
   **Tennessee Williams, *Camino Real*, 1953**

There is one way to find out if a man is honest – ask him. If he says 'Yes', you know he is crooked.
   **Groucho Marx, 1954**

Experience teaches you that the man who looks you straight in the eye, particularly if he adds a firm handshake, is hiding something.
   **Clifton Fadiman, *Enter, Conversing*, 1962**

The only guy who is honest is the guy who sings in the shower. Everyone else is a prostitute.
   **Kim Fowley**

It's better to be quotable than to be honest.
   **Tom Stoppard, in the *Guardian*, 1973**

*See also* DECENCY, TRUTH

# HOPE

We promise according to our hopes, and perform according to our fears.
   **François, Duc de La Rochefoucauld, *Maxims*, 1665**

Gratitude is merely a secret hope of further favours.
   **François, Duc de La Rochefoucauld, *Maxims*, 1665**

Men should do with their Hopes as they do with tame Fowl, cut their Wings that they may not fly over the Wall.
   **George Savile, Marquis of Halifax, *Political, Moral and Miscellaneous Thoughts and Reflexions*, c.1694**

Hope is the worst of evils, for it prolongs the torment of man.
   **Friedrich Wilhelm Nietzsche, *Human, All Too Human*, 1878**

It is well known that we should not expect something for nothing but we do – and call it Hope.
   **Edgar Watson Howe, *Country Town Sayings*, 1911**

Hope is a pathological belief in the occurrence of the impossible.
**H.L. Mencken,** *Sententiae,* **1916**

Hope must feel that the human breast is amazingly tolerant.
**Henry Haskins,** *Meditations in Wall Street,* **1940**

Hope is an illusion for squares.
**Colin Johnson,** *Wild Cat Falling*

The hope that springs eternal
Springs right up your behind.
**Ian Dury,** *This Is What We Find,* **1979**

*See also* OPTIMISM

# HUMANITY

Two things only the people anxiously desire: bread and the Circus games.
**Juvenal,** *Satires*

In brief, we are all monsters, that is, a composition of man and beast.
**Sir Thomas Browne,** *Religio Medici,* **1642**

The truest wild beasts live in the most populous places.
**Baltasar Gracian,** *The Art of Worldly Wisdom,* **1647**

The reason why fools and knaves thrive better in the world than wiser and honester men is because they are nearer to the general temper of mankind, which is nothing but a mixture of cheat and folly.
**Samuel Butler,** *Prose Observations 1660–1680,* **ed. Hugh de Quehen, 1980**

It is the Fools and Knaves that make the Wheels of the World turn. *They* are *the World;* those few who have Sense or Honesty sneak up and down single, but never go in Herds.
**George Savile, Marquis of Halifax,** *Political, Moral and Miscellaneous Thoughts and Reflexions,* **c.1694**

The most necessary in the World, and yet the least usual, is to reflect that those we deal with may know how to be as arrant knaves as ourselves.
**George Savile, Marquis of Halifax,** *Political, Moral and Miscellaneous Thoughts and Reflexions,* **c.1694**

The World is nothing but Vanity cut into several Shapes.
**George Savile, Marquis of Halifax, *Political, Moral and Miscellaneous Thoughts and Reflexions*, c.1694**

The more I see of men the more I admire dogs.
**Marie de Rabutin-Chantal, Marquise de Sévigné, 1725**

The world is a vast temple dedicated to Discord.
**Voltaire, letter, 1752**

That observation which is called knowledge of the world will be found more frequently to make men cunning than good.
**Samuel Johnson, *The Rambler*, 1749–52**

The world, in its best state, is nothing more than a large assembly of beings, combining to counterfeit happiness, which they do not feel, employing every art and contrivance to embellish life, and to hide their real condition from the eyes of one another.
**Samuel Johnson, *The Adventurer*, 1753–4**

The first man to fence in a piece of land saying 'This is mine' and who found people simple enough to believe him, was the real founder of civil society.
**Jean-Jacques Rousseau, *Discourse on the Origin and Bases of Inequality among Men*, 1755**

No sooner are we supplied with everything that nature can demand, than we sit down to contrive artificial appetites.
**Samuel Johnson, *The Idler*, 1758–60**

All men are born with a sufficiently violent liking for domination, wealth and pleasure, and with much taste for idleness; consequently all men want the money and the wives or daughters of others, to be their master, to subject them to all their caprices, and to do nothing, or at least to do only very agreeable things.
**Voltaire, *Philosophical Dictionary*, 1764**

Once the people begin to reason, all is lost.
**Voltaire, letter, 1766**

We are to consider mankind not as we wish them, but as we find them, frequently corrupt and always fallible.
**Samuel Johnson, *Works* vol. xi, 1787**

The only thing that stops God sending a second Flood is that the first one was useless.
  **Nicolas de Chamfort, *Characters and Anecdotes*, 1771**

The people are that part of the state which does not know what it wants.
  **Georg Wilhelm Friedrich Hegel**

Mankind are an incorrigible race. Give them but bugbears and idols – it is all that they ask.
  **William Hazlitt, *Lectures on the English Comic Writers*, 1819**

Never pity people because they are ill-used. They only wait the opportunity to use others just as ill.
  **William Hazlitt**

That great baby, the world, however it may cry up and pretend to admire its idols, is just like the little girl who, after dressing up her doll in all its finery, and caressing it until she is tired, is not easy until she has pulled it to pieces again and reduced it to its original rags and wool.
  **William Hazlitt, *The Ruling Passion*, 1829**

Human beings cling to their delicious tyrannies and to their exquisite nonsense like a drunkard to his bottle and go on until death stares them in the face.
  **Sydney Smith**

It is an error to suppose that no man understands his own character. Most persons know even their failings very well, only they persist in giving them names different from those usually assigned by the rest of the world.
  **Sir Arthur Helps, *Thoughts in the Cloister and the Crowd*, 1835**

Believe everything you hear about the world; nothing is too impossibly bad.
  **Honoré de Balzac**

Society is a hospital of incurables.
  **Ralph Waldo Emerson, 1843**

The general average of mankind are not only moderate in intellect, but also moderate in inclinations: they have no taste or wishes strong enough to incline them to do anything unusual, and they consequently do not understand those who have, and class all such with the wild and intemperate upon whom they are accustomed to look down.

**John Stuart Mill,** *On Liberty*, **1859**

It is hard for a pure and thoughtful man to live in a state of rapture at the spectacle afforded him by his fellow-creatures.

**Matthew Arnold**

The Lord prefers common-looking people. That is the reason He makes so many of them.

**Abraham Lincoln**

Tell me what you think you are and I will tell you what you are not.

**Henri-Frédéric Amiel,** *Journal intime*, **1866**

Whatever you may be sure of, be sure of this: that you are dreadfully like other people.

**James Russell Lowell,** *My Study Windows*, **1871**

That all men should be brothers is the dream of people who have no brothers.

**Charles Chincholles,** *Pensées de tout le monde*, **1880**

People who have no faults are terrible – there is no way of taking advantage of them.

**Anatole France**

I sometimes think that God, in creating man, somewhat overestimated his ability.

**Oscar Wilde**

Humanity is a pigsty where liars, hypocrites and the obscene in spirit congregate.

**George Moore,** *Confessions of a Young Man*, **1888**

'Every man has his price.' This is not true. But for every man there exists a bait which he cannot resist swallowing.

**Friedrich Wilhelm Nietzsche**

Man is a dog's ideal of what God should be.

**Holbrook Jackson**

It is only shallow people who do not judge by appearances.
  **Oscar Wilde, *The Picture of Dorian Gray*, 1891**

It is absurd to divide people into good and bad. People are either charming or tedious.
  **Oscar Wilde, *Lady Windermere's Fan*, 1892**

The great merit of society is to make one appreciate solitude.
  **Charles Chincholles, quoted in *Reflections on the Art of Life* by J.R. Solly, 1902**

Most people are other people. Their thoughts are someone else's opinions, their lives a mimicry, their passions a quotation.
  **Oscar Wilde, *De Profundis*, 1905**

The self-made man is often proud of a poor job.
  **Addison Mizner and Oliver Herford, *The Entirely New Cynic's Calendar*, 1905**

In each human heart there are a tiger, a pig, an ass and a nightingale. Diversity of character is due to their unequal activity.
  **Ambrose Bierce, *The Devil's Dictionary*, 1911**

The devil is an optimist if he thinks he can make people meaner.
  **Karl Kraus, in *Karl Kraus* by H. Zohn, 1971**

The world is a prison in which solitary confinement is preferable.
  **Karl Kraus, *Half Truths and One and a Half Truths*, 1986**

Man, biologically considered, . . . is the most formidable of all beasts of prey, and, indeed, is the only one that preys systematically on its own species.
  **William James, *Memories and Studies*, 1911**

We think as we do, mainly because other people think so.
  **Samuel Butler, *Notebooks*, 1912**

The fixity of a habit is generally in direct proportion to its absurdity.
  **Marcel Proust, *Remembrance of Things Past*, 1913–27**

The world, like an accomplished hostess, pays most attention to those whom it will soonest forget.
  **John Churton Collins, in *The English Review*, 1914**

Men are the only animals that devote themselves, day in and day out, to making one another unhappy. It is an art like any other. Its virtuosi are called altruists.

**H.L. Mencken, *Sententiae*, 1916**

The Plain People are worth dying for until you bunch them and give them the cold Once-Over, and then they impress the impartial Observer as being slightly Bovine, with a large Percentage of Vegetable Tissue.

**George Ade, *Hand-Made Fables*, 1920**

Most human beings are quite likeable if you do not see too much of them.

**Robert Lynd**

Considering how bad men are, it is wonderful how well they behave.

**Salvador de Madariaga**

Many people believe they attracted by God, or by Nature, when they are only repelled by man.

**William R. Inge, *More Lay Thoughts of a Dean*, 1931**

The world consists of the dangerously insane and such that are not.

**Mark Twain, *Notebooks*, 1935**

I'll give you my opinion of the human race in a nutshell . . . their heart's in the right place, but their head is a thoroughly inefficient organ.

**W. Somerset Maugham, *The Summing Up*, 1938**

Happy that few of us are aware of the world until we are already in league with it.

**Elizabeth Bowen, *The Death of the Heart*, 1938**

Most people are such fools that it is really no great compliment to say that a man is above the average.

**W. Somerset Maugham, *A Writer's Notebook*, 1949**

Humanity, let us say, is like people packed in an automobile which is travelling downhill without lights at terrific speed and driven by a small four-year-old child. The signposts along the way are all marked 'Progress'.

**Lord Dunsany, 1954**

What men value in this world is not rights, but privileges.

**H.L. Mencken,** *Minority Report*, **1956**

Mankind . . . will not willingly admit that its destiny can be revealed by the breeding of flies or the counting of chiasmata.

**Cyril Dean Darlington, lecture, 1960**

In a crisis that forces a choice to be made among alternative courses of action, most people will choose the worst one possible.

**S.A. Rudin, in the** *New Republic*, **1961**

He who despairs over an event is a coward, but he who holds hopes for the human condition is a fool.

**Albert Camus,** *Notebooks*, **1962**

Mankind has collected together all the wisdom of his ancestors, and can see what a fool man is.

**Elias Canetti**

Nothing is the history of the world viewed from a suitable distance. Revolution is a trivial shift in the emphasis of suffering; the capacity for self-indulgence changes hands. But the world does not alter its shape or its course . . . Against such immutability the human struggle takes place on the same scale as the insect movements in the grass.

**Tom Stoppard,** *Lord Malquist and Mr Moon*, **1966**

Human beings seem to have an almost unlimited capacity to deceive themselves and to deceive themselves into taking their own lies for truth.

**R.D. Laing,** *The Politics of Experience*, **1967**

We are all murderers and prostitutes. No matter to what culture, society, class, nation one belongs, no matter how normal, moral or mature one takes oneself to be.

**R.D. Laing,** *The Politics of Experience*, **1967**

If one looks with a cold eye at the mess man has made of his history, it is difficult to avoid the conclusion that he has been afflicted by some built-in mental disorder which drives him towards self-destruction. Murder within the species on an individual or collective scale is a phenomenon unknown in the whole animal kingdom, except for man, and a few varieties of ants and rats.

**Arthur Koestler, in the** *Observer*, **1968**

Though the strongest resist all temptation, all human beings who suffer from any deficiency, real or imagined, are under compulsion to draw attention to it.

**Quentin Crisp, *The Naked Civil Servant*, 1968**

There is no such thing as a situation so intolerable that human beings must necessarily rise up against it. People can bear anything, and the longer it exists the more placidly they will bear it.

**Philip Slater, *The Pursuit of Loneliness*, 1970**

People will swim through shit if you put a few bob in it.

**Peter Sellers**

In the fight between you and the world, back the world.

**Frank Zappa**

People are always talking about tradition, but they forget we have a tradition of a few hundred years of nonsense and stupidity, that there is a tradition of idiocy, incompetence and crudity.

**Hugo Demartini, quoted in *Contemporary Artists*, 1977**

Everyone becomes the thing they most despise.

**Robert Benchley, quoted in *Wits End* by J.R. Gaines, 1977**

All God's children are not beautiful. Most of God's children are, in fact, barely presentable.

**Fran Lebowitz, *Metropolitan Life*, 1978**

The human race never solves any of its problems. It merely outlives them.

**David Gerrold, in *Starlog* magazine, 1978**

That old question 'Who are we?' receives a disappointing answer in the world in which we must live. Actually, we are merely the subject of this so-called civilised world, in which intelligence, baseness, heroism and stupidity get on very well together and are alternately being pushed to the fore.

**René Magritte, quoted in *Magritte: The True Art of Painting*, ed. H. Torczyner, 1979**

We . . . make the modern error of dignifying the Individual. We do everything we can to butter him up. We give him a name, assure him that he has certain inalienable rights, educate him, let him pass on his name to his brats and when he dies we give him a special hole in the ground . . . But after all, he's only a seed, a bloom and a withering stalk among pressing billions. Your Individual is a pretty disgusting, vain, lewd little bastard . . . By God, he has only one right guaranteed to him in Nature, and that is the right to die and stink to Heaven.

**Ross Lockridge, quoted in** *Short Lives* **by Katinka Matson, 1980**

If ignorance is bliss, why aren't more people happy.

**Leonard Rossiter**

People (a group that in my opinion has always attracted an undue amount of attention) have often been likened to snowflakes. This analogy is meant to suggest that each is unique – no two alike. This is quite patently not the case. People . . . are quite simply a dime a dozen. And, I hasten to add, their only similarity to snowflakes resides in their invariable and lamentable tendency to turn, after a few warm days, to slush.

**Fran Lebowitz,** *Social Studies***, 1981**

More than any other time in history, mankind faces a crossroads. One path leads to despair and utter hopelessness. The other, to total extinction. Let us pray we have the wisdom to choose correctly.

**Woody Allen,** *Side Effects***, 1981**

It seemed the world was divided into good and bad people. The good ones slept better . . ., while the bad ones seemed to enjoy the waking hours much more.

**Woody Allen,** *Side Effects***, 1981**

*See also* LIFE, MEN, WOMEN

# HUSBANDS

The bachelor is a peacock, the engaged man a lion, and the married man a jackass.

**German proverb**

The majority of husbands remind me of an orangutang trying to play the violin.

**Honoré de Balzac,** *The Physiology of Marriage***, 1829**

If there were no husbands, who would look after our mistresses.

**George Moore, *Confessions of a Young Man*, 1888**

A woman who takes her husband about with her everywhere is like a cat that goes on playing with a mouse long after she's killed it.

**Saki (H.H. Munro), *The Watched Pot*, 1924**

No woman can endure a gambling husband, unless he is a steady winner.

**Lord Thomas Dewar**

I know many married men, I even know a few happily married men, but I don't know one who wouldn't fall down the first open coal-hole running after the first pretty girl who gave him a wink.

**George Jean Nathan**

The man she had was kind and clean
And well enough for everyday,
But, oh, dear friends,
You should have seen
The one that got away.

**Dorothy Parker, *The Fisherwoman*, 1931**

There you are you see, quite simply, if you cannot have your dear husband for a comfort and a delight, for a breadwinner and a crosspatch, for a sofa, a chair or a hotwater bottle, one can use him as a Cross to be borne.

**Stevie Smith**

The opera is like a husband with a foreign title – expensive to support, hard to understand and therefore a supreme social challenge.

**Cleveland Amory, on NBC-TV, 1961**

All husbands are alike, but they have different faces so you can tell them apart.

**Anonymous, quoted in *Cassell Book of Humorous Quotations*, 1968**

A husband is simply a lover with two days' growth of beard, his collar off and a bad cold in the head.

**Anonymous, quoted in *Cassell Book of Humorous Quotations*, 1968**

Virginity is supposed to be something you give to your husband, like engraved cufflinks, on your wedding day.

**Jilly Cooper, *Super Women*, 1974**

*See also* AFFAIRS, DIVORCE, LOVE, LOVERS, MARRIAGE, WIVES

# HYPOCRISY

It is of great consequence to disguise your inclination, and to play the hypocrite well; and men are so simple in their temper and so submissive to their present necessities, that he that is neat and cleanly in his collusions shall never want people to practise them upon.

**Niccolò Machiavelli, *The Prince*, 1513**

Hypocrisy is the homage that vice pays to virtue.

**François, Duc de La Rochefoucauld, *Maxims*, 1665**

He must be a perfect *complete hypocrite*, if he will be a *complete tradesman*.

**Daniel Defoe, *The Complete English Tradesman*, 1726**

Remorse is nothing save the anticipation of the pain to which our offence has exposed us.

**C.A. Helvétius, *De l'homme*, 1773**

General Good is the plea of the scoundrel, hypocrite and flatterer.

**William Blake, *Jerusalem*, 1804–20**

Man is no angel. He is sometimes more of a hypocrite and sometimes less, and then fools say he has or has not principles.

**Honoré de Balzac, *Old Goriot*, 1835**

It is a very noble hypocrisy not to talk of oneself.

**Friedrich Wilhelm Nietzsche, *Human, All Too Human*, 1878**

What people call insincerity is simply a method by which we can multiply our personalities.

**Oscar Wilde, *The Critic as Artist*, 1891**

A little sincerity is a dangerous thing, and a great deal of it is absolutely fatal.

**Oscar Wilde, *The Critic as Artist*, 1891**

There is a good deal to be said for blushing, if one can do it at the proper moment.

**Oscar Wilde, *A Woman of No Importance*, 1893**

A sentimentalist is simply one who desires to have the luxury of an emotion without paying for it.

**Oscar Wilde**

To be natural is such a very difficult pose to keep up.

**Oscar Wilde, *An Ideal Husband*, 1895**

Hypocrite, n: One who, professing virtues that he does not respect, secures the advantage of seeming to be what he despises.

**Ambrose Bierce, *The Devil's Dictionary*, 1911**

Hypocrisy is the most difficult and nerve-racking vice that any man can pursue; it needs an unceasing vigilance and a rare detachment of spirit. It cannot, like adultery or gluttony, be practised at spare moments; it is a wholetime job.

**W. Somerset Maugham, *Cakes and Ale*, 1930**

Sentimentality is a superstructure covering brutality.

**C.G. Jung, *Reflections*, 1953**

We live behind our faces, while they front for us.

**Michael Korda, *Power in the Office*, 1976**

A hypocrite is a person who . . . but who isn't?

**Don Marquis, quoted in *The Oxford Book of Aphorisms*, ed. J. Gross, 1983**

*See also* BELIEF, FAITH, IDEALS, MORALS, RELIGION, TRUE BELIEVERS, TRUTH

# IDEALS

The idealist is incorrigible: if he be thrown out of Heaven, he makes an ideal of his Hell.

**Friedrich Wilhelm Nietzsche, *Human, All Too Human*, 1878**

Do not use that foreign word 'ideals'. We have that excellent native word 'lies'.

**Henrik Ibsen, *The Wild Duck*, 1884**

Man is a dog's ideal of what God should be.
  **Holbrook Jackson**

An idealist is one who helps the other fellow to make a profit.
  **Henry Ford**

An idealist is one who, on noticing that a rose smells better than a cabbage, concludes that it will also make better soup.
  **H.L. Mencken, *Sententiae*, 1916**

Idealism increases in direct proportion to one's distance from the problem.
  **John Galsworthy**

It seems to be the fate of idealists to obtain what they have struggled for in a form which destroys their ideals.
  **Bertrand Russell, *Marriage and Morals*, 1929**

When they come downstairs from their ivory towers, idealists are apt to walk straight into the gutter.
  **Logan Pearsall Smith, *Afterthoughts*, 1931**

We are all inclined to judge ourselves by our ideals; others by their acts.
  **Harold Nicolson**

Positive ideals . . . can seldom be achieved without someone being killed or maimed or interned.
  **E.M. Forster, *Two Cheers for Democracy*, 1951**

Idealism is the noble toga that political gentlemen drape over their will to power.
  **Aldous Huxley, 1963**

Idealism is fine, but as it approaches reality the cost becomes prohibitive.
  **William F. Buckley Jr**

An idealist – that implies you aren't going to achieve something.
  **Arthur Scargill, 1974**

Rigorous ideological committment is of greatly negative value for governing a country . . . and is a positive threat to economic tranquility and well-being. Economic and social institutions are in a constant process of change; ideological committment, by its nature and strongly avowed virtue, is static. Accordingly, guidance therefrom is likely to be obsolete, obsolescent or irrelevant.

**John Kenneth Galbraith, quoted in the *New York Review of Books*, 1986**

*See also* BELIEF, FAITH, IDEAS, MORALS, RELIGION, TRUE BELIEVERS, TRUTH

# IDEAS

A nice man is a man of nasty ideas.

**Jonathan Swift, *Thoughts on Various Subjects*, 1706**

We use ideas merely to justify our evil, and speech merely to conceal our ideas.

**Voltaire**

All universal moral principles are idle fancies.

**Donatien Alphonse François, Marquis de Sade, *The 120 Days of Sodom*, 1785**

One of the greatest pains to human nature is the pain of a new idea.

**Walter Bagehot, *Physics and Politics*, 1872**

As soon as an idea is accepted it is time to reject it.

**Holbrook Jackson**

To die for an idea is to place a pretty high price upon conjectures.

**Anatole France, *The Revolt of the Angels*, 1914**

An idea is putting truth in checkmate.

**José Ortega y Gasset, *The Revolt of the Masses*, 1932**

Nothing is more dangerous than an idea, when a man has only one idea.

**Alain, *Propos de la Réligion*, 1938**

Man is ready to die for an idea, provided that idea is not quite clear to him.

**Paul Eldridge, *Horns of Glass*, 1943**

Few things are as immutable as the addiction of political groups to the ideas by which they have once won office.

**John Kenneth Galbraith, *The Affluent Society*, 1958**

Let's remind ourselves that last year's fresh idea is today's cliché.

**Austen Briggs**

As a rule, the most dangerous ideas are not the ones that divide people but those on which they agree.

**Stephen Vizinczey, *The Rules of Chaos*, 1970**

Of all political ideas, perhaps the most dangerous is the wish to make people perfect and happy. The attempt to realise heaven on earth has always produced a hell.

**Karl Popper, 1971**

*See also* BELIEF, FAITH, IDEALS, MORALS, RELIGION, TRUE BELIEVERS, TRUTH

# INTELLECTUALS

Be wiser than other people if you can, but do not tell them so.

**Lord Chesterfield, *Letters to his Son*, 1774**

Clever men are the tools with which bad men work.

**William Hazlitt, *Collected Works*, 1904**

An intellectual is a parasite that exudes culture.

**Tadeusz Kotarbinski**

What is a highbrow? It is a man who has found something more interesting than women.

**Edgar Wallace, interview, 1931**

A class made up solely of intellectuals will always have a guilty conscience.

**Adolf Hitler, on schoolmasters**

Intellectuals are like women – they go for the military.

**André Malraux**

To the man-in-the-street, who, I'm sorry to say
Is a keen observer of life,
The word 'intellectual' suggests right away
A man who's untrue to his wife.

**W.H. Auden, *New Year Letter*, 1941**

Intellectuals can tell themselves anything, sell themselves any bill of goods, which is why they are so often patsies for the ruling classes.

**Lillian Hellman, *An Unfinished Woman*, 1969**

Intellectuals are people who believe that ideas are more important than values. That is to say, their own ideas and other people's values.

**Gerald Brenan, *Thoughts in a Dry Season*, 1978**

If you are sure you understand everything that is going on, you are hopelessly confused.

**Walter Mondale, 1978**

One time you let people know how much sense you got, right away they quit having anything to do with you.

**Chester Burnett (Howlin' Wolf)**

Wisdom is deepest platitude.

**Gore Vidal, on London Weekend Television, 1981**

*See also* GENIUS

# JOURNALISM

News is something someone, somewhere doesn't want you to print – the rest is advertising.

**Anonymous**

A newswriter is a man without virtue, who writes lies at home for his own profit.

**Samuel Johnson, *The Idler*, 1758–60**

Perhaps an editor might divide his paper into four chapters, heading the first, Truths; the second, Probabilities; the third, Possibilities and the fourth, Lies.

**Thomas Jefferson**

A newspaper writer is one who has failed in his calling.

**Otto von Bismarck, 1862**

There is much to be said in favour of modern journalism. By giving us the opinions of the uneducated, it keeps us in touch with the ignorance of the community.

**Oscar Wilde,** *The Critic as Artist,* **1891**

The public have an insatiable curiosity to know everything. Except what is worth knowing. Journalism, conscious of this, and having tradesman-like habits, supplies their demands.

**Oscar Wilde,** *The Soul of Man under Socialism,* **1891**

Journalism largely consists in saying 'Lord Jones Dead' to people who never knew Lord Jones was alive.

**G.K. Chesterton,** *The Wisdom of Father Brown,* **1914**

Newspapers have roughly the same relationship to life as fortune-tellers to metaphysics.

**Karl Kraus,** *Half Truths and One and a Half Truths,* **1986**

Journalists write because they have nothing to say, and have something to say because they write.

**Karl Kraus**

Journalism: a profession whose business is to explain to others what it personally doesn't understand.

**Lord Northcliffe**

Editor . . . a person employed on a newspaper, whose business it is to separate the wheat from the chaff, and to see that the chaff is printed.

**Elbert Hubbard,** *Roycroft Dictionary,* **1923**

All newspaper editorial writers ever do is come down from the hills after the battle is over and bayonet the wounded.

**Anonymous**

You cannot hope
To bribe or twist,
Thank God! the
British journalist.
But seeing what
That man will do
Unbribed, there's
No occasion to.

**Humbert Wolfe,** *The Uncelestial City,* **1930**

There is more joy in Fleet Street over one sinner that cuts his sweet-heart's throat than over the ninety and nine just men who marry and live happily ever after.

**A.P. Herbert, *Mild and Bitter*, 1936**

There is but one way for a newspaper man to look at a politician, and that is down.

**Frank H. Simonds, quoted in *H.L. Mencken's Dictionary of Quotations*, 1941**

To a newspaper man a human being is an item with skin wrapped around it.

**Fred Allen**

A [newspaper] editor should have a pimp for a brother so he'd have someone to look up to.

**Gene Fowler**

Journalism . . . drawing sketches in the sand that the sea will wash away.

**Walter Lippmann, *The New Republic*, 1915**

Freedom of the press in Britain is freedom to print such of the proprietor's prejudices as the advertisers don't object to.

**Hannen Swaffer, 1902**

[The] constant yelping about a free press means, with a few honourable exceptions, freedom to peddle scandal, crime, sex, sensationalism, hate, innuendo and the political and financial uses of propaganda. A newspaper is a business out to make money through advertising revenue. That is predicated on its circulation and you know what circulation depends on.

**Raymond Chandler, *The Long Goodbye*, 1953**

The press conference is the politician's way of being informative without actually saying anything.

**Emery Kelen**

The interview is an intimate conversation between journalist and politician wherein the journalist seeks to take advantage of the garrulity of the politician and the politician of the credulity of the journalist.

**Emery Kelen**

People everywhere confuse what they read in the newspapers with news.

**A.J. Liebling, in the *New Yorker* magazine, 1956**

The media, far from being a conspiracy to dull the political sense of the people, could be viewed as a conspiracy to disguise the extent of political indifference.

**David Riesman**

Journalism – an ability to meet the challenge of filling the space.

**Rebecca West, in the *New York Herald Tribune*, 1956**

I read the newspaper avidly. It is my one form of continuous fiction.

**Aneurin Bevan, 1960**

You know very well that whether you are on page one or page thirty depends on whether [the press] fear you. It is just as simple as that.

**Richard M. Nixon**

The important thing about the so-called 'communications industry' is that it is basically concerned with merchandising. News is a kind of by-product and if you want to sell things, you don't want to offend anybody.

**I.F. Stone, in *The Listener* magazine, 1963**

There are honest journalists like there are honest politicians. When bought they stay bought.

**Bill Moyers**

To the majority of [newspapermen] a woman is either somebody's mother or a whore.

**Alexander King, *Rich Man, Poor Man, Freud and Fruit*, 1965**

It is part of the social mission of every great newspaper to provide a refuge and a home for the largest possible number of salaried eccentrics.

**Baron Thomson of Fleet**

Everything you read in the newspapers is absolutely true, except for that rare story of which you happen to have first-hand knowledge.

**Erwin Knoll**

The only qualities for real success in journalism are ratlike cunning, a plausible manner and a little literary ability. The capacity to steal other people's ideas and phrases . . . is also invaluable.

**Nicholas Tomalin, *Stop the Press, I Want to Get On*, 1969**

Most rock journalism is people who can't write interviewing people who can't talk for people who can't read.

**Frank Zappa**

Journalism is organised gossip.

**Edward Egglestone**

The First Law of Journalism: to confirm existing prejudice, rather than contradict it.

**Alexander Cockburn, *(more)* magazine, 1974**

We should always tell the Press, freely and frankly, anything they can easily find out.

**Antony Jay and Jonathan Lynn, *Yes, Prime Minister*, 1986**

Journalists are notoriously easy to kid. All you have to do is speak to a journalist in a very serious tone of voice and he will be certain that you are either telling the truth or a big, important lie. It has never occurred to any journalist that he is having his leg pulled.

**P.J. O'Rourke, *Parliament of Whores*, 1991**

After politics, journalism has always been the preferred career of the ambitious but lazy second-rater.

**Gore Vidal, *A View from the Diners Club*, 1991**

Never trust a smiling reporter.

**Ed Koch**

Journalism could be described as turning one's enemies into money.

**Craig Brown, 1993**

*See also* TELEVISION & RADIO

# JUSTICE

The love of justice in most men is nothing more than the fear of suffering injustice.

**François, Duc de La Rochefoucauld, *Maxims*, 1665**

To talk of not acting from fear is mere parliamentary cant. From what motive but . . . have all the improvements in our constitution proceeded. I question if justice has ever been done to large masses of mankind from any other motive.

**Sydney Smith,** *The Letters of Peter Plymley***, 1807**

The only way to make the mass of mankind see the beauty of justice is by showing them in pretty plain terms the consequence of injustice.

**Sydney Smith, quoted in** *Roads to Ruin***, by E.S. Turner, 1950**

Justice is the sanction of established injustice.

**Anatole France,** *Crainquebille***, 1901**

Justice, n. A commodity which in a more or less adulterate condition the State sells to the citizen as a reward for his allegiance, taxes and personal service.

**Ambrose Bierce,** *The Devil's Dictionary***, 1911**

Justice is being allowed to do whatever I like; injustice is whatever prevents me from doing it.

**Samuel Butler,** *Notebooks***, 1912**

In the Halls of Justice the only justice is in the halls.

**Lenny Bruce**

Justice is like a train that's nearly always late.

**Yevgeny Yevtushenko,** *A Precocious Autobiography***, 1963**

*See also* CRIME, LAW, LAWYERS

# LAUGHTER

He who laughs at everything is as big a fool as he who weeps at everything.

**Baltasar Gracian,** *The Art of Worldly Wisdom***, 1647**

Laughter is nothing else but sudden glory arising from some sudden conception of some eminency in ourselves, by comparison with the infirmity of others, or with our own formerly.

**Thomas Hobbes,** *On Human Nature***, 1650**

Laughter is the hiccup of a fool.

**John Ray,** *A Collection of English Proverbs***, 1670**

Laughter is little more than an expression of self-satisfied shrewdness.
  **Georg Wilhelm Friedrich Hegel, *The Philosophy of Right*, 1820**

He who laughs has not yet heard the bad news.
  **Bertolt Brecht**

Nothing shortens a journey so pleasantly as an account of misfortunes at which the hearer is permitted to laugh.
  **Quentin Crisp, *How To Become a Virgin*, 1981**

*See also* HAPPINESS

# LAW

Laws are like spiders' webs which, if anything small falls into them they ensnare it, but large things break through and escape.
  **Solon, quoted in *Lives and Opinions of Eminent Philosophers* by Diogenes Laertius, *c.*AD225**

Sir, executions are intended to draw spectators. If they do not draw spectators they don't answer their purpose.
  **Samuel Johnson, quoted in *The Life of Samuel Johnson* by J. Boswell, 1791**

Laws are now maintained in credit, not because they are essentially just, but because they are laws. It is the mystical foundation of their authority; they have none other. They are often made by fools; more often by men who in hatred of equality have want of equity; but ever by men who are vain and irresolute. There is nothing so grossly and largely offending, nor so ordinarily wrongful, as the laws.
  **Michel de Montaigne, *Essays*, 1595**

Necessity hath no law.
  **Oliver Cromwell, 1654**

Law is but a heathen word for power.
  **Daniel Defoe, *The History of the Kentish Rebellion*, 1701**

Liberty is the right to do what the laws permit.
  **Charles de Secondat, Baron de Montesquieu, *De l'ésprit des lois*, 1748**

The law doth punish man or woman
That steals the goose from off the common,
But lets the greater felon loose,
That steals the common from the goose.
  **Anonymous**

Laws are always useful to persons of property.
  **Jean-Jacques Rousseau,** *The Social Contract*, **1762**

The mass of the people have nothing to do with the laws but to obey them.
  **Bishop Samuel Horsley, 1795**

Every law which originated in ignorance and malice, and gratifies the passions from which it sprang, we call the wisdom of our ancestors.
  **Sydney Smith,** *The Letters of Peter Plymley*, **1807**

What are laws but the expression of some class which has power over the rest of the community?
  **Thomas Babington Macaulay, Baron Macaulay,** *Southey's Colloquies*, **1830**

People say law but they mean wealth.
  **Ralph Waldo Emerson,** *Journals*, **1909–14**

We bury men when they are dead, but we try to embalm the dead body of laws, keeping the corpse in sight long after the vitality has gone. It usually takes a hundred years to make a law; and then, after it has done its work, takes a hundred years to get rid of it.
  **Henry Ward Beecher,** *Life Thoughts*, **1858**

If a man stay away from his wife for seven years, the law presumes the separation to have killed him; yet according to our daily experience, it might well prolong his life.
  **Charles Darling,** *Scintillae Juris*, **1877**

A jury is composed of twelve men of average ignorance.
  **Herbert Spencer**

A reasonable man can get out of most any trouble, except marriage, without going to law.
  **Reflections of a Bachelor, 1878**

The law has no claim to human respect. It has no more civilizing mission; its only purpose is to protect exploitation.

**Peter Kropotkin,** *Paroles d'un révolté,* **1884**

The law, in all its majestic equality, forbids the rich as well as the poor to sleep under bridges.

**Anatole France,** *The Red Lily,* **1894**

Law is the expression of the will of the strongest for the time being.

**Henry Brooks Adams**

Of course there's a different law for the rich and the poor; otherwise, who would go into business.

**E. Ralph Stewart**

A judge is a lawyer who once knew a politician.

**Anonymous**

Where there's a will, there's a lawsuit.

**Addison Mizner and Oliver Herford,** *The Cynic's Calendar,* **1901**

Lawful, adj. Compatible with the will of a judge having jurisdiction.

**Ambrose Bierce,** *The Devil's Dictionary,* **1911**

Judge: a law student who marks his own papers.

**H.L. Mencken,** *Sententiae,* **1916**

It has long been noticed that juries are pitiless for robbery and full of indulgence for infanticide. A question of interest, my dear Sir! The jury is afraid of being robbed and has passed the age when it could be a victim of infanticide.

**Edmond About, quoted in** *A Cynic's Breviary* **by J.R. Solly 1925**

The Reasonable Man . . . is devoid of any human weaknesses, with not a single saving vice . . . This excellent but odious character stands like a monument in the Courts of Justice.

**A.P. Herbert,** *Misleading Cases in the Common Law,* **1929**

The law, as manipulated by clever and highly respectable rascals, still remains the best avenue for a career of honourable and leisurely plunder.

**Gabriel Chevallier,** *Clochemerle,* **1936**

The law isn't justice. It's a very imperfect mechanism. If you press exactly the right buttons and are also lucky, justice may also turn up in the answer.

**Raymond Chandler, *The Long Goodbye*, 1953**

Cops never say goodbye. They're always hoping to see you again in the line-up.

**Raymond Chandler, *The Long Goodbye*, 1953**

I have never seen a situation so dismal that a policeman couldn't make it worse.

**Brendan Behan**

The dispensing of injustice is always in the right hands.

**Stanislaw J. Lec, *Unkempt Thoughts*, 1962**

A man's respect for law and order exists in precise relationship to the size of his pay cheque.

**Adam Clayton Powell, *Keep the Faith Baby*, 1967**

The police and so forth only exist insofar as they can demonstrate their authority. They say they're here to preserve order, but in fact they'd go absolutely mad if all the criminals of the world went on strike for a month. They'd be on their knees begging for a crime. That's the only existence they have.

**William S. Burroughs, in the *Guardian*, 1969**

One of the greatest delusions in the world is the hope that the evils of this world can be cured by legislation.

**Thomas B. Reed**

To the right wing 'law and order' is often just a code phrase, meaning 'get the niggers'. To the left wing it often means political oppression.

**Gore Vidal, 1975**

The quality of legislation passed to deal with a problem is inversely proportional to the volume of media clamour that brought it on.

**G. Ray Funkhouser, quoted in *The Official Rules*
by P. Dickson, 1978**

Guilty is what the man says when your luck runs out.

**Joseph Wambaugh, screenplay for *The Onion Field*, 1979**

I don't care what the law is – just tell me who the judge is.

**Roy Cohn, quoted in *Citizen Cohn* by Nicholas Von Hoffman, 1988**

The Metropolitan Police Force is abbreviated to the 'Met' to give more members a chance of spelling it.

**Mike Barfield, in *The Oldie* magazine, 1992**

*See also* CRIME, JUSTICE, LAWYERS

# LAWYERS

A bad agreement is better than a good lawyer.

**Italian proverb**

Lawyers' houses are built on the heads of fools.

**George Herbert, *Jacula Prudentum*, 1651**

A man without money need no more fear a crowd of lawyers than a crowd of pickpockets.

**William Wycherley, *The Plain Dealer*, 1674**

Sometimes a man who deserves to be looked down upon because he is a fool is despised only because he is a lawyer.

**Charles de Secondat, Baron de Montesquieu, *Persian Letters*, 1721**

God works wonders now and then
Behold! a lawyer, an honest man.

**Benjamin Franklin, *Poor Richard's Almanack*, 1733–58**

Lawyers are the only persons in whom ignorance of the law is not punished.

**Jeremy Bentham**

Lawyers are the only civil delinquents whose judges must of necessity be chosen from themselves.

**Charles Caleb Colton, *Lacon*, 1820**

A lawyer is a learned gentleman who rescues your estate from your enemies and keeps it for himself.

**Henry, Baron Brougham**

Whether you're an honest man or whether you're a thief
Depends on whose solicitor has given me my brief.
    **W.S. Gilbert,** *Utopia Ltd,* **1893**

Lawyer – one who protects us against robbers by taking away the temptation.
    **H.L. Mencken,** *Sententiae,* **1916**

A lawyer: the only man in whom ignorance of the law is not punished.
    **Elbert Hubbard,** *Book of Epigrams,* **1923**

Litigation: a form of hell whereby money is transferred from the pockets of the proletariat into those of lawyers.
    **Kin Hubbard, 1923**

Be frank and explicit with your lawyer . . . it is his business to confuse the issue afterwards.
    **Anonymous, quoted in** *A Cynic's Breviary* **by J.R. Solly, 1925**

There is no better way of exercising the imagination as the study of law. No poet ever interpreted nature as freely as a lawyer interprets truth.
    **Jean Giraudoux,** *Tiger at the Gates,* **1955**

A jury consists of twelve persons chosen to decide who has the better lawyer.
    **Robert Frost**

A lawyer is a learned gentleman who rescues your estate from your enemies and keeps it for himself.
    **David Lodge,** *The British Museum is Falling Down,* **1965**

The best client is a scared millionaire.
    **Anonymous**

*See also* JUSTICE, LAW

# LEADERS

Rulers are a scourge through whom God punishes those whom he decides to punish.
    **Abu Yusuf,** *Kitab Al-Khara,* **850**

A prince who desires to maintain his position must learn to be not always good, but to be so or not, as needs require.

**Niccolò Machiavelli, *The Prince*, 1513**

The people resemble a wild beast, which, naturally fierce and accustomed to live in the woods, has been brought up, as it were, in a prison and in servitude, and having by accident got its liberty, not being accustomed to search for its food, and not knowing where to conceal itself, easily becomes the prey of the first who seeks to incarcerate it again.

**Niccolò Machiavelli, *Discourse upon the First Ten Books of Livy*, 1518**

Princes are generous enough if they take nothing from me; and do me much good if they do me no hurt.

**Michel de Montaigne, *Essays*, 1595**

They say princes learn no art truly, but the art of horsemanship. The reason is, the brave beast is no flatterer. He will throw a prince as soon as his groom.

**Ben Jonson, *Timber; or Discoveries Made upon Men and Matter*, 1640**

The people would be just as noisy if they were going to see me hanged.

**Oliver Cromwell, remarking on the crowds cheering his progress**

A prince who writes against flattery is as strange as a pope who writes against infallibility.

**Voltaire, letter, 1740**

Princes, like beauties, from their youth
Are strangers to the voice of truth.

**John Gay, *Fables*, 1727**

Whoever is foremost leads the herd.

**Johann Christoff Friedrich von Schiller**

To succeed in chaining the multitude you must seem to wear the same fetters.

**Voltaire, *Philosophical Dictionary*, 1764**

It is a general error to suppose the loudest complainer for the public to be the most anxious for its welfare.

**Edmund Burke, *Observations on a Publication, 'The present state of the nation'*, 1769**

All oppressors attribute the frustration of their desires to the want of sufficient rigour. Then they redouble the efforts of their impotent cruelty.

**Edmund Burke, *The Impeachment of Warren Hastings*, 1788**

Tyrants seldom want pretexts.

**Edmund Burke, *Letter to a Member of the National Assembly*, 1791**

When we think we lead most, we are most led.

**George Gordon, Lord Byron, *The Two Foscari*, 1821**

The conduct and opinions of public men at different periods of their careers must not be curiously contrasted in a free and aspiring society.

**Benjamin Disraeli, speech, 1834**

To be a leader of men one must turn one's back on men.

**Havelock Ellis**

There are three sorts of despots. There is the despot who tyrannizes over the body. There is the despot who tyrannizes over the soul. There is the despot who tyrannizes over the soul *and* body alike. The first is called the Prince. The second is called the Pope. The third is called the People.

**Oscar Wilde, *The Soul of Man under Socialism*, 1891**

The demagogue is one who preaches doctrines he knows to be untrue to men he knows to be idiots.

**H.L. Mencken**

What luck for the rulers that men do not think.

**Adolf Hitler**

It is the curse of the great that they have to step over corpses to create new life.

**Heinrich Himmler**

So long as you suffer any man to call himself your shepherd, sooner or later you will find a crook around your ankle.

**H.G. Wells, *Experiment in Autobiography*, 1934**

As long as men worship the Caesars and Napoleons, the Caesars and Napoleons will duly rise and make them miserable.

**Aldous Huxley, *Ends and Means*, 1937**

Those who have had no share in the good fortunes of the mighty
Often have a share in their misfortunes.

**Bertolt Brecht, *The Caucasian Chalk Circle*, 1945**

A leader is a man who has the ability to get other people to do what
they don't want to do and like it.

**Harry S. Truman**

When smashing monuments, save the pedestals – they always come in
handy.

**Stanislaw J. Lec, *Unkempt Thoughts*, 1962**

If Presidents don't do it to their wives, they do it to the country.

**Mel Brooks, as the 'Two Thousand Year Old Man', 1962**

If someone tells you he is going to make a 'realistic decision', you
immediately understand that he has resolved to do something bad.

**Mary McCarthy, *On the Contrary*, 1962**

The benevolent despot who sees himself as a shepherd of the people still
demands from others the obedience of sheep.

**Eric Hoffer, *The Ordeal of Change*, 1964**

People, like sheep, tend to follow a leader – occasionally in the right
direction.

**Alexander Chase, *Perspectives*, 1966**

When you hear the word 'inevitable', watch out! An enemy of humanity has revealed himself.

**Stephen Vizinczey, *The Rules of Chaos*, 1970**

Here comes the new boss
Same as the old boss.

**Pete Townshend, *Won't Get Fooled Again*, 1971**

Anybody that wants the presidency so much that he'll spend two
years organising and campaigning for it is not to be trusted with the
office.

**David Broder, in the *Washington Post*, 1973**

*See also* DEMOCRACY, GOVERNMENT, POLITICIANS, POLITICS,
POWER, VOTING

# LIBERALS

What is called liberality is often merely the vanity of giving.
**François, Duc de La Rochefoucauld, *Maxims*, 1665**

I hate liberality – nine times out of ten it is cowardice, and the tenth time lack of principle.
**Henry Addington, Viscount Sidmouth**

A liberal is a man who leaves a room when the fight begins.
**Heywood Broun**

Liberal – a power worshipper without power.
**George Orwell**

We who are liberal and progressive know that the poor are our equals in every sense except that of being equal to us.
**Lionel Trilling, *The Liberal Imagination*, 1950**

A liberal is a man too broadminded to take his own side in a quarrel.
**Robert Frost**

It's easier to be a liberal a long way from home.
**Don K. Price**

We know what happens to people who stay in the middle of the road: they get run over.
**Aneurin Bevan, speech, 1953**

A liberal is a person whose interests aren't at stake at the moment.
**Willis Player**

The liberals can understand everything but people who don't understand them.
**Lenny Bruce**

A rich man told me recently that a liberal is a man who tells other people what to do with their money.
**Imamu Amiri Baraka (Everett Leroi Jones), *Kulchur*, 1962**

What the liberal really wants is to bring about change that will not in any way endanger his position.
**Stokeley Carmichael**

The liberal [on pornography] . . . is like a man who loathes whore-houses in practice, but doesn't mind them in principle, providing they are designed by Mies van der Rohe and staffed by social workers in Balenciaga dresses.

**Kenneth Tynan, in *Esquire* magazine, 1968**

Hell hath no fury like a liberal scorned.

**Dick Gregory**

If God had been a Liberal there wouldn't have been ten command-ments, there would have been ten suggestions.

**Malcolm Bradbury and Christopher Bigsby, *After Dinner Game*, 1982**

I have often been called a Nazi, and although it is unfair, I don't let it bother me. I don't let it bother me for one simple reason. No-one has *ever* had a fantasy about being tied to a bed and sexually ravished by someone dressed as a liberal.

**P.J. O'Rourke, *Give War a Chance*, 1992**

*See also* CONSERVATIVES, GOVERNMENT, PARTIES, POLITICS

# LIFE

Life is an hereditary disease.

**Graffito**

What do baths bring to your mind? Oil, sweat, dirt, greasy water and everything that is disgusting. Such, then, is life in all its parts and such is every material thing in it.

**Marcus Aurelius Antoninus, *Meditations*, AD150**

During the time men live without a common power to keep them all in awe, . . . the life of man [is] solitary, poor, nasty, brutish and short.

**Thomas Hobbes, *Leviathan*, 1651**

The majority of men employ the first part of life in making the rest miserable.

**Jean de La Bruyère, *The Characters*, 1688**

If thou intendest to live happy, thou must make but few Reflections on Life.

**Thomas Fuller, M.D., *Introductio ad Prudentiam*, 1727**

We are born crying, live complaining and die disappointed.
**Thomas Fuller, M.D., *Gnomologia*, 1732**

In the great game of human life one begins by being a dupe and ends by being a rogue.
**Voltaire**

Human life is everywhere a state in which much is to be endured and little to be enjoyed.
**Samuel Johnson, *Rasselas*, 1759**

Such is the state of life, that none are happy but by the anticipation of change: the change itself is nothing; when we have made it the next wish is to change again.
**Samuel Johnson, *Rasselas*, 1759**

Life can then little else supply
But a few good fucks and then we die.
**Thomas Potter, *The Essay on Woman*, 1763 (usually attrib. to John Wilkes)**

Nothing can exceed the vanity of our existence but the folly of our pursuits.
**Oliver Goldsmith, *The Good-Natured Man*, 1768**

Life is barren enough surely with all her trappings; let us therefore be careful how we strip her.
**Samuel Johnson, *Johnsonian Miscellanies*, ed. G.B. Hills, 1897**

Life is a pill which none of us can bear to swallow without gilding.
**Samuel Johnson, *Johnsonian Miscellanies*, ed. G.B. Hills, 1897**

That kind of life is most happy which affords us most opportunities of gaining our own esteem.
**Samuel Johnson**

The whole of life is but keeping away the thoughts of death.
**Samuel Johnson, *The Life of Samuel Johnson* by J. Boswell, 1791**

Life to the great majority is only a constant struggle for mere existence – with the certainty of losing it.
**Arthur Schopenhauer, *The World as Will and Idea*, 1819**

To desire immortality is to desire the perpetuation of a great mistake.
**Arthur Schopenhauer,** *The World as Will and Idea,* **1819**

To what point of insignificance may human life not dwindle! To what fine, agonizing threads will it not cling!
**William Hazlitt,** *Literary Remains,* **ed. W. Hazlitt Jr, 1836**

Life is an apprenticeship to constant renunciations, to the steady failure of our claims, our hopes, our powers, our liberty.
**Henri-Frédéric Amiel,** *Journal,* **1856**

If God were suddenly condemned to live the life which he has inflicted upon men, he would kill himself.
**Alexander Dumas fils**

Life is a hospital is which every patient is possessed by the desire to change his bed.
**Charles Baudelaire**

A man's worst difficulties begin when he is able to do as he likes.
**T.H. Huxley**

Life is a fatal complaint, and an eminently contagious one.
**Oliver Wendell Holmes,** *The Poet at the Breakfast-Table,* **1872**

The great pleasure in life is doing what people say you cannot do.
**Walter Bagehot,** *Literary Studies,* **1879–95**

Life is much too important a thing to talk seriously about it.
**Oscar Wilde,** *Vera, or the Nihilists,* **1880**

All you need in life is ignorance and confidence and then success is sure.
**Mark Twain, letter, 1887**

Life is one long process of getting tired.
**Samuel Butler,** *Notebooks,* **1912**

Almost every person, if you will believe himself, holds a quite different theory of life from the one on which he is patently acting.
**Robert Louis Stevenson,** *Virginibus Puerisque,* **1881**

All ways end at the same point . . . Disillusion.
**Oscar Wilde,** *The Picture of Dorian Gray,* **1891**

In this world there are only two tragedies. One is not getting what one wants and the other is getting it.

**Oscar Wilde, *Lady Windermere's Fan*, 1892**

The first duty in life is to be as artificial as possible. What the second duty is no one has as yet discovered.

**Oscar Wilde, *Phrases and Philosophies for the Use of the Young*, 1894**

Life is a predicament that precedes death.

**Henry James**

There is always a right and a wrong way, and the wrong way always seems the more reasonable.

**George Moore**

Life is like an onion: you peel off layer after layer and then you find there is nothing in it.

**James Gibbons Huneker**

Once your reputation's done
You can live a life of fun.

**Wilhelm Busch**

Life being what it is, one dreams of revenge.

**Paul Gauguin**

Experience is a good teacher, but she sends in terrific bills.

**Minna Antrim, *Naked Truth and Veiled Allusions*, 1902**

Life is a lease imposed upon the occupant without previous communication of the conditions in the contract.

**Guy Delaforest, quoted in *Reflections on the Art of Life* by J.R. Solly, 1902**

To pass through life tranquilly, one must not be too clear-sighted.

**Gustave Droz, quoted in *Reflections on the Art of Life* by J.R. Solly, 1902**

The great secret in life . . . [is] not to open your letters for a fortnight. At the expiration of that period you will find that nearly all of them have answered themselves.

**Arthur Binstead, *Pitcher's Proverbs*, 1909**

The meaning of life is that it stops.
**Franz Kafka**

Society is a madhouse where the wardens are the officials and police.
**August Strindberg, *Zones of the Spirit*, 1913**

There is no cure for birth and death save to enjoy the interval.
**George Santayana, *Soliloquies in England*, 1922**

To repent, and then to start all over again, such is life.
**Victor Cherbuliez, quoted in *A Cynic's Breviary* by J.R. Solly, 1925**

Life is a glorious cycle of song
A medley of extemporanea
And love is a thing that can never go wrong
And I am Marie of Roumania
**Dorothy Parker, *Comment*, 1927**

Don't take life too seriously – you will never get out of it alive.
**Elbert Hubbard, *The Notebook*, 1927**

The one dependable law of life: everything is always worse than you thought it was going to be.
**Dorothy Parker, *The Waltz*, 1936**

Life is not a spectacle or a feast; it is a predicament.
**George Santayana, *Articles and Essays*, 1936–7**

Why should not things be largely absurd, futile and transitory? They are so, and we are so, and they and we go very well together.
**George Santayana**

There are two things to aim at in life: first, to get what you want, and after that to enjoy it. Only the wisest of mankind achieve the second.
**Logan Pearsall Smith, *Afterthoughts*, 1931**

As a remedy to life in society I would suggest the big city. Nowadays it is the only desert within our means.
**Albert Camus, *Notebooks*, 1935–42**

What is life? Life is stepping down a step or sitting in a chair. And it isn't there.

**Ogden Nash, *Good Intentions*, 1942**

We give people a box in the suburbs, it's called a house, and every night they sit in it staring at another box; in the morning they run off to another box called an office, and at the weekends they get into another box, on wheels this time, and grope their way through endless traffic jams.

**Caroline Kelly**

For the ordinary man is passive. Within a narrow circle . . . he feels himself master of his fate, but against major events he is as helpless as against the elements. So far from endeavouring to influence the future, he simply lies down and lets things happen to him.

**George Orwell**

Human life begins on the other side of despair.

**Jean-Paul Sartre, *The Flies*, 1942**

Life is a maze in which we take the wrong turning before we have learnt to walk.

**Cyril Connolly (Palinurus), *The Unquiet Grave*, 1944**

We are all serving a life-sentence in the dungeon of life.

**Cyril Connolly (Palinurus), *The Unquiet Grave*, 1944**

If you want a picture of the future, imagine a boot stamping on the human face – forever . . . And remember that is for ever.

**George Orwell, *Nineteen Eighty-Four*, 1948**

Most people get a fair amount of fun out of their lives, but on balance life is suffering and only the very young or the very foolish imagine otherwise.

**George Orwell, *Shooting an Elephant*, 1950**

To have a grievance is to have a purpose in life.

**Eric Hoffer, *The Passionate State of Mind*, 1954**

Take the socalled 'standardofliving'. What do most people mean by 'living'? They don't mean living. They mean the latest and closest plural approximation to the singular prenatal passivity which science, in its finite but unbounded wisdom, has succeeded in selling their wives.

**e.e. cummings, *Poems*, 1923–54**

Life always comes to a bad end.

**Marcel Aymé, *Les oiseaux de lune*, 1955**

A man can look upon his life and accept it as good or evil; it is far, far harder for him to confess that it has been unimportant in the sum of things.

**Murray Kempton, *Part of Our Time*, 1955**

Since all life is futility, then the decision to exist must be the most irrational of all.

**E.M. Cioran, *The Temptation to Exist*, 1956**

We're all of us sentenced to solitary confinement inside our own skins, for life.

**Tennessee Williams, *Orpheus Descending*, 1957**

We cry when we are born, and what follows can only be an attenuation of this cry.

**Françoise Sagan, in the *Sunday Express*, 1957**

Life is an unbroken succession of false situations.

**Thornton Wilder, in the *Observer*, 1957**

It takes a kind of shabby arrogance to survive in our time, and a fairly romantic nature to want to.

**Edgar Z. Friedenberg, *The Vanishing Adolescent*, 1959**

For most men life is a search for the proper manila envelope in which to get themselves filed.

**Clifton Fadiman, 1960**

Life is like a sewer. What you get out of it depends on what you put into it.

**Tom Lehrer, *An Evening Wasted with Tom Lehrer*, 1953**

The messiness of experience, that may be what we mean by life.

**Daniel J. Boorstin, *The Image*, 1961**

Human life is mainly a process of filling in time until the arrival of death, or Santa Claus, with very little choice, if any, of what kind of business one is going to transact during the long wait.

**Eric Berne, *Games People Play*, 1964**

Life is a game at which everybody loses.

**Leo Sarkadi-Schuller**

Human life . . . is only theatre, and mostly cheap melodrama at that.

**Malcolm Muggeridge, *Tread Softly For You Tread on My Jokes*, 1966**

I have always felt that concentration camps . . . are the logical conclusion of contemporary life.

**Arthur Miller, in *Writers at Work* 3rd series, 1967**

Life is a gamble at terrible odds – if it was a bet you wouldn't take it.

**Tom Stoppard, *Rosencrantz and Guildenstern Are Dead*, 1967**

What is there to say, finally, except that pain is bad and pleasure good, life all, death nothing.

**Gore Vidal, in *Esquire* magazine, 1970**

Most people's lives aren't complex – they're just complicated.

**L. Rust Hills, in *Esquire* magazine, 1970**

Our daily life is a bad serial by which we let ourselves be bewitched.

**Michel Butor, *Répertoire II*, 1969**

No one recovers from the disease of being born, a deadly wound if ever there was one.

**E.M. Cioran, *The Fall into Time*, 1971**

All that shimmers on the surface of the world, all that we call interesting, is the fruit of ignorance and inebriation.

**E.M. Cioran, *The Fall into Time*, 1971**

Life is first boredom, then fear.
Whether or not we use it, it goes,
And leaves what something hidden from us chose,
And age, and then the only end of age.

**Philip Larkin, *Dockery and Son*, 1974**

If you just try long enough and hard enough, you can always manage to boot yourself in the posterior.

**A.J. Liebling, *The Press*, 1975**

Sometimes it seems like that is the choice – either kick ass or kiss ass.

**James Caan, in *Playboy* magazine, 1976**

Being frustrated is disagreeable, but the real disasters in life begin when you get what you want.

**Irving Kristol, 1977**

Life is a concentration camp. You're stuck here and there's no way out and you can only rage impotently against your persecutors.

**Woody Allen, in *Esquire* magazine, 1977**

Life is divided into the horrible and the miserable.

**Woody Allen, *Annie Hall*, 1977**

Life is what happens to you while you're busy making other plans.

**John Lennon, *Beautiful Boy*, 1979**

'After she was dead, I loved her.' That is the story of every life – and death.

**Gore Vidal, in the *New York Review of Books*, 1980**

The very purpose of existence is to reconcile the glowing opinion we hold of ourselves with the appalling things that other people think about us.

**Quentin Crisp, *How To Become a Virgin*, 1981**

Life is a meaningless comma in the sentence of time.

**Chris Garratt and Mick Kidd, *The Essential Biff*, 1982**

In my youth I hoped to do great things; now I shall be satisfied to get through without scandal.

**Walter Bagehot, quoted in *Selected Letters of Raymond Chandler*, ed. F. MacShane, 1981**

Life is an effort that deserves a better cause.

**Karl Kraus, *Half Truths and One and a Half Truths*, 1986**

The problems of the world, AIDS, cancer, nuclear war, pollution are, finally, no more solvable than the problems of a tree which has borne fruit: the apples are overripe and they are falling – what can be done? . . . What can be done about the problems that beset our life? *Nothing* can be done, and nothing needs to be done.

**David Mamet, *Writing in Restaurants*, 1988**

Life is generally something that happens elsewhere.

**Alan Bennett, *Talking Heads*, 1989**

*See also* EXPERIENCE, HUMANITY, TIME

# LOVE

In love there is always one who kisses and one who offers the cheek.

**French proverb**

Love is the affection of a mind that has nothing better to engage it.

**Theophrastus, *c*.300BC**

Hunger stops love, or if not hunger, time.

**Crates, quoted in *Lives and Opinions of Eminent Philosophers* by Diogenes Laertius, *c*.AD225**

Love lasteth as long as the money endureth.

**William Caxton, *The Game and Playe of Chesse*, 1474**

Oh love will make a dog howl in tune.

**Francis Beaumont and John Fletcher, *The Queen of Corinth*, *c*.1612**

Out upon it, I have loved
Three whole days together
And am like to love three more
If it prove fair weather.

**Sir John Suckling, *Fragmenta Aurea*, 1646**

Admiration is a very short-lived passion, that immediately decays upon growing familiar with its object.

**Joseph Addison, *The Spectator*, 1711**

When poverty comes in at the door, love creeps out at the window.

**Thomas Fuller M.D., *Gnomologia*, 1732**

The only victory in love is flight.

**Napoleon Bonaparte, *Maxims*, 1804–15**

Love, in present day society, is just the exchange of two momentary desires and the contact of two skins.

**Nicolas de Chamfort, _Maximes et pensées_, 1805**

He who cannot love must learn to flatter.

**Johann Wolfgang von Goethe**

Constancy has nothing virtuous in itself, independently of the pleasure it confers.

**Percy Bysshe Shelley, _Queen Mab_ (notes), 1813**

As that gallant can best affect a pretended passion for one woman, who has no true love for another, so he that has no real esteem for any of the virtues, can best assume the appearance of them all.

**Charles Caleb Colton, _Lacon_, 1820**

Love is an alchemist that can transmute poison into food – and a spaniel that prefers even punishment from one hand to caresses from another.

**Charles Caleb Colton, _Lacon_, 1820**

The power of love consists mainly in the privilege that Potentate possesses of coining, circulating, and making current those falsehoods between man and woman, that would not pass for one moment, either between woman and woman, or man and man.

**Charles Caleb Colton, _Lacon_, 1820**

Love matches are made by people who are content, for a month of honey, to condemn themselves to a life of vinegar.

**Marguerite, Countess of Blessington**

What is irritating about love is that it is a crime that requires an accomplice.

**Charles Baudelaire**

The magic of our first love is our ignorance that it can ever end.

**Benjamin Disraeli**

We study ourselves three weeks, we love each other three months, we squabble three years, we tolerate each other thirty years, and then the children start all over again.

**Hippolyte Taine, _Vie et opinions de Thomas Graingorge_, 1868**

Love is the desire to prostitute oneself. There is, indeed, no exalted pleasure that cannot be related to prostitution.

**Charles Baudelaire,** *Intimate Journals,* **1887**

Love matches, so called, have illusion for their father and need for their mother.

**Friedrich Wilhelm Nietzsche**

Women are well aware that what is commonly called sublime and poetical love depends not upon moral qualities, but on frequent meetings, and on the style in which the hair is done up, and on the colour and the cut of the dress.

**Leo Tolstoy,** *The Kreutzer Sonata,* **1889**

The only true love is love at first sight; second sight dispels it.

**Israel Zangwill**

There is only one way to be happy by means of the heart – to have none.

**Paul Bourget,** *La Physiologie de l'amour moderne,* **1890**

There is always something ridiculous about the passions of people whom one has ceased to love.

**Oscar Wilde,** *The Picture of Dorian Gray,* **1891**

Always! that is a dreadful word . . . it is a meaningless word too. The only difference between a caprice and a life-long passion is that the caprice lasts a little longer.

**Oscar Wilde,** *The Picture of Dorian Gray,* **1891**

When one is in love one begins by deceiving oneself. And one ends by deceiving others. This is what the world calls a romance.

**Oscar Wilde,** *A Woman of No Importance,* **1893**

Romance should never begin with sentiment. It should begin with science and end with a settlement.

**Oscar Wilde,** *An Ideal Husband,* **1895**

It is well to write love letters. There are certain things it is not easy to ask your mistress for face to face, like money, for instance.

**Henri de Régnier**

The fickleness of the women whom I love is only equalled by the infernal constancy of the women who love me.

**George Bernard Shaw,** *The Philanderer,* **1898**

When we want to read of the deeds that are done for love, whither do we turn? To the murder column.

**George Bernard Shaw**

First love is only a little foolishness and a lot of curiosity, no really self-respecting woman would take advantage of it.

**George Bernard Shaw,** *John Bull's Other Island*, **1904**

Protestations of undying affection are never ridiculous when they are accompanied by emeralds.

**W. Somerset Maugham,** *Lady Frederick*, **1907**

Romance: once upon a time. Seldom twice.

**Oliver Herford and John Clay,** *Cupid's Cyclopedia*, **1910**

Women in love are less ashamed than men; they have less to be ashamed of.

**Ambrose Bierce,** *The Devil's Dictionary*, **1911**

No woman ever falls in love with a man unless she has a better opinion of him than he deserves.

**Edgar Watson Howe,** *Country Town Sayings*, **1911**

Cupid, n. The so-called god of love. This bastard creation of a barbarous fancy . . . of all unbeautiful and inappropriate conceptions, this is the most reasonless and offensive.

**Ambrose Bierce,** *The Devil's Dictionary*, **1911**

Love, n. A temporary insanity curable by marriage or the removal of the patient from the influences under which he incurred the disease . . . it is sometimes fatal, but more frequently to the physician than to the patient.

**Ambrose Bierce,** *The Devil's Dictionary*, **1911**

To live is like to love: all reason is against it and all healthy instinct is for it.

**Samuel Butler,** *Notebooks*, **1912**

A woman we love rarely satisfies all our needs and we deceive her with a woman we do not love.

**Marcel Proust,** *Remembrance of Things Past*, **1913–27**

Love is the delusion that one woman differs from another.
   **H.L. Mencken, *Sententiae*, 1916**

To be in love is merely to be in a state of perpetual anaesthesia – to mistake an ordinary young man for a Greek god, or an ordinary young woman for a goddess.
   **H.L. Mencken, *Prejudices* 1st series, 1920**

The only love letters which are of any use are those of goodbye.
   **Etienne Rey**

It's no compliment to be loved by a man who has had no experience.
   **Ian Hay**

Love is what happens to a man and woman who don't know each other.
   **W. Somerset Maugham**

Love is based upon a view of women that is impossible to any man who has had experience of them.
   **H.L. Mencken, *Prejudices* 4th series, 1924**

You must not love animals, they don't last long enough. You must not love humans, they last too long.
   **Anonymous, quoted in *A Cynic's Breviary* by J. R. Solly, 1925**

Lady, lady, should you meet
One whose ways are all discreet,
One who murmers that his wife
Is the lodestar of his life,
One who keeps assuring you
That he never was untrue,
Never loved another one . . .
Lady, lady, better run!
   **Dorothy Parker, *Social Note*, 1927**

My soul is crushed, my spirit sore;
I do not like me anymore,
I cavil, quarrel, grumble, grouse,
I ponder on the narrow house
I shudder at the thought of men . . .
I'm due to fall in love again.
   **Dorothy Parker, *Symptom Recital*, 1927**

By the time you swear you're his
Shivering and sighing
And he vows his passion is
Infinite, undying –
Lady, make a note of this:
One of you is lying.

**Dorothy Parker, *Unfortunate Coincidence*, 1927**

When you're away, I'm restless, lonely,
Wretched, bored, dejected, only
Here's the rub, my darling dear
I feel the same when you are here.

**Samuel Hoffenstein, *Poems in Praise of Practically Nothing*,
1929**

A husband is what's left of the lover once the nerve has been extracted.

**Helen Rowland, *A Guide to Men*, 1929**

Love . . . a burnt match skating in a urinal.

**Hart Crane, *The Bridge*, 1930**

The ideal love affair is conducted by post.

**George Bernard Shaw**

Every love's the love before
In a duller dress.

**Dorothy Parker, *Summary*, 1931**

We hate the people we love because they're the only ones that can hurt
us.

**Lyn Starling, screenplay for *Private Worlds*, 1935**

The first man who can think of how he's going to stay in love with
his wife and another woman is going to win that prize they're always
talking about in Sweden.

**Clare Booth Luce, *The Women*, 1936**

Love is something that hangs up behind the bathroom door and smells
of Lysol.

**Ernest Hemingway, *To Have and Have Not*, 1937**

The word 'love' bridges for us those chasms of momentary indifference
and boredom which gape from time to time between even the most
ardent lovers.

**Aldous Huxley, *The Olive Tree*, 1937**

The voyage of love is all the sweeter for an outside stateroom and a seat at the Captain's table.

**Henry Haskins,** *Meditations in Wall Street*, **1940**

You study one another for three weeks, you love each other for three months, you fight for three years and you tolerate the situation for thirty.

**André de Misson**

Oh, love is real enough, you will find it some day, but it has one arch-enemy – and that is life.

**Jean Anouilh,** *Ardèle*, **1948**

Love is only a dirty trick played on us to achieve the continuation of the species.

**W. Somerset Maugham,** *A Writer's Notebook*, **1949**

If two people love each other, there can be no happy end to it.

**Ernest Hemingway**

Love is a hole in the heart.

**Ben Hecht,** *Winkelberg*, **1950**

Love is simple to understand if you haven't got a mind soft and full of holes. It's a crutch, and there isn't one of us who doesn't need a crutch.

**Norman Mailer,** *Barbary Shore*, **1951**

The credulity of love is the most fundamental source of authority.

**Sigmund Freud,** *Collected Works*, **1955**

Many a man has fallen in love with a girl in a light so dim he would not have chosen a suit by it.

**Maurice Chevalier, 1955**

Every little girl knows about love. It is only her capacity to suffer because of it that increases.

**Françoise Sagan, in the** *Daily Express*, **1957**

Is that what love is? Using people? And maybe that's what hate is. Not being able to use people.

**Gore Vidal and Tennessee Williams, screenplay for** *Suddenly Last Summer*, **1959**

Romance, like alcohol, should be enjoyed, but should not be allowed to become necessary.

**Edgar Z. Friedenberg, *The Vanishing Adolescent*, 1959**

Human love is often but the encounter of two weaknesses.

**François Mauriac, *Cain, Where Is Your Brother?*, 1962**

A man in love, like Romeo, can no more join his beloved between the sheets than push his dear mother off a roof, at least, not for some time.

**Ben Hecht, *Letters from Bohemia*, 1964**

The best love affairs are those we never had.

**Norman Lindsay, *Bohemians of the Bulletin*, 1965**

Of course it's possible to love a human being if you don't know them too well.

**Charles Bukowski, *Notes of a Dirty Old Man*, 1969**

Love, love, love – all the wretched cant of it, masking egotism, lust, masochism, fantasy under a mythology of sentimental postures, a welter of self-induced miseries and joys, blinding and masking the essential personalities in the frozen gestures of courtship, in the kissing and the dating and the desire, the compliments and the quarrels which vivify its barrenness.

**Germaine Greer, *The Female Eunuch*, 1970**

Love is what makes the world go round – that and clichés.

**Michael Symons, in the *Sydney Morning Herald*, 1970**

Romance, like the rabbit at the dog track, is the elusive, fake, and never attained reward which, for the benefit and amusement of our masters, keeps us running and thinking in safe circles.

**Beverly Jones, *The Florida Paper on Women's Liberation*, 1970**

That desert of loneliness and recrimination that men call love.

**Samuel Beckett, quoted in *The New York Review of Books*, 1971**

Love is the victim's response to the rapist.

**Ti-Grace Atkinson**

What we're all looking for is someone who doesn't live there, just pays for it.

**Andy Warhol, *From A to B and Back Again*, 1975**

Perhaps at fourteen every boy should be in love with some ideal woman to put on a pedestal and worship. As he grows up, of course, he will put her on a pedestal the better to view her legs.

**Barry Norman, quoted in *The Listener* magazine, 1978**

'All I want is us to share the occasional candle-lit dinner and a bit of slap and tickle when your old man's away on business. No involvement. No strings. No complications.' 'Oh Myles, this is too wonderful.' Relief flooded her entire being. Here at last was the casual fling she had always dreamed of.

**Posy Simmonds, *True Love*, 1981**

Love is like cheap wine . . . it leads you to the stars, but leaves you with the gutrot of tomorrow.

**Chris Garratt and Mick Kidd, *The Rainy Day Biff*, 1983**

*See also* AFFAIRS, DIVORCE, HUSBANDS, LOVERS, MARRIAGE, SEX, WIVES

# LOVERS

The reason that lovers never weary each other is because they are always talking about themselves.

**François, Duc de La Rochefoucauld, *Maxims*, 1665**

'Tis an unhappy circumstance that . . . the man so often should outlive the lover.

**William Congreve, *The Way of the World*, 1700**

All men are thieves in love, and like a woman the better for being another's property.

**John Gay, *The Beggar's Opera*, 1728**

Wisely a woman prefers to a lover a man who neglects her. This one may love her some day, some day the lover will not.

**John Hay**

Don't give to lovers you will replace irreplaceable presents.

**Logan Pearsall Smith**

The sweeter the apple, the blacker the core –
Scratch a lover and find a foe!

**Dorothy Parker, *Ballade of a Great Weariness*, 1927**

When from time to time I have seen the persons with whom the great lovers satisfied their desires, I have often been more astonished by the robustness of their appetites than envious of their successes. It is obvious that you need not often go hungry if you are willing to dine off mutton hash and turnip tops.

**W. Somerset Maugham,** *The Summing Up*, 1938

There is no fury like an ex-wife searching for a new lover.

**Cyril Connolly (Palinurus),** *The Unquiet Grave*, 1944

*See also* AFFAIRS, DIVORCE, HUSBANDS, LOVE, MARRIAGE, SEX, WIVES

# LYING

To know how to dissemble is the knowledge of kings.

**Cardinal Richelieu,** *Mirame*, c.1625

When you say you agree to a thing on principle, you mean that you have not the slightest intention of carrying it out in practice.

**Otto von Bismarck**

The most common sort of lie is that by which a man deceives himself; the deception of others is a relatively rare offence.

**Friedrich Wilhelm Nietzsche,** *The Antichrist*, 1888

A lie with a purpose is one of the worst kind, and the most profitable.

**Finley Peter Dunne,** *Mr Dooley's Opinions*, 1901

A little inaccuracy sometimes saves tons of explanation.

**Saki (H.H. Munro),** *The Comments of Moung Ka*, 1924

Four-fifths of the perjury in the world is expended on tombstones, women and competitors.

**Lord Thomas Dewar**

The greater the lie, the greater the chance that it will be believed.

**Adolf Hitler,** *Mein Kampf*, 1924

Lying is an indispensable part of making life tolerable.

**Bergan Evans**

When a man you like switches from what he said a year ago, or four years ago, he is a broad-minded person who has courage enough to change his mind with changing conditions. When a man you don't like does it, he is a liar who has broken his promises.

**Franklin P. Adams (F.P.A.),** *Nods and Becks*, **1944**

The system of organised lying on which society is founded.

**George Orwell, outline for** *Nineteen Eighty-Four*, **1946**

A lie is an abomination unto the Lord and a very present help in trouble.

**Adlai Stevenson, 1951**

Society can only exist on the basis that there is some amount of polished lying and that no one says exactly what he thinks.

**Lin Yutang**

Fraud is the homage that force pays to reason.

**Charles P. Curtis,** *A Commonplace Book*, **1957**

Conversation is more often likely to be an attempt at deliberate evasion, deliberate confusion, rather than communication. We are all cheats and liars, really.

**James Jones, in** *Writers at Work* **3rd series, 1957**

The art of living is the art of knowing how to believe lies.

**Cesare Pavese,** *The Burning Brand*, **1961**

Don't lie if you don't have to.

**Leo Szilard, quoted in** *Science*, **1972**

You don't tell deliberate lies, but sometimes you have to be evasive.

**Margaret Thatcher, 1976**

The camera cannot lie. But it can be an accessory to untruth.

**Harold Evans,** *Pictures on a Page*, **1978**

*See also* HONESTY, TRUTH

# MADNESS

The first step towards madness is to think oneself wise.

**Fernando de Rojas,** *Celestina, or the Tragi-Comedy of Calisto and Melibea*, **1499–1502**

Men will always be mad, and those who think they can cure them are the maddest of all.

**Voltaire, letter, 1762**

Mad, adj. Affected with a high degreee of intellectual independence; not conforming to standards of thought, speech and action derived by the conformants from the study of themselves; at odds with the majority; in short, unusual.

**Ambrose Bierce, *The Devil's Dictionary*, 1911**

A man who is 'of sound mind' is one who keeps the inner madman under lock and key.

**Paul Valéry, *Mauvaises pensées et autres*, 1942**

To think contrary to one's era is heroism. But to speak against it is madness.

**Eugène Ionesco**

Whom the mad would destroy, first they make Gods.

**Bernard Levin, 1967**

Insanity – a perfectly rational adjustment to the insane world.

**R.D. Laing, quoted in the *Guardian*, 1972**

A madman is also a man whom society did not want to hear and whom it wanted to prevent from uttering certain intolerable truths.

**Antonin Artaud, *Selected Writings*, 1976**

# MANNERS

Politeness is fictitious benevolence.

**Samuel Johnson, *The Journal of a Tour to the Hebrides*
by J. Boswell, 1785**

Manners are the hypocrisy of a nation.

**Honoré de Balzac**

Politeness is a tacit agreement that peoples' miserable defects, whether moral or intellectual, shall on either side be ignored and not be made the subject of reproach.

**Arthur Schopenhauer, *Our Relation to Others*, 1851**

A lady: that monster of European civilization and Teutonico-Christian stupidity.
**Arthur Schopenhauer, *Parerga und Paralipomena*, 1851**

That roguish and cheerful vice, politeness.
**Friedrich Wilhelm Nietzsche, *Beyond Good and Evil*, 1886**

Politeness, n. The most acceptable hypocrisy.
**Ambrose Bierce, *The Devil's Dictionary*, 1911**

Politeness is organised indifference.
**Paul Valéry, *Tel quel*, 1943**

Rudeness is the weak man's imitation of strength.
**Eric Hoffer, *The Passionate State of Mind*, 1954**

Tact is the art of convincing people that they know more than you do.
**Raymond Mortimer**

Manners are especially the need of the plain. The pretty can get away with anything.
**Evelyn Waugh, in the *Observer*, 1962**

Tact consists in knowing how far to go in going too far.
**Jean Cocteau, quoted in *The Faber Book of Aphorisms*, ed. W.H. Auden and L. Kronenberger, 1964**

Manners are the lowest common denominator of ethical experience.
**Victor S. Navasky, *Naming Names*, 1980**

# MARRIAGE

A wife is one who stands by a man in all the trouble he wouldn't have had if he hadn't married her.
**Anonymous**

Marriage is the only evil that men pray for.
**Greek proverb**

Marriage is a romance in which the hero dies in the first chapter.
**Anonymous**

Asked when a man should marry: For a young man, not yet; for an old man, never at all.
    **Diogenes, c.350BC**

The man who marries for money earns it.
    **Jewish proverb**

Women, deceived by men, want to marry them; it is a kind of revenge as good as any other.
    **Philip de Remi Beaumanoir**

A good marriage would be between a blind wife and a deaf husband.
    **Michel de Montaigne, Essays, 1595**

Marriage is good for nothing but to make friends fall out.
    **Thomas Shadwell, The Sullen Lovers, 1668**

Marriage is a desperate thing. The frogs in Aesop were extreme wise; they had a great mind to some water, but they would not leap into the well, because they could not get out again.
    **John Selden, Table Talk, 1689**

Courtship to marriage, as a very witty prologue to a very dull play.
    **William Congreve, The Old Bachelor, 1693**

Every man plays the fool once in his life, but to marry is to play the fool all one's life long.
    **William Congreve, The Old Bachelor, 1693**

Tho' marriage makes man and wife one flesh, it leaves 'em still two fools.
    **William Congreve, The Double Dealer, 1694**

What cloying meat is love, when matrimony's the sauce to it.
    **John Vanbrugh, The Provok'd Wife, 1697**

Never marry a widow unless her first husband was hanged.
    **James Kelly, Scottish proverbs, 1721**

Keep thy Eyes wide open before Marriage, and half shut afterwards.
    **Thomas Fuller, M.D., Introductio ad Prudentiam, 1727**

Marriage is the only adventure open to the cowardly.
**Voltaire, *Thoughts of a Philosopher*, 1734**

His designs were strictly honourable, as the phrase is: that is, to rob a lady of her fortune by way of marriage.
**Henry Fielding, *The History of Tom Jones*, 1749**

There is, indeed, nothing that so much seduces reason from vigilance, as the thought of passing life with an amiable woman.
**Samuel Johnson, *The Idler*, 1758–60**

Love is blind, but marriage restores its sight.
**Georg Christoph Lichtenberg, *Aphorisms*, 1764–99**

It is possible, though not very probable, that there may be joy in marriage.
**Lord Chesterfield, *Letters to his Son*, 1774**

'Tis safest in matrimony to begin with a little aversion.
**Richard Brinsley Sheridan, *The Rivals*, 1775**

A gentleman who had been very unhappy in marriage married immediately after his wife died: Johnson said it was the triumph of hope over experience.
**Samuel Johnson, *The Life of Samuel Johnson* by J. Boswell, 1791**

Love is an ideal thing, marriage a real thing; a confusion of the real with the ideal never goes unpunished.
**Johann Wolfgang von Goethe**

Marriage is a good thing, and so is a bone for a dog; but if you tied it to his tail it will drive him mad.
**Colonel George Hanger, *The Life and Adventures and Opinions of Col. George Hanger*, 1801**

For the butterfly, mating and propagation involve the sacrifice of life, for the human being, the sacrifice of beauty.
**Johann Wolfgang von Goethe**

Next to being married a girl likes to be crossed in love now and then.
**Jane Austen, *Pride and Prejudice*, 1813**

A system could not well have been devised more studiously hostile to human happiness than marriage.

**Percy Bysshe Shelley, *Queen Mab* (notes), 1813**

Marriage is a feast where the grace is sometimes better than the dinner.

**Charles Caleb Colton, *Lacon*, 1820**

Marriage must incessantly contend with a monster that devours everything: familiarity.

**Honoré de Balzac, *The Physiology of Marriage*, 1829**

The married woman is a slave whom one must be able to set upon a throne.

**Honoré de Balzac, *The Physiology of Marriage*, 1829**

The music at a wedding procession always reminds me of the music of soldiers going into battle.

**Heinrich Heine**

The most happy marriage I can picture or imagine to myself would be the union of a deaf man to a blind woman.

**Samuel Taylor Coleridge, quoted in *Recollections*,
ed. T. Allsop, 1836**

Advice to persons about to marry – don't.

**Mr Punch's Almanac, 1845**

It doesn't much signify whom one marries, for one is sure to find out the next morning that it was someone else.

**Samuel Rogers, *Table Talk*, ed. A. Dyce, 1856**

Marriage is at best a dangerous experiment.

**Thomas Love Peacock, *Gryll Grange*, 1860–1**

No man is regular in his attendance at the House of Commons until he is married.

**Benjamin Disraeli**

Marriage: a ceremony in which rings are put on the finger of the lady and through the nose of the gentleman.

**Herbert Spencer**

Every woman should marry – and no man.
  **Benjamin Disraeli, *Lothair*, 1870**

If we take matrimony at its lowest . . . if we regard it as no more than a sort of friendship recognised by the police.
  **Robert Louis Stevenson, *Virginibus Puerisque*, 1881**

You may carve it on his tombstone, you may cut it on his card
That a young man married is a young man marred.
  **Rudyard Kipling, *The Story of the Gadsbys*, 1889**

A man can be happy with any woman as long as he does not love her.
  **Oscar Wilde, *The Picture of Dorian Gray*, 1891**

One should always be in love. That is the reason why one should never marry.
  **Oscar Wilde**

Men marry because they are tired, women because they are curious. Both are disappointed.
  **Oscar Wilde, *A Woman of No Importance*, 1893**

The honeymoon is the period when the bride still trusts the groom's word of honour.
  **Anonymous**

I am not in favour of long engagements. They give people the oporunity of finding out each other's character before marriage, which I think is never advisable.
  **Oscar Wilde, *The Importance of Being Earnest*, 1895**

If we men married the women we deserve, we should have a very bad time of it.
  **Oscar Wilde, *An Ideal Husband*, 1895**

Just because a girl's married ain't no sign she hasn't loved and lost.
  **Kin Hubbard, *Abe Martin on Things in General*, 1926–30**

If you are afraid of loneliness, don't marry.
  **Anton Chekhov**

I think it can be stated without denial that no man ever saw a man he would be willing to marry if he were a woman.
  **George Gibbs, *How to Stay Married*, 1925**

It is most unwise for people in love to marry.
  **George Bernard Shaw**

If it were not for the presents, an elopement would be preferable.
  **George Ade, *Forty Modern Fables*, 1901**

When you see what some girls marry, you realise how much they must hate to work for a living.
  **Helen Rowland, *Reflections of a Bachelor Girl*, 1909**

Even if a man was delightful, no woman would marry him if she knew what he was like.
  **E.F. Benson, *Paul*, 1906**

Marriage: the conventional ending of a love affair. A lonesome state.
  **Oliver Herford and John Clay, *Cupid's Cyclopedia*, 1910**

In olden times sacrifices were made at the altar – a practice which is still continued.
  **Helen Rowland**

It isn't tying himself to one woman that a man dreads when he thinks of marrying; it's separating himself from all the others.
  **Helen Rowland**

Marriage – a souvenir of love.
  **Helen Rowland**

Bride, n. A woman with a fine prospect of happiness behind her.
  **Ambrose Bierce, *The Devil's Dictionary*, 1911**

Marriage, n. The state or condition of a community consisting of a master, a mistress and two slaves, making in all, two.
  **Ambrose Bierce, *The Devil's Dictionary*, 1911**

Wedding, n. A ceremony at which two persons undertake to become one, one undertakes to become nothing, and nothing undertakes to become supportable.
  **Ambrose Bierce, *The Devil's Dictionary*, 1911**

Marriage is a good deal like a circus: there is not as much in it as is represented in the advertising.

**Edgar Watson Howe, *Country Town Sayings*, 1911**

Marriage is distinctly and repeatedly excluded from heaven. Is this because it is thought likely to mar the general felicity?

**Samuel Butler, *Notebooks*, 1912**

In matrimony to hesitate is sometimes to be saved.

**Samuel Butler, *Notebooks*, 1912**

The conjugal bedroom is the coexistence of brutality and martyrdom.

**Karl Kraus, *Half Truths and One and a Half Truths*, 1986**

He marries best who puts it off until it is too late.

**H.L. Mencken, *Sententiae*, 1916**

If people waited to know each other before they were married, the world wouldn't be so grossly over-populated.

**W. Somerset Maugham**

When a man marries it is no more than a sign that the feminine talent for persuasion and intimidation . . . has forced him into a more or less abhorrent compromise with his own honest inclinations and best interests.

**H.L. Mencken**

Marriage, in life, is like a duel in the midst of a battle.

**Edmond About, quoted in *A Cynic's Breviary* by J.R. Solly, 1925**

Women are always anxious to urge bachelors to matrimony; is it from charity or revenge?

**Gustave Vapereau, quoted in *A Cynic's Breviary* by J.R. Solly, 1925**

The woman who does not marry makes a blunder than can only be compared to that of the man who does.

**Gyp, quoted in *A Cynic's Breviary* by J.R. Solly, 1925**

To marry a woman who you love and who loves you is to lay a wager with her as to who will stop loving the other first.

**Alfred Capus, *Notes et pensées*, 1926**

A man who marries a woman to educate her falls victim to the same fallacy as the woman who marries a man to reform him.

**Elbert Hubbard, *The Notebook*, 1927**

A marriage is likely to be what is called happy if neither party ever expected to get much happiness out of it.

**Bertrand Russell, *Marriage and Morals*, 1929**

Many a necklace becomes a noose.

**Paul Eldridge**

There are various forms of a certain disease, the victim of which is unable to say, 'No'. Some of these forms are more serious than others and often lead to electrocution or marriage.

**Robert Benchley**

Marriage is the waste paper basket of the emotions.

**Sidney Webb, Baron Passfield, quoted in *Autobiography* by Lord Russell, 1967**

Marriage always demands the greatest understanding of the art of insincerity possible between two human beings.

**Vicki Baum, *Results of an Accident*, 1931**

And so they were married – to be more together –
And found they were never again so much together –
Divided by the morning tea,
By the evening paper,
By children and tradesmen's bills.

**Louis MacNeice, *Les Sylphides*, 1941**

Very few modern women either like or desire marriage, especially after the ceremony has been performed. Primarily women wish attention and affection. Matrimony is something they accept when there is no alternative. Really, it is a waste of time, and hazardous, to marry them. It leaves one open to a rival. Husbands, good or bad, always have rivals. Lovers, never.

**Helen Lawrenson, in *Esquire* magazine, 1939**

Marriage is like paying an endless visit in your worst clothes.

**J.B. Priestley, quoted in *Frank Muir Goes Into* by F. Muir, 1978**

The dread of loneliness is greater than the fear of bondage, so we get married.

**Cyril Connolly (Palinurus), *The Unquiet Grave*, 1944**

The complaints which anyone voices against his mate indicate exactly the qualities which stimulated attraction before marriage.

**Dr Rudolf Dreikurs, *The Challenge of Marriage*, 1946**

All married women should make a habit of saying, 'In spite of everything dear, I'm still devoted to you.'

**Eric Linklater, *Private Angelo*, 1946**

Bachelors know more about women than married men. If they didn't, they would be married too.

**H.L. Mencken, *A Mencken Chrestomathy*, 1949**

An egotist is a man who expects a woman to marry him for himself alone.

**Raymond Mortimer**

Marriage is a lottery in which men stake their liberty and women their happiness.

**Virginie des Rieux**

There is probably nothing like living together for blinding people to each other.

**Ivy Compton-Burnett, *Mother and Son*, 1955**

Love, for too many people in our time, consists of sleeping with a seductive woman, one who is properly endowed with the right distribution of curves and conveniences, and one upon whom a permanent lien has been acquired through the institution of marriage.

**Ashley Montagu, *The Natural Superiority of Women*, 1953**

Marriage is a vulgar effort on the part of dull people to bring boredom to a fine art.

**J.B. Morton ('Beachcomber')**

Marriage is based on the theory that when a man discovers a brand of beer exactly to his taste he should at once throw up his job and go to work in the brewery.

**George Jean Nathan, 1958**

Marriage is give and take. You'd better give it to her, or she'll take it anyway.

**Joey Adams, *Cindy and I*, 1959**

A man in love is incomplete until he is married. Then he is finished.

**Zsa Zsa Gabor, in *Newsweek* magazine, 1960**

If you're going to break up with your old lady and you live in a small town, make sure you don't break up at three in the morning. Because you're screwed – there's nothing to do . . . So make it about nine in the morning, . . . bullshit around, worry her a little, then come back at seven in the night.

**Lenny Bruce**

It is easier to live through someone else than to become complete yourself.

**Betty Friedan, *The Feminine Mystique*, 1963**

Marriage is a triumph of habit over hate.

**Oscar Levant, *Memoirs of an Amnesiac*, 1965**

When you're married to someone, they take you for granted . . . when you're living with someone it's fantastic . . . they're so frightened of losing you they've got to keep you satisfied all the time.

**Nell Dunn, *Poor Cow*, 1967**

The only real argument for marriage is that it remains the best method for getting acquainted.

**Heywood Broun, quoted in *Wits End*, ed. R. Drennan, 1968**

When you're bored with yourself, marry, and be bored with someone else.

**David Pryce-Jones, *Owls and Satyrs*, 1960**

Marriage . . . the most advanced form of warfare in the modern world.

**Malcolm Bradbury, *The History Man*, 1975**

Bigamy is having one husband too many. Monogamy is the same.

**Anonymous woman, quoted as epigraph to *Fear of Flying* by Erica Jong, 1975**

Marriage is an arrangement by which two people start by getting the best out of each other and often end by getting the worst.

**Gerald Brenan, *Thoughts in a Dry Season*, 1978**

The glances over cocktails
That seemed to be so sweet
Don't seem quite so amorous
Over Shredded Wheat.

**Anonymous rhyme, quoted in *Frank Muir Goes Into* by Frank Muir, 1978**

Marriage is an attempt to change a night owl into a homing pigeon.

**Anonymous, quoted in *The Penguin Book of Modern Quotations*, ed. Cohen and Cohen, 1981**

Marriage is two people agreeing to tell the same lie.

**Karen Durbin, 1981**

It is explained that all relationships require a little give and take. This is untrue. Any partnership demands that we give and give and give and at the last, as we flop into our graves exhausted, we are told that we didn't give enough.

**Quentin Crisp, *How To Become a Virgin*, 1981**

After your marriage, my dear, unpleasant things are bound to happen, but take no notice. I never did.

**Anonymous aristocrat, advice to her daughter, quoted in *Victorian Women* by Joan Perkin, 1993**

*See also* AFFAIRS, DIVORCE, HUSBANDS, LOVE, LOVERS, WIVES

# THE MASSES

A wise fellow who is also worthless always charms the rabble.

**Euripides, *Hippolytus*, 428BC**

Happy are those who are convinced so as to be of the general Opinions.

**George Savile, Marquis of Halifax, *Political, Moral and Miscellaneous Thoughts and Reflexions*, c.1694**

If the multitude ever deviate into the right, it is always for the wrong reasons.

**Lord Chesterfield, *Letters to his Son*, 1774**

About things on which the public thinks long, it commonly attains to think right.

**Samuel Johnson, *Works* vol. vii, 1787**

Every numerous assembly is *mob*, let the individuals who compose it be what they will . . . Understanding they have collectively none; but they have ears and eyes which must be flattered and seduced.

**Lord Chesterfield,** *Letters to his Son*, **1774**

Ten million ignorances do not constitute one knowledge.

**Clemens von Metternich, on democracy**

The public is an old woman. Let her maunder and mumble.

**Thomas Carlyle,** *Journal*, **1835**

What the crowd requires is mediocrity of the highest order.

**Auguste Préault**

Unanimity is almost an indication of servitude.

**Charles de Rémusat**

Leave this hypocritical prating about the masses. Masses are rude, lame, unmade, pernicious in their demands and influence, and need not to be flattered but to be schooled.

**Ralph Waldo Emerson,** *The Conduct of Life*, **1860**

The majority is always wrong.

**Israel Zangwill**

When all think alike, then no one is thinking.

**Walter Lippmann, quoted in** *The Book of Laws* **by H. Faber, 1980**

Hatred is the most accessible and comprehensive of all unifying agents. Mass movements can rise and spread without belief in a God, but never without belief in a devil.

**Eric Hoffer,** *The True Believer*, **1951**

Mass democracy, mass morality and the mass media thrive independently of the individual, who joins them at a cost of at least a partial perversion of his instinct and insights. He pays for his social ease with what used to be called his soul, his discriminations, his uniqueness, his psychic energy, his self.

**Al Alvarez, in** *The Listener* **magazine, 1971**

There's a whiff of the lynch mob or the lemming migration about any over-large concentration of like-thinking individuals, no matter how virtuous their cause.

**P.J. O'Rourke,** *Parliament of Whores*, **1991**

Altruism, a quality as hated by the generality as it is rare.
  **Gore Vidal, *A View from the Diner's Club*, 1991**

A mob . . . is an ugly thing to see. The audience that's easily moved
to tears is as easily moved to sadistic dementia.
  **P.J. O'Rourke, *Give War a Chance*, 1992**

*See also* CLASS

# MAXIMS

If you would live innocently seek solitude.
  **Publilius Syrus, *Moral Sayings*, c.50BC**

All bad precedents began as justifiable measures.
  **Gaius Julius Caesar, quoted in *The Conspiracy of Catiline*
  by Sallust, c.50BC**

Severities should be dealt out all at once, so that their suddenness give
less offence; benefits ought to be handed out drop by drop, so that they
may be relished the more.
  **Niccolò Machiavelli, *The Prince*, 1513**

There are three things that are not to be credited: a woman when she
weeps, a merchant when he swears, nor a drunkard when he prays.
  **Barnaby Rich, *My Lady's Looking Glass*, 1616**

Do pleasant things yourself, but unpleasant things do through others.
  **Baltasar Gracian, *The Art of Worldly Wisdom*, 1647**

Fish and visitors smell after three days.
  **Benjamin Franklin, *Poor Richard's Almanack*, 1733–58**

Promises and pie-crust are made to be broken.
  **Jonathan Swift, *A Complete Collection of Polite and Ingenious
  Conversation*, 1738**

One of the pleasures of reading old letters is the knowledge that they
need no answer.
  **George Gordon, Lord Byron, quoted in *The Oxford Book of
  Aphorisms*, ed. J. Gross, 1983**

Grant graciously what you cannot refuse safely, and conciliate those you cannot conquer.

**Charles Caleb Colton, *Lacon*, 1820**

Nothing is so useless as a general maxim.

**Thomas Babington Macaulay, Baron Macaulay, in the *Edinburgh Review*, 1827**

When you talk to the half-wise, twaddle; when you talk to the ignorant, brag; when you talk to the sagacious, look very humble and ask their opinion.

**Edward George Bulwer-Lytton, Baron Lytton, *Paul Clifford*, 1830**

We should distrust any enterprise that requires new clothes.

**Henry David Thoreau, *Walden*, 1854**

The Eleventh Commandment: Thou shalt not be found out.

**George Whyte-Melville, *Holmby House*, 1860**

There are not many joys in human life equal to the joy of the sudden birth of a generalization.

**Peter Kropotkin, 1884**

Look for the ridiculous in everything and you will find it.

**Jules Renard, *Journal*, 1890**

Murder is always a mistake – one should never do anything one cannot talk about after dinner.

**Oscar Wilde, *The Picture of Dorian Gray*, 1891**

In this world there are only two tragedies. One is not getting what one wants, and the other is getting it. The last is much the worst, the last is a real tragedy.

**Oscar Wilde, *Lady Windermere's Fan*, 1892**

One should always play fairly when one has the winning cards.

**Oscar Wilde, *An Ideal Husband*, 1895**

Nothing matters very much, and few things matter at all.

**Arthur James, Earl Balfour, attributed**

Ade's Law: Anyone can win – unless there happens to be a second entry.

**George Ade, *Forty Modern Fables*, 1901**

The most delightful day after the one on which you buy a cottage in the country is the one on which you resell it.

**J. Brécheux, quoted in *Reflections on the Art of Life* by J.R. Solly, 1902**

Take care to get what you like or you will be forced to like what you like.

**George Bernard Shaw, *Man and Superman*, 1903**

It is dangerous to be sincere unless you are also stupid.

**George Bernard Shaw, *Man and Superman*, 1903**

It is far better to know too little than to know too much.

**Samuel Butler, *Notebooks*, 1912**

Always mistrust a subordinate who never finds fault with his superior.

**John Churton Collins, in the *English Review*, 1914**

Treat a whore like a lady and a lady like whore.

**Wilson Mizner, quoted in *The Incredible Mizners* by A. Johnson, 1953**

Never gamble – except with a little of the best of it.

**Wilson Mizner, quoted in *The Incredible Mizners* by A. Johnson, 1953**

'Necessity is the mother of invention' is a silly proverb. 'Necessity is the mother of futile dodges' is much nearer the truth.

**Alfred North Whitehead, quoted in *The Faber Book of Aphorisms*, ed. W.H. Auden and L. Kronenberger, 1964**

Living well is the best revenge.

**Anonymous, 1925**

Right or wrong is all the same
When baby needs new shoes.
It isn't how you play the game,
It's whether you win or lose.

**John Lardner, replying to Grantland Rice's famous 'It matters not who lost or won . . . but how you played the game'**

Don't ever make the same mistake twice – unless it pays.

**Mae West**

If you aren't rich you should always look useful.
  **Louis-Ferdinand Céline,** *Journey to the End of the Night,* **1932**

The race is not always to the swift, nor the battle to the strong, but that's the way to bet.
  **Damon Runyon**

The finest plans have always been spoiled by the littleness of them that should carry them out.
  **Bertolt Brecht,** *Mother Courage,* **1941**

If it's good, they'll stop making it.
  **Herbert Block ('Herblock')**

You should make a point of trying every experience once – except incest and folk-dancing.
  **Anonymous Scot, quoted in** *Farewell My Youth* **by A. Bax, 1943**

Never eat at a place called Mom's. Never play cards with a man named Doc. And never lie down with a woman who's got more troubles than you.
  **Nelson Algren**

Mistakes are always initial.
  **Cesare Pavese, quoted in** *The Faber Book of Aphorisms,*
  **ed. W.H. Auden and L. Kronenberger, 1964**

Intimacy has its conventions as well as ordinary social intercourse. There are three cardinal rules: don't take somebody's else's boyfriend unless you've been specifically invited to do so, don't take a drink without being asked, and keep a scrupulous accounting in financial matters.
  **W.H. Auden,** *The Table-Talk of W. H. Auden,*
  **ed. Alan Ansen, 1990**

Always fornicate between clean sheets and spit on a well-scrubbed floor.
  **Christopher Fry,** *The Lady's Not for Burning,* **1949**

If you want to get along, go along.
  **Sam Rayburn, political credo**

Be nice to people on the way up, because you'll meet them on your way down.
    **Wilson Mizner, quoted in *The Incredible Mizners* by A. Johnson, 1953**

To be modern is to potter about in the terminal ward.
    **E.M. Cioran, *Syllogismes de l'amertume*, 1952**

Logic is the art of going wrong with confidence.
    **Joseph Wood Krutch**

Gumperson's Law: the probability of anything happening is in inverse ratio to its desirability.
    **John W. Hazard, *Changing Times*, 1957**

A little inaccuracy saves a world of explanation.
    **C.E. Ayres**

More will mean worse.
    **Kingsley Amis, in *Encounter* magazine, 1960**

The final delusion is the belief that one has lost all delusions.
    **Maurice Chapelain**

Be careful what you set your heart upon – for it will surely be yours.
    **James Baldwin, *Nobody Knows My Name*, 1961**

Beware of Greeks bearing gifts, coloured men looking for loans, and whites who understand the negro.
    **Adam Clayton Powell Jr**

The way to a man's heart is through his wife's belly, and don't you forget it.
    **Edward Albee, *Who's Afraid of Virginia Woolf?*, 1962**

1. Never give anything away for nothing. 2. Never give more than you have to (always catch the buyer hungry and always make him wait). 3. Always take back everything if you possibly can.
    **William S. Burroughs, on drug pushing in the *Daily Telegraph*, 1964**

If you've got them by the balls, their hearts and minds will follow.
    **The Green Berets, military motto, c.1965**

Never sleep three in a bed – or you'll wake up three in a bed.
  **Günter Grass, *Dog Years*, 1963**

Standards are always out of date – that's what makes them standards.
  **Alan Bennett, *Forty Years On*, 1968**

A paranoid is a man who knows a little of what's going on.
  **William S. Burroughs, in *Friends* magazine, 1970**

The chief cause of problems is solutions.
  **Eric Sevareid, 1970**

Ninety-nine per cent of everything is crap.
  **Theodore Sturgeon**

If it works, it's obsolete.
  **Marshall McLuhan, in *The Listener* magazine, 1971**

Do not assume the other fellow has intelligence to match yours. He may have more.
  **Terry-Thomas**

When in doubt, mumble; when in trouble, delegate; when in charge, ponder.
  **James H. Boren, quoted in *The Official Rules* by Paul Dickson, 1972**

Blessed is he who expects no gratitude, for he shall not be disappointed.
  **W.C. Bennett, quoted in *The Official Rules* by Paul Dickson, 1972**

Unhappiness is best defined as the difference between our talents and our expectations.
  **Edward de Bono, in the *Observer*, 1977**

When anyone says they often think something it means they've just thought of it now.
  **Michael Frayn, *Alphabetical Order*, 1975**

If anything can go wrong, it will.
  **Murphy's Law, quoted in *The Official Rules* by Paul Dickson, 1972**

The three questions of greatest concern are – 1. Is it attractive? 2. Is it amusing? 3. Does it know its place?

**Fran Lebowitz, *Metropolitan Life*, 1978**

You know what they say – the sweetest word in the English language is revenge.

**Peter Beard, in *Interview* magazine, 1978**

1. You can't win. 2. You can't break even. 3. You can't even quit the game.

**Ginsberg's Theorem, quoted in *Murphy's Law* by A. Bloch, 1979**

The whole world is a scab. The point is to pick it constructively.

**Peter Beard, quoted in *Loose Talk*, ed. L. Botts, 1980**

A conclusion is the place where you got tired of thinking.

**Matz's Maxim, in *Murphy's Law Book Two* by A. Bloch, 1980**

When a man speaks of the need for realism one may be sure that this is always the prelude to some bloody deed.

**Sir Isaiah Berlin, quoted in *The Times*, 1981**

A good terminology is half the game.

**Anonymous, quoted in *Bricks to Babel* by A. Koestler, 1981**

Always be nice to those younger than you, because they are the ones who will be writing about you.

**Cyril Connolly, *Journal 1928–1937*, ed. D. Pryce-Jones, 1983**

Only two things are worth having – money, which you have not had the trouble of earning, and irresponsibility.

**Cyril Connolly, *Journal 1928–1937*, ed. D. Pryce-Jones, 1983**

So long as there is anything to be gained by saying nothing, it is always better to say nothing than anything.

**Antony Jay and Jonathan Lynn, script for *Yes, Prime Minister*, 1986**

If you can keep your head when all about you are losing theirs, perhaps you have misunderstood the situation.

**Graffito**

What you can't have, abuse.
**Italian proverb**

# MEDICINE

He that sinneth before his Maker, Let him fall into the hands of the physician.
**The Bible,** *Ecclesiasticus (Apocrypha),* **c.AD100**

There are more old drunkards than there are old physicians.
**François Rabelais,** *Gargantua,* **1535**

Diseases are the interests of pleasures.
**John Ray,** *A Collection of English Proverbs,* **1670**

Doctors allow one to die; charlatans kill.
**Jean de La Bruyère,** *The Characters,* **1688**

The patient is not likely to recover who makes the doctor his heir.
**Thomas Fuller, M.D.,** *Gnomologia,* **1732**

He who was never sick dies the first fit.
**Thomas Fuller, M.D.,** *Gnomologia,* **1732**

The art of medicine consists in amusing the patient while nature cures the disease.
**Voltaire**

Philosophy, like medicine, has plenty of drugs, few good remedies, and hardly any specific cures.
**Nicolas de Chamfort,** *Maximes et pensées,* **1805**

Doctors are the same as lawyers; the only difference is that lawyers merely rob you, wheras doctors rob you and kill you too.
**Anton Chekhov**

One knows so well the popular idea of health. The English country gentleman galloping after a fox. The unspeakable in full pursuit of the uneatable.
**Oscar Wilde,** *A Woman of No Importance,* **1893**

The animals are not as stupid as one thinks – they have neither doctors nor lawyers.

**L. Docquier, quoted in *Reflections on the Art of Life* by J.R. Solly, 1902**

You can always read a doctor's bill and you can never read his prescription.

**Finley Peter Dunne, *Mr Dooley Says*, 1910**

Cured yesterday of my disease
I died last night of my physician.

**Matthew Prior**

Every man who feels well is a sick man neglecting himself.

**Jules Romains, *Knock*, 1923**

A really conscientious doctor ought to die with his patient. The captain goes down with his ship, He doesn't survive the wreck!

**Eugène Ionesco, *The Bald Prima Donna*, 1948**

If Patient turns out to be really ill, after all, it is always possible to look grave at the same time and say 'You realise, I suppose, that twenty-five years ago you'd have been dead.'

**Stephen Potter, *One-Upmanship*, 1952**

Sociology . . . the study of people who do not need to be studied by people who do.

**E.S. Turner**

I have a perfect cure for a sore throat – cut it.

**Alfred Hitchcock**

The beneficient effects of the regular quarter-hour's exercise before breakfast is more than offset by the mental wear-and-tear in getting out of bed fifteen minutes earlier than one otherwise would.

**Simeon Strunsky**

I don't believe the kindliest of men ever learned about the death of his doctor without a feeling of smugness.

**Richard Gordon**

Now a Jew, in the dictionary, is one who is descended from the ancient tribes of Judea . . . but you and I know what a Jew is – one who killed

Our Lord . . . A lot of people say to me 'Why did you kill Christ?'
'I dunno, it was one of those parties, got out of hand, you know . . .'
We killed him because he didn't want to become a doctor, that's
why we killed him.

**Lenny Bruce, quoted in *The Essential Lenny Bruce*,
ed. J. Cohen, 1967**

There's no fun in medicine, but there's a lot of medicine in fun.

**Anonymous, quoted in *The Wit of Medicine*, ed. L. and
M. Cowan, 1972**

A drug is a substance that when injected into a guinea pig produces a
scientific paper.

**Anonymous, quoted in *The Wit of Medicine*, ed. L. and
M. Cowan, 1972**

If a patient is poor he is committed to a public hospital as a 'psychotic'.
If he can afford a sanatorium, the diagnosis is 'neurasthenia'. If he is
wealthy enough to be in his own home under the constant watch of
nurses and physicians, he is simply 'an indisposed eccentric'.

**Pierre Janet, quoted in *The Wit of Medicine*, ed. L. and
M. Cowan, 1972**

There is no human activity, eating, sleeping, drinking or sex which
some doctor somewhere won't discover leads directly to cardiac arrest.

**John Mortimer, in the *Observer*, 1978**

I have always said that exercise is a short cut to the cemetery.

**John Mortimer, *Rumpole of the Bailey*, 1978**

A young physician can expect nothing but trouble from an important
and original discovery made early in his career. Such an individual
would be wise to attribute his discovery to luck rather than ability. An
even more cynical thought is that a pioneer should develop some
physical handicap (a limp, a stutter or a an eye patch).

**Adrian Upton, in *The Vital Probe* by I.S. Cooper, 1982**

Medicine: 'Your money and your life!'

**Karl Kraus, *Half Truths and One and a Half Truths*, 1986**

A virus is a Latin word translated by doctors to mean 'Your guess is
as good as mine'.

**Anonymous**

Some doctors make the same mistakes for twenty years and call it clinical experience.

**Noah Fabricant**

Why live like an invalid to die as a healthy man?

**Italian proverb**

# MEN

A man must learn to endure patiently that which he cannot avoid conveniently.

**Michel de Montaigne, *Essays*, 1595**

Never battle with a man who has nothing to lose, for then the conflict is unequal.

**Baltasar Gracian, *The Art of Worldly Wisdom*, 1647**

To make a Man tell of some private Grievance, pretend the like Uneasiness, and seem sick of the same Disease.

**Thomas Fuller, M.D., *Introductio ad Prudentiam*, 1727**

Animals have these advantages over man: they have no theologians to instruct them, their funerals cost them nothing, and no one starts law suits over their wills.

**Voltaire**

Questioner: 'I wonder what pleasure men can take in making beasts of themselves?'
Johnson: 'He who makes a beast of himself gets rid of the pain of being a man.'

**Samuel Johnson, *Murray's Johnsoniana*, 1836**

Man's chief merit consists in resisting the impulses of his nature.

**Samuel Johnson, *Johnsonian Miscellanies*, ed. G. B. Hill, 1897**

Man originates in muck, wades a while in muck, makes muck and in the end returns to muck.

**Johann Christoff Friedrich von Schiller, *The Robbers*, 1781**

Depend upon it that if a man talks of his misfortunes, there is something in them that is not disagreeable to him.

**Samuel Johnson, *The Life of Samuel Johnson* by J. Boswell, 1791**

A man can be so much of everything that he is nothing of any thing.

**Samuel Johnson, *The Life of Samuel Johnson* by J. Boswell, 1791**

Let a man admire himself, and he will infallibly find plenty of simpletons to admire him.

**William Hazlitt, *Butts of Different Sorts*, 1829**

Yield to a man's tastes and he will yield to your interests.

**Edward George Bulwer-Lytton, Baron Lytton, *Paul Clifford*, 1830**

If every man were straightforward in his opinions, there would be no conversation.

**Benjamin Disraeli**

If you pick up a starving dog and make him prosperous, he will not bite you. That is the principal difference between a dog and a man.

**Mark Twain**

One never dives into the water to save a drowning man more eagerly than when there are others present who dare not take the risk.

**Friedrich Wilhelm Nietzsche**

I sometimes think that God, in creating man, somewhat overestimated his ability.

**Oscar Wilde**

It is only the superficial qualities that last. Man's deeper nature is soon found out.

**Oscar Wilde, *Phrases and Philosophies for the Use of the Young*, 1894**

Why did nature create Man? Was it to show that she is big enough to make mistakes, or was it pure ignorance?

**Holbrook Jackson**

Man is the only animal that strikes his women-folk.

**Jeannie Gunn**

[A] 'Grand Old Man'. That means on our continent any one with snow white hair who has kept out of jail till eighty.

**Stephen Leacock**

Male, n. A member of the unconsidered, or negligible sex. The male of the human race is commonly known to the female as Mere Man. The genus has two varieties: good providers and bad providers.
**Ambrose Bierce, *The Devil's Dictionary*, 1911**

Never trust a man who speaks well of everybody.
**John Churton Collins, in *The English Review*, 1914**

Too often the strong, silent man is silent only because he does not know what to say, and is reputed strong only because he has remained silent.
**Sir Winston Churchill, 1924**

Man is a clever animal who behaves like an imbecile.
**Albert Schweitzer**

How does a man live? By completely forgetting he is a human being.
**Bertolt Brecht, *The Threepenny Opera*, 1928**

The only really masterful noise a man makes in a house is the noise of his key, when he is still on the landing, fumbling for the lock.
**Colette**

If man had created man, he would be ashamed of his performance.
**Mark Twain, *Notebooks*, 1935**

Man is a useless passion.
**Jean-Paul Sartre, *Being and Nothingness*, 1943**

Most of us grow up to be the kind of men our mothers warned us against.
**Brendan Behan**

What is man? A miserable little pile of secrets.
**André Malraux**

If man is only a little lower than the angels, the angels should reform.
**Mary Wilson Little**

The only real threat to man is man himself.
**Dr Brock Chisholm**

There are no great men, buster. There are only men.
   **Charles Schnee, screenplay for *The Bad and the Beautiful*, 1952**

You may be sure that when a man begins to call himself a realist he is preparing to do something that he is secretly ashamed of doing.
   **Sydney J. Harris**

Men are those creatures with two legs and eight hands.
   **Jayne Mansfield**

Always suspect the man who seems to fit every need.
   **Sir James Darling**

Women think of being a man as a gift. It is a duty. Even making love can be a duty. A man has always got to get it up, and love isn't always enough.
   **Norman Mailer, in *Nova* magazine, 1969**

It is chiefly through the instinct to kill that man achieves intimacy with the life of nature.
   **Lord Clark**

Probably the only place where a man can feel really secure is in a maximum security prison, except for the imminent threat of release.
   **Germaine Greer, *The Female Eunuch*, 1970**

Don't accept rides from strange men – and remember that all men are as strange as hell.
   **Robin Morgan, *Sisterhood is Powerful*, 1970**

If you catch a man, throw him back.
   **Women's Liberation slogan, *c*.1975**

*See also* HUMANITY, WOMEN

# THE MILITARY

It is the blood of the soldier that makes the general great.
   **Anonymous**

If my soldiers began to think, not one would remain in the ranks.
   **Frederick the Great, attributed**

The greatest general is he who makes the fewest mistakes.
**Napoleon Bonaparte,** *Maxims,* **1804–15**

There is nothing on earth as stupid as a gallant officer.
**Arthur Wellesley, Duke of Wellington**

Generals have never risen from the very learned or erudite class of
officers but have mostly been men who, from the circumstances of their
position, could not have obtained any great amount of knowledge.
**Karl von Clausewitz,** *On War,* **1832**

The louder he talked of his honour, the faster we counted our spoons.
**Ralph Waldo Emerson,** *The Conduct of Life,* **1860**

No plan survives contact with the enemy.
**Field-Marshal Helmuth von Moltke**

When the military man approaches the world locks up its spoons and
packs off its womankind.
**George Bernard Shaw,** *Major Barbara,* **1907**

'He's a cheerful old card', grunted Harry to Jack
As they slogged up to Arras with rifle and pack.
. . .
But he did for them both with his plan of attack.
**Siegfried Sassoon,** *The General,* **1917**

Nothing raises morale better than a dead general.
**John Masters,** *The Road Past Mandalay,* **1961**

We are the unwilling, led by the unqualified, doing the unnecessary
for the ungrateful.
**Graffito, Vietnam War, 1970**

The army works like this: if a man dies when you hang him, keep hang-
ing him until he gets used to it.
**Spike Milligan**

There are three kinds of intelligence – the intelligence of man, the
intelligence of animals, and the intelligence of the military. In that order.
**Gottfried Reinhardt**

*See also* BRAVERY

# MONEY

There is no fortress so strong that money cannot take it.
**Marcus Tullius Cicero**

A son might bear with composure the death of his father, but the loss of his inheritance might drive him to despair.
**Niccolò Machiavelli, *The Prince*, 1513**

There are but two families in the world: Have-much and Have-little.
**Miguel de Cervantes, *Don Quixote*, 1615**

Plenty of people despise money, but few know how to give it away.
**François, Duc de La Rochefoucauld, *Maxims*, 1665**

Those who lack money when they come to borrow will also lack money when they come to pay.
**Oliver Goldsmith, *The Citizen of the World*, 1762**

I would rather trust my money to a man who has no hands, and so a physical impossibility to steal, than to a man of the most honest principles.
**Samuel Johnson, *The Life of Samuel Johnson* by J. Boswell, 1791**

Is not a Patron . . . one who looks with unconcern on a man struggling for life in the water, and, when he has reached ground, encumbers him with help?
**Samuel Johnson, *The Life of Samuel Johnson* by J. Boswell, 1791**

The jingling of the guinea helps the hurt that honour feels.
**Alfred, Lord Tennyson, *Locksley Hall*, 1842**

Few rich men own their property: their property owns them.
**Robert G. Ingersoll, 1896**

Cash: a sort of window-fastener to keep Love from flying out.
**Oliver Herford and John Clay, *Cupid's Cyclopedia*, 1910**

Love may laugh at locksmiths, but he has a profound respect for money bags.
**Sidney Paternoster, *The Folly of the Wise*, 1907**

The most important thing in life is not to have money, but that others have it.
**Sacha Guitry**

The two most beautiful words in the English language are 'Cheque Enclosed'.
**Dorothy Parker**

Kissing your hand may make you feel very good, but a diamond and safire bracelet lasts for ever.
**Anita Loos, *Gentlemen Prefer Blondes*, 1925**

What is robbing a bank compared with founding a bank?
**Bertolt Brecht, *The Threepenny Opera*, 1928**

The chief value of money is that one lives in a world in which it is over-estimated.
**H.L. Mencken**

The most sensitive part of a man is not his skin but his wallet.
**Adolf Hitler**

The avoidance of taxes is the only pursuit that still carries any reward.
**John Maynard Keynes**

There are few sorrows, however poignant, in which a good income is of no avail.
**Logan Pearsall Smith, *Afterthoughts*, 1931**

A 'sound' banker, alas, is not one who sees danger and avoids it, but one who, when he is ruined, is ruined in a conventional and orthodox way along with his fellows, so that no one can really blame him.
**John Maynard Keynes, *Essays in Persuasion*, 1933**

An economist's guess is likely to be as good as anyone else's.
**Will Rogers**

No woman marries for money: they are all clever enough, before marrying a millionaire, to fall in love with him first.
**Cesare Pavese, *The Business of Living: Diaries*, 1935–50**

Where there is money, there is fighting.
**Marian Anderson, quoted in *Marian Anderson: A Portrait* by Kosti Vehanen, 1941**

Money cannot buy
The fuel of love
But is excellent kindling.

**W.H. Auden**

Economists are people who work with numbers but don't have the personality to be accountants.

**Anonymous**

An economist is a person who talks about something he doesn't understand and makes you feel you are ignorant.

**Herbert Prochnow**

A bank is a place where they lend you an umbrella in fair weather and ask for it back when it begins to rain.

**Robert Frost**

If you would know what the Lord God thinks of money, you have only to look at those to whom he gives it.

**Maurice Baring, quoted in _Writers at Work_ 1st series, 1958**

Wealth is not without its advantages, and the case to the contrary, although it has often been made, has never proved widely persuasive.

**John Kenneth Galbraith, _The Affluent Society_, 1958**

Economy: cutting down on other people's wages.

**J.B. Morton ('Beachcomber')**

The most popular labour-saving device today is still a husband with money.

**Joey Adams, _Cindy and I_, 1959**

Gentility is what is left over from rich ancestors after the money is gone.

**John Ciardi**

There is no stronger craving in the world than that of the rich for titles, except that of the titled for riches.

**Hesketh Pearson, _The Marrying Americans_, 1961**

Credit . . . is the only enduring testimonial to man's confidence in man.

**James Blish**

Those who have some means think that the most important thing in the world is love. The poor know that it is money.

**Gerald Brenan,** *Thoughts in a Dry Season***, 1978**

No one would remember the Good Samaritan if he had only had good intentions. He had money as well.

**Margaret Thatcher, quoted in** *The Spectator* **magazine, 1980**

A lot of pain and nuisance might be avoided if the rich would only appreciate the point where love becomes money.

**Cyril Connolly,** *Journal 1928–1937***, ed. D. Pryce-Jones, 1983**

The rich, particularly rich women, exist to facilitate things.

**Cyril Connolly,** *Journal 1928–1937***, ed. D. Pryce-Jones, 1983**

The trouble about a free market economy is that it requires so many policemen to make it work.

**Neal Ascherson, in the** *Observer***, 1985**

In all recorded history there has not been one economist who had to worry about where the next meal would come from.

**Peter Drucker**

*See also* BUSINESS, POVERTY & THE POOR, THE RICH

# MORALS

If we resist our passions, it is more from their weakness than from our strength.

**François, Duc de La Rochefoucauld,** *Maxims***, 1665**

We reprove others not so much to correct them as to persuade them that we ourselves are free from their faults.

**François, Duc de La Rochefoucauld,** *Maxims***, 1665**

Repentance is not so much remorse for what we have done as the fear of consequences.

**François, Duc de La Rochefoucauld,** *Maxims***, 1665**

When vices give us up we flatter ourselves that we are giving them up.

**François, Duc de La Rochefoucauld,** *Maxims***, 1665**

We often do good that we may do evil with impunity.
  **François, Duc de La Rochefoucauld, *Maxims*, 1665**

Humility is a virtue all preach, none practise, and yet everybody is content to hear. The master thinks it is good doctrine for his servant, the laity for the clergy and the clergy for the laity.
  **John Selden, *Table Talk*, 1689**

Leave morals and honesty to the poor, as they do in London.
  **John Gay, *The Beggar's Opera*, 1728**

It is easier to bear what's amiss than go about to reform it.
  **Thomas Fuller, M.D., *Gnomologia*, 1732**

Be not too hasty to trust or admire the teachers of morality; they discourse like angels but they live like men.
  **Samuel Johnson, *Rasselas*, 1759**

All universal moral principles are idle fancies.
  **Donatien Alphonse François, Marquis de Sade, *The 120 Days of Sodom*, 1785**

It is essential to the triumph of reform that it should never succeed.
  **William Hazlitt**

If I knew for a certainty that man was coming to my house with the conscious design of doing me good, I should run for my life.
  **Henry Thoreau, *Walden*, 1854**

In judging others folks will work overtime for no pay.
  **Charles Carrothers**

We blame in others only those faults by which we do not profit.
  **Alexander Dumas, père**

When Dr Johnson defined patriotism as the last refuge of a scoundrel, he ignored the enormous possibilities of the word 'reform'.
  **Senator Roscoe Conkling, 1876**

Fear is the mother of morality.
  **Friedrich Wilhelm Nietzsche, *The Genealogy of Morals*, 1887**

Morality is the best of all devices for leading mankind by the nose.
**Friedrich Wilhelm Nietzsche, *The Antichrist*, 1888**

Scandal is gossip made tedious by morality.
**Oscar Wilde**

A man who moralises is usually a hypocrite and a woman who moralises is invariably plain.
**Oscar Wilde, *Lady Windermere's Fan*, 1892**

Nothing so needs reforming as other people's habits.
**Mark Twain, 1894**

Wickedness is a myth invented by good people to account for the curious attractiveness of others.
**Oscar Wilde, *Phrases and Philosophies for the Use of the Young*, 1894**

I never came across anyone in whom the moral sense was dominant who was not heartless, cruel, vindictive, log-stupid and entirely lacking in the smallest sense of humanity. Moral people, as they are termed, are simply beasts. I would sooner have fifty unnatural vices than one unnatural virtue.
**Oscar Wilde, letter to Leonard Smithers, 1897**

Morality is simply the attitude we adopt to people whom we personally dislike.
**Oscar Wilde, *An Ideal Husband*, 1895**

Vice is a creature of such hideous mien that the more you see it the better you like it.
**Finley Peter Dunne, *Mr Dooley's Opinions*, 1901**

Morality consists in suspecting other people of not being legally married.
**George Bernard Shaw, *The Doctor's Dilemma*, 1908**

Moral, adj. Conforming to a local and mutable standard of right. Having the quality of general expediency.
**Ambrose Bierce, *The Devil's Dictionary*, 1911**

Fool, n. A person who pervades the domain of intellectual speculation and diffuses himself through the channels of moral activity.
**Ambrose Bierce, *The Devil's Dictionary*, 1911**

Immoral, adj. Inexpedient.

**Ambrose Bierce, *The Devil's Dictionary*, 1911**

If you can't answer a man's argument, all is not lost. You can still call him vile names.

**Elbert Hubbard**

Moral indignation is jealousy with a halo.

**H.G. Wells**

Immorality is the morality of those who are having a better time.

**H.L. Mencken, *Sententiae*, 1916**

Remorse – regret that one waited so long to do it.

**H.L. Mencken, *Sententiae*, 1916**

The difference between a moral man and a man of honour is that the latter regrets a discreditable act, even when it has worked and he has not been caught.

**H.L. Mencken, *Sententiae*, 1916**

Morality . . . is what the majority then and there happen to like and immorality is what they dislike.

**Alfred North Whitehead**

A sense of humour always withers in the presence of the messianic delusion, like justice and truth in front of patriotic passion.

**H.L. Mencken, *Prejudices* 1919–27**

We like to moralise when we are old because it makes a merit of many deprivations which have become a necessity.

**Mme de Salm-Dyck, quoted in *A Cynic's Breviary*
by J.R. Solly, 1925**

Many people think that virtue consists of severity towards others.

**Alphonse Karr, quoted in *A Cynic's Breviary* by J.R. Solly, 1925**

We have, in fact, two kinds of morality side by side; one which we preach but do not practise, and another which we practise but seldom preach.

**Bertrand Russell, *Sceptical Essays*, 1928**

Eats first, morals after.

**Bertolt Brecht, *The Threepenny Opera*, 1928**

A concern with the perfectibility of mankind is always a symptom of thwarted or perverted development.

**Hugh Kingsmill**

Fearful is the seductive power of goodness.

**Bertolt Brecht, *The Caucasian Chalk Circle*, 1947**

Half the harm that is done in this world
Is due to people who want to feel important.

**T.S. Eliot, *The Cocktail Party*, 1950**

Righteous people terrify me . . . virtue is its own punishment.

**Aneurin Bevan**

A woman can look both moral and exciting – if she also looks as if it were quite a struggle.

**Edna Ferber, in the *Reader's Digest*, 1954**

The urge to save humanity is almost always a false front for the urge to rule.

**H.L. Mencken, *Minority Report*, 1956**

It is in the interest of [film] producers to maintain a certain moral standard since, if they don't do this, the immoral films won't sell.

**Jean Renoir**

Moral indignation is in most cases two per cent moral, forty-eight per cent indignation and fifty per cent envy.

**Vittorio De Sica, in the *Observer*, 1961**

Morality's not practical. Morality's a gesture. A complicated gesture learnt from books.

**Robert Bolt, *A Man for All Seasons*, 1960**

Things have got to be wrong in order that they may be deplored.

**Whitney Griswold, quoted in the *New York Times*, 1963**

Moral responsibility is what is lacking in a man when he demands it of a woman.

**Karl Kraus, *Half Truths and One and a Half Truths*, 1986**

Chastity always takes its toll: in some it produces pimples, in others sex laws.

**Karl Kraus, *Half Truths and One and a Half Truths*, 1986**

The Moral Majority is deeply anti-semitic and will always remain so because the Jews killed our Lord (proving that no good deed goes unpunished . . . ).

**Gore Vidal, *Armageddon*, 1987**

Nor is it remarkable to find a papal encyclical upholding the existence of objective moral standards. A belief in the existence of objective moral standards, authoritatively explained, is, after all, the heritage of all Christians; indeed, of all Jews and Muslims. It helps to explain why they have been able to wage war on each other with good consciences.

**Andrew Brown, in the *Independent*, 1993**

*See also* BELIEF, THE CLERGY, FAITH, GOD, IDEALS, IDEAS, RELIGION, TRUE BELIEVERS, TRUTH

# MUSIC

The main thing the public demands of a composer is that he be dead.

**Arthur Honegger**

Song is the licensed medium for bawling in public things too silly or sacred to be uttered in ordinary speech.

**Oliver Herford**

Composers shouldn't think too much – it interferes with their plagiarism.

**Howard Dietz**

Classical music is the kind we keep thinking will turn into a tune.

**Kin Hubbard, *Abe Martin's Sayings*, 1915**

Opera is a loosely connected series of songs designed to make a full evening's entertainment out of an overture.

**Miles Kington**

# NATIONALISM

The first man to fence in a piece of land saying 'This is mine' and who found people simple enough to believe him, was the real founder of civil society.

**Jean-Jacques Rousseau, *Discourse on the Origin and Bases of Inequality among Men*, 1754**

Happy is the nation that has no history.
   **Cesare Beccaria, *Of Crimes and Punishments*, 1764**

To find a new country and invade it has always been the same thing.
   **Samuel Johnson, *Works* vol. v, 1787**

Kings are for nations in their swaddling clothes.
   **Victor Hugo, speech, 1848**

Immigrant: an unenlightened person who thinks one country better than another.
   **Ambrose Bierce, *The Devil's Dictionary*, 1911**

Nationalism is an infantile disease. It is the measles of mankind.
   **Albert Einstein, letter, 1921**

I know of no existing nation that deserves to live. And I know of very few individuals.
   **H.L. Mencken**

The chief business of the nation, as a nation, is the setting up of heroes, mostly bogus.
   **H.L. Mencken, *Prejudices* 3rd series, 1922**

Countries are like fruit – the worms are always inside.
   **Jean Giraudoux, *Siegfried*, 1922**

Freeing oppressed nationalities is perhaps the most dangerous of all philanthropic enterprises.
   **William Bolitho, *Twelve Against the Gods*, 1929**

The world is divided into two groups of nations: those which want to expel the Jews, and those which do not want to receive them.
   **Chaim Weizmann, 1938**

Unhappy the land that needs heroes.
   **Bertolt Brecht, *Galileo*, 1937–9**

Gratitude, like love, is never a dependable international emotion.
   **Joseph Alsop, in the *Observer*, 1952**

The great nations have always acted like gangsters and the small nations like prostitutes.
   **Stanley Kubrick, 1963**

The hour of their crime does not strike simultaneously for all nations. This explains the permanence of history.

**E.M. Cioran, quoted in *The Faber Book of Aphorisms*, ed. W.H. Auden and L. Kronenberger, 1964**

History teaches us that men and nations behave wisely once they have exhausted all other alternatives.

**Abba Eban, 1970**

In any country there must be people who have to die. They are the sacrifices any nation has to make to achieve law and order.

**Idi Amin Dada, 1976**

The length of a country's national anthem is inversely proportional to the importance of that country.

**Allen L. Otten, quoted in *The Book of Laws* by H. Faber, 1980**

I am always fascinated when people talk about 'the forging of a nation'. Most nations are forgeries, perpetrated in the last century or so.

**Neal Ascherson, in the *Observer*, 1985**

The unattractive thing about chauvinism is not so much aversion to other nations, but the love of one's own.

**Karl Kraus, *Half Truths and One and a Half Truths*, 1986**

*See also* PATRIOTISM

# NEIGHBOURS

Love your neighbour, yet don't pull down your hedge.

**Benjamin Franklin**

Philosophy may teach us to bear with equanimity the misfortunes of our neighbours.

**Oscar Wilde, lecture, 1882**

Do not love your neighbour as yourself. If you are on good terms with yourself it as impertinence; if on bad, an injury.

**George Bernard Shaw, *Man and Superman*, 1903**

Comfort, n. A state of mind produced by contemplation of a neighbour's uneasiness.

**Ambrose Bierce, *The Devil's Dictionary*, 1911**

Do unto yourself as your neighbours do unto themselves and look pleasant.

**George Ade, *Hand-Made Fables*, 1920**

The propriety of some persons seems to consist in having improper thoughts about their neighbours.

**F.H. Bradley, *Aphorisms*, 1930**

It's a recession when your neighbour loses his job; it's a depression when you lose yours.

**Harry S. Truman, 1958**

Don't shout for help at night. You might wake your neighbours.

**Stanislaw J. Lec, *Unkempt Thoughts*, 1962**

Never keep up with the Jones. Drag them down to your level, it's cheaper.

**Quentin Crisp, 1978**

*See also* CHARITY

# OPINIONS

Public opinion is a compound of folly, weakness, prejudice, wrong feeling, right feeling, obstinacy and newspaper paragraphs.

**Robert Peel**

We follow the world in approving others, but go before it in approving ourselves.

**Charles Caleb Colton, *Lacon*, 1820**

What is a theory but an imperfect generalization caught up by a predisposition.

**J.A. Froude, *The Lives of the Saints*, 1852**

What we call public opinion is generally public sentiment.

**Benjamin Disraeli, speech, 1880**

The public buys its opinions as it buys its meat, or takes in its milk, on the principle that it is cheaper to do this than to keep a cow. So it is – but the milk is more likely to be watered.

**Samuel Butler, *Notebooks*, 1912**

Sound opinions are valueless. What matters is who holds them.

**Karl Kraus,** *Half Truths and One and a Half Truths,* **1986**

Deliberation, n. The act of examining one's bread to see which side it is buttered on.

**Ambrose Bierce,** *The Devil's Dictionary,* **1911**

One should respect public opinion insofar as is necessary to avoid starvation and keep out of prison, but anything that goes beyond this is voluntary submission to an unnecessary tyranny.

**Bertrand Russell,** *The Conquest of Happiness,* **1930**

There is no tyranny so despotic as that of public opinion among a free people.

**Donn Platt**

*See also* ADVICE

# OPTIMISM

Optimism, n. An intellectual disorder, yielding to no treatment but death. It is hereditary, but fortunately not contagious.

**Ambrose Bierce,** *The Devil's Dictionary,* **1911**

The optimist proclaims we live in the best of all possible worlds; and the pessimist fears this is true.

**James Branch Cabell,** *The Silver Stallion,* **1926**

An optimist is a guy that never had much experience.

**Don Marquis,** *Archy and Mehitabel,* **1927**

Optimism is the content of small men in high places.

**F. Scott Fitzgerald,** *The Crack-Up,* **1936**

The optimist thinks that this is the best of all possible worlds, and the pessimist knows it.

**J. Robert Oppenheimer, in** *The Bulletin of the Atomic Scientists,* **1951**

What passes for optimism is most often the effect of an intellectual error.

**Raymond Aron,** *The Opium of the Intellectuals,* **1957**

An optimist is one who knows exactly how bad a place the world can be; a pessimist is one who finds out anew every morning.

**Peter Ustinov, in *The Illustrated London News*, 1968**

The man who smiles when things go wrong has thought of someone he can blame it on.

**Jones' Law, quoted in *Murphy's Law* by A. Bloch, 1979**

*See also* PESSIMISM

# PARENTS

A man doesn't shoot himself when he's going to be made a lawful father for the first time, unless he can see a long way into the future.

**Henry Lawson**

A father is a banker provided by nature.

**Anonymous, quoted in *The Oxford Book of Aphorisms*,
ed. J. Gross, 1983**

The first half of our lives is ruined by our parents, and the second half by our children.

**Clarence Darrow**

The fundamental defect of fathers is that they want their children to be a credit to them.

**Bertrand Russell**

Kath: Can he be present at the birth of his child?
Ed: It's all any reasonable child can expect if the dad is present at the conception.

**Joe Orton, *Entertaining Mr Sloane*, 1964**

The mother of the year should be a sterilised woman with two adopted children.

**Paul Ehrlich**

From the moment of birth, when the Stone Age baby confronts the 20th century mother, the baby is subjected to these forces of violence, called love, as its father and mother, and their parents and their parents before them, have been. These forces are mainly concerned with destroying most of its potential.

**R.D. Laing, *The Politics of Experience*, 1967**

They fuck you up, your Mum and Dad.
They may not mean to, but they do.
And give you all the faults they had
And add some extra, just for you.
  **Philip Larkin, *This Be The Verse*, 1974**

Parents are the bones on which children sharpen their teeth.
  **Peter Ustinov, *Dear Me*, 1977**

Your responsibility as a parent is not as great as you might imagine.
You need not supply the world with the next conqueror of disease or
major motion picture star. If your child simply grows up to be someone
who does not use the word 'collectible' as a noun, you can consider
yourself an unqualified success.
  **Fran Lebowitz, *Social Studies*, 1981**

Spoil the child
Spare the rod
Open up the caviar and say
Thank God!
  **Noël Coward, quoted in *Ritz* magazine, 1984**

A father's pride, laid on thick, always makes me wish that the fellow
had at least experienced some pain during procreation.
  **Karl Kraus, *Half Truths and One and a Half Truths*, 1986**

*See also* ADULTS, CHILDREN, FAMILIES

# PARTIES

Party loyalty lowers the greatest of men to the petty level of the masses
  **Jean de La Bruyère, *The Characters*, 1688**

The best Party is but a kind of conspiracy against the rest of the
nation . . . Ignorance maketh men go into a party, and shame keepeth
them from going out of it.
  **George Savile, Marquis of Halifax, *Political, Moral and
  Miscellaneous Thoughts and Reflexions*, c.1694**

All political parties die at last of swallowing their own lies.
  **John Arbuthnot, 1735**

There is no act of treachery or mean-ness of which a political party is not capable; for in politics there is no honour.
  **Benjamin Disraeli, *Vivian Grey*, 1826–7**

A Conservative government is an organised hypocrisy.
  **Benjamin Disraeli, speech, 1845**

A sect or party is an elegant incognito devised to save a man from the vexation of thinking.
  **Ralph Waldo Emerson, *Journals*, 1909–14**

English experience indicates that when two great political parties agree about something, it is generally wrong.
  **G.K. Chesterton, 1919**

Party is the madness of the many for the gain of the few.
  **Alexander Pope**

Cease being the slave of a party and you become its deserter.
  **Jules Simon**

The two party system . . . is a triumph of the dialectic. It showed that two could be one and one could be two and had probably been fabricated by Hegel for the American market on a subcontract from General Dynamics.
  **I.F. Stone, 1968**

*See also* CONSERVATIVES, DEMOCRACY, GOVERNMENT, LIBERALS, POLITICS, VOTING

# PATRIOTISM

Patriot: a candidate for place. Politics: the art of getting one.
  **Henry Fielding, *The Covent Garden Journal*, 1752**

A Patriot is a Fool in ev'ry age.
  **Alexander Pope, *Epistles and Satires of Horace Imitated*, 1733–8**

Patriotism is the last refuge of a scoundrel.
  **Samuel Johnson, *The Life of Samuel Johnson* by J. Boswell, 1791**

'God save the King' . . . too often means God save my pension and my place, God give my sisters an allowance out of the privy purse, make me clerk of the irons, let me survey the meltings, let me live upon the fruits of other men's industry, and fatten upon the plunder of the public.

**Sydney Smith,** *The Letters of Peter Plymley*, **1807**

Talking of patriotism, what humbug it is; it is a word which always commemorates a robbery. There isn't a foot of land in the world which doesn't represent the ousting and re-ousting of a long line of successive owners.

**Mark Twain,** *A Connecticut Yankee at King Arthur's Court*, **1889**

Patriotism is the virtue of the vicious.

**Oscar Wilde**

Patriotism is one of the Monopolist Instincts. And the Monopolist Instincts are the greatest enemies of social life in humanity. They are what we have got in the end to outlive. The test of a man's place in the scale of being is how far he has outlived them.

**Grant Allen, quoted in** *The Westminster Gazette*, **1894**

The less a statesman amounts too, the more he loves the flag.

**Kin Hubbard**

'My country, right or wrong' is a thing that no patriot would think of saying, except in a desperate case. It is like saying 'My mother, drunk or sober.'

**G.K. Chesterton**

To be patriotic, hate all nations but your own; to be religious, all sects but your own; to be moral, all pretences but your own.

**Lionel Strachey**

Whenever you hear a man speak of his love for his country, it is a sign that he expects to be paid for it.

**H.L. Mencken,** *Sententiae*, **1916**

Patriotism is often an arbitrary veneration of real estate above principles.

**George Jean Nathan**

Patriotism is your conviction that this country is superior to all other countries because you were born in it.

**George Bernard Shaw**

Love makes fools, marriage cuckolds, and patriotism malevolent imbeciles.

**Paul Léautaud**

This is the devilish thing about foreign affairs: they are foreign and will not always conform to our whim.

**James Reston, 1964**

# PEACE

Peace, n. In international affairs, a period of cheating between two periods of fighting.

**Ambrose Bierce, *The Devil's Dictionary*, 1911**

Everlasting peace will come to the world when the last man has slain the last but one.

**Adolf Hitler**

There is no such thing as inner peace. There is only nervousness or death. Any attempt to prove otherwise constitutes unacceptable behaviour.

**Fran Lebowitz, *Metropolitan Life*, 1978**

'Peace' is when nobody's shooting. A 'just peace' is when our side gets what it wants.

**Bill Mauldin, quoted in *Loose Talk*, ed. L. Botts, 1980**

Peace on earth would mean the end of civilization as we know it.

**Joseph Heller, *Picture This*, 1986**

# PESSIMISM

Blessed is he who expects nothing, for he shall never be disappointed.

**Alexander Pope, letter, 1727**

A pessimist is a man who thinks everybody is as nasty as himself and hates them for it.

**George Bernard Shaw, *An Unsocial Socialist*, 1883**

It is a matter for regret that so many mean, low suspicions turn out to be well-founded.

**Edgar Watson Howe, *Country Town Sayings*, 1911**

The most prolific period of pessimism comes at twenty-one, or there-abouts, when the first attempt is made to translate dreams into reality.
**Heywood Broun,** *Pieces of Hate*, 1922

A pessimist is a man who has been compelled to live with an optimist.
**Elbert Hubbard,** *The Notebook*, 1927

To be a prophet it is sufficient to be a pessimist.
**Elsa Triolet**

Rowe's Rule: the odds are five to six that the light at the end of the tunnel is the headlight of an oncoming train.
**Paul Dickson,** *The Official Rules*, 1978

*See also* OPTIMISM

# PHILOSOPHY

The only difference between graffiti and philosophy is the word 'fuck'.
**Graffito**

There is nothing so absurd or ridiculous that has not at some time been said by some philosopher.
**Marcus Tullius Cicero**

There was never yet philosopher
That could endure the toothache patiently.
**William Shakespeare,** *Much Ado About Nothing*, 1598

When he who hears doesn't understand him who speaks, and when he who speaks doesn't know what he himself means – that is philosophy.
**Voltaire,** *Candide*, 1759

Metaphysics is the finding of bad reasons for what we believe upon instinct.
**F.H. Bradley,** *Appearance and Reality*, 1893

Only the shallow know themselves.
**Oscar Wilde,** *Phrases and Philosophies for the Use of the Young*, 1894

The more conscious a philosopher is of the weak spots of his theory, the more certain he is to speak with an air of final authority.

**Don Marquis**

Metaphysics is almost always an attempt to prove the incredible by an appeal to the unintelligible.

**H.L. Mencken, *Minority Report*, 1956**

Any philosophy that can be put 'in a nutshell' belongs there.

**Sydney J. Harris, *Leaving the Surface*, 1968**

Being wrong is just an occupational hazard of being a philosopher.

**Ronald Laura**

# PLAGIARISM

Men who borrow their opinions can never repay their debts.

**George Savile, Marquis of Halifax, *Political, Moral and Miscellaneous Thoughts and Reflexions*, c.1694**

Originality is nothing but judicious imitation.

**Voltaire**

If we steal thoughts from the moderns, it will be cried down as plagiarism; if from the ancients it will be cried up as erudition.

**Charles Caleb Colton, *Lacon*, 1820**

About the most originality that any writer can hope to achieve honestly is to steal with good judgement.

**Josh Billings**

If you steal from one author it's plagiarism; if you steal from many it's research.

**Wilson Mizner**

Originality is undetected plagiarism.

**William R. Inge**

We prefer to believe that the absence of inverted commas guarantees the originality of a thought, whereas it may be merely that the utterer has forgotten its source.

**Clifton Fadiman, *Any Number Can Play*, 1957**

Original thought is like original sin: both happened before you were born to people you could not have possibly met.

**Fran Lebowitz, *Social Studies*, 1981**

*See also* AUTHORS, BOOKS, WRITING

# POETS & POETRY

Poetry is the stuff in books that doesn't quite reach the margins.

**Anonymous**

All poets pretend to write for immortality, but the whole tribe have no objection to present pay and present praise.

**Charles Caleb Colton, *Lacon*, 1820**

Immature poets imitate, mature poets steal.

**T.S. Eliot, *Philip Massinger*, 1920**

The ideal audience the poet imagines consist of the beautiful who go to bed with him, the powerful who invite him to dinner and tell him secrets of state, and his fellow-poets. The actual audience he gets consists of myopic schoolteachers, pimply young men who eat in cafeterias, and his fellow-poets. This means, in fact, he writes for his fellow-poets.

**W.H. Auden, *Poets at Work*, 1948**

It is a sad fact about our culture that a poet can earn much more money writing or talking about his art than he can by practising it.

**W.H. Auden, *The Dyer's Hand*, 1963**

If you are of the opinion that the contemplation of suicide is sufficient evidence of a poetic nature, do not forget that actions speak louder than words.

**Fran Lebowitz, *Metropolitan Life*, 1978**

The romantic is a spoilt priest, just as the novelist is a spoilt poet.

**Cyril Connolly, *Journal 1928–1937*, ed. D. Pryce-Jones, 1983**

*See also* AUTHORS, BOOKS, WRITING

# POLITICIANS

A horrible voice, bad breath, and a vulgar manner – the characteristics of a popular politician.
   **Aristophanes**

Persistence in one opinion has never been considered a merit in political leaders.
   **Marcus Tullius Cicero, *Ad Familiares*, c.50BC**

It is easier for a camel to go through the eye of a needle, or for a rich man to enter the kingdom of heaven than for a politician to lay aside disguise.
   **James Caulfeild, Earl Charlemont, letter, 1767**

An honest politician is one who when he is bought will stay bought.
   **Simon Cameron, 1860**

A politician divides mankind into two classes: tools and enemies. That means he knows only one class – enemies.
   **Friedrich Wilhelm Nietzsche**

The first duty, if not the whole duty, of a private member of the House of Commons is to speak as little and to vote as often as he can.
   **Herbert Asquith, First Earl of Oxford, speech, 1890**

Only people who look dull ever get into the House of Commons, and only people who are dull ever succeed there.
   **Oscar Wilde, *An Ideal Husband*, 1895**

Politicians speak for their parties, and parties never are, never have been and never will be wrong.
   **Walter Dwight**

The politician is an acrobat: he keeps his balance by saying the opposite of what he does.
   **Maurice Barrès**

He knows nothing and thinks he knows everything. That points clearly to a political career.
   **George Bernard Shaw, *Major Barbara*, 1907**

The House of Lords: five hundred men, ordinary men, chosen accidentally from among the unemployed.

**David Lloyd George, speech, 1909**

The fact of a man's having proclaimed (as leader of a political party, or in any other capacity) that it is wicked to lie obliges him as a rule to lie more than other people.

**Marcel Proust, *Remembrance of Things Past*, 1913–27**

A gentleman will blithely do in politics what he would kick a man downstairs for doing in ordinary life.

**Earl of Rosebery, 1914**

It is easy to settle the world upon a soap box.

**David Lloyd George**

Politician – any man with influence enough to get his old mother a job as a charwoman at City Hall.

**H.L. Mencken, *Sententiae*, 1916**

The nauseous sham goodfellowship our democratic public men get up for shop use.

**George Bernard Shaw, *Back to Methuselah*, 1921**

The conception of an 'honest' politician is not altogether a simple one. The most tolerant definition is: one whose political actions are not dictated by a desire to increase his own income.

**Bertrand Russell, Presidential Address to LSE students, 1923**

When I was a boy I was told that anyone could become President. I'm beginning to believe it.

**Clarence Darrow**

A wise politician will never grudge a genuflexion or a rapture if it is expected of him by the prevalent opinion.

**F.S. Oliver, *The Endless Adventure*, 1930**

There's just one rule for politicians all over the world. Don't say in power what you say in opposition. If you do, you'll only have to carry out what the other fellows have found impossible.

**John Galsworthy, *Maid in Waiting*, 1931**

A politician is a person with whose politics you don't agree; if you agree with him he is a statesman.

**David Lloyd George, 1935**

Dictators always look good until the last minutes.

**Thomas Masaryk**

The trouble with this country is that there are too many politicians who believe, with a conviction based on experience, that you can fool all of the people all of the time.

**Franklin P. Adams (F.P.A.),** *Nods and Becks***, 1944**

When the political columnists say 'every thinking man' they mean themselves; and when the candidates appeal to 'every intelligent voter', they mean everybody who is going to vote for them.

**Franklin P. Adams (F.P.A.),** *Nods and Becks***, 1944**

A politician is an arse upon which everyone has sat except a man.

**e.e. cummings,** *One Times One***, 1944**

Have you ever read *Mein Kampf*? It's really the most honest book any politician has ever written.

**W.H. Auden,** *The Table-Talk of W.H. Auden***,
ed. Alan Ansen, 1990**

Politicians, like prostitutes, are held in contempt. But what man does not run to them when he needs their services?

**Brendan Francis**

Anyone who says he isn't going to resign, four times, definitely will.

**John Kenneth Galbraith**

Successful democratic politicians are insecure and intimidated men. They advance politically only as they placate, appease, bribe, seduce, bamboozle or otherwise manage to manipulate the demanding and threatening elements in their constituencies.

**Walter Lippmann,** *The Public Philosophy***, 1955**

A good politician is quite as unthinkable as an honest burglar.

**H.L. Mencken,** *Minority Report***, 1956**

The statesman shears the sheep, the politician skins them.

**Austin O'Malley**

The Left is a group of people who will never be happy unless they can convince themselves that they are about to be betrayed by their leaders.
   **Richard Crossman, diary, 1959**

Politicians are the same all over. They promise to build a bridge even where there is no river.
   **Nikita Khruschev, 1960**

Old politicians, like old actors, revive in the limelight.
   **Malcolm Muggeridge, in *Esquire* magazine, 1961**

Exhortation of other people to do something is the last resort of politicians who are at a loss to know what to do themselves.
   **Sir Paul Chambers, 1961**

Since a politician never believes what he says, he is surprised when others believe him.
   **Charles de Gaulle, 1962**

Don't take a nickel, just hand them your business card.
   **Richard M. Daley, advising on the safe enjoyment of graft**

Congress – these, for the most part, illiterate hacks whose fancy vests are spotted with gravy and whose speeches, hypocritical, unctuous and slovenly, are spotted also with the gravy of political patronage.
   **Mary McCarthy, *On the Contrary*, 1962**

Politics and the fate of mankind are shaped by men without ideals and without greatness. Men who have greatness within them don't go in for politics.
   **Albert Camus, *Notebooks*, 1962**

A little nonsense now and then is not a bad thing. Where would we politicians be if we were not allowed to talk it sometimes?
   **J. Enoch Powell, 1965**

The House of Lords, an illusion to which I have never been able to subscribe – responsibility without power, the prerogative of the eunuch throughout the ages.
   **Tom Stoppard, *Lord Malquist and Mr Moon*, 1965**

Render any politician down and there's enough fat to fry an egg.
   **Spike Milligan, 1968**

These presidential ninnies should stick to throwing out baseballs, and leave the important matters to serious people.

**Gore Vidal**

The most distinctive characteristic of the successful politician is selective cowardice.

**Richard Harris, in the *New Yorker* magazine, 1968**

It is dangerous for a national candidate to say things that people might remember.

**Senator Eugene McCarthy**, 1968

In order to become the master, the politician poses as the servant.

**Charles de Gaulle, 1969**

A politician is an acrobat: he keeps his balance by saying the opposite of what he does.

**Maurice Barrès**

A dilemma is a politician trying to save both of his faces at once.

**John A. Lincoln**

Any American who is prepared to run for President should automatically, by definition, be disqualified from ever doing so.

**Gore Vidal**

Wisdom is essential in a President; the appearance of wisdom will do in a candidate.

**Eric Sevareid**

The effectiveness of a politician varies in inverse proportion to his commitment to a principle.

**Sam Shaffer, in *Newsweek* magazine, 1971**

Politicians who wish to succeed must be prepared to dissemble, at times to lie. All deceit is bad. In politics some deceit or moral dishonesty is the oil without which the machinery would not work.

**Woodrow Wyatt, in the *Sunday Times*, 1973**

A statesman is a politician who places himself at the service of the nation. A politician is a statesman who places the nation at his service.

**Georges Pompidou, in the *Observer*, 1973**

Take our politicians: they're a bunch of yo-yos. The presidency is now a cross between a popularity contest and a high school debate, with an encyclopedia of clichés as the first prize.

**Saul Bellow, 1980**

If you hear someone in public life say that he is going to stand firmly on principle, you should take cover and warn others to do the same. There is going to be suffering.

**John Kenneth Galbraith, in *The New York Review of Books*, 1986**

In an age of television one must steer clear of presidents who may not know how to act president, and go instead for the best actor available for the job, the one who can read with warm plausibility the commercials that have been written for him.

**Gore Vidal, *Armageddon*, 1987**

Above any other position of eminence, that of Prime Minister is filled by fluke.

**J. Enoch Powell, in the *Observer*, 1987**

*See also* GOVERNMENT, LEADERS, PARTIES, POLITICS, POWER, VOTING

# POLITICS

Politics, as the word is commonly understood, are nothing but corruptions.

**Jonathan Swift, *Thoughts on Various Subjects*, 1706**

Boswell: So, Sir, you laugh at schemes of political improvement.
Johnson: Why, Sir, most schemes of political improvement are very laughable things.

**Samuel Johnson**

Politics are . . . nothing more than a means of rising in the world.

**Samuel Johnson, 1775**

In politics, as on the sickbed, people toss fom side to side, thinking they will be more comfortable.

**Johann Wolfgang von Goethe**

The duty of an opposition [is] very simple – to oppose everything and propose nothing.
  **Lord Derby, 1841**

A Parliament is nothing less than a big meeting of more or less idle people.
  **Walter Bagehot, *The English Constitution*, 1867**

Our differences are policies, our agreements principles.
  **William McKinley**

We have a single system and in that system the only question is the price at which the proletariat is to be bought and sold, the bread and circuses.
  **Henry Brooks Adams, *The Education of Henry Adams*, 1907**

Politics, as a practice, whatever its professions, has always been the systematic organisation of hatreds.
  **Henry Brooks Adams, *The Education of Henry Adams*, 1907**

Practical politics consists in ignoring facts.
  **Henry Brooks Adams, *The Education of Henry Adams*, 1907**

Politics, n. The conduct of public affairs for private advantage.
  **Ambrose Bierce, *The Devil's Dictionary*, 1911**

Alliance, n. In international politics, the union of two thieves who have their hands so deeply inserted into each other's pocket that they cannot safely plunder a third.
  **Ambrose Bierce, *The Devil's Dictionary*, 1911**

Politics, n. A strife of interests masquerading as a contest of principles.
  **Ambrose Bierce, *The Devil's Dictionary*, 1911**

Where you stand depends on where you sit.
  **Rufus Miles, on political opinions**

Communism, like any other revealed religion, is largely made up of prophecies.
  **H.L. Mencken**

A man should always be drunk when he talks of politics – it's the only way in which to make them important.
  **Sean O'Casey, *The Shadow of a Gunman*, 1923**

Politics, as hopeful men practise it in the world, consists mainly of the delusion that a change in form is a change in substance.

**H.L. Mencken, *Prejudices* 4th series, 1924**

Socialism . . . is little better than a dusty survival of a plan to meet the problems of fifty years ago based on a misunderstanding of what some-one said a hundred years ago.

**John Maynard Keynes**

The whole aim of practical politics is to keep the populace alarmed (and hence clamorous to be led to safety) by menacing it with an endless series of hobgoblins, all of them imaginary.

**H.L. Mencken**

In a political fight, when you've got nothing in favour of your side, start a row in the opposition camp.

**Huey P. Long**

Politics is the art of preventing people from taking part in affairs which properly concern them.

**Paul Valéry, *Tel quel*, 1943**

In our time, political speech and writing are largely the defence of the indefensible.

**George Orwell, *Politics and the English Language*, 1950**

Political language . . . is designed to make lies sound truthful and murder respectable and to give an appearance of solidarity to pure wind.

**George Orwell, *Politics and the English Language*, 1950**

Political thinking consists in deciding upon the conclusion first and then finding good arguments for it. An open mind is considered irresponsible – and perhaps it really is.

**Richard Crossman, diary, 1959**

Politics is the diversion of trivial men who, when they succeed at it, become important in the eyes of more trivial men.

**George Jean Nathan, 1954**

Nothing is so admirable in politics as a short memory.

**John Kenneth Galbraith**

In any assembly the simplest way to stop the transacting of business and split the ranks is to appeal to a principle.

**Jacques Barzun, *The House of Intellect*, 1959**

Vote for the man who promises least – he'll be the least disappointing.

**Bernard Baruch, quoted in *Meyer Berger's New York*, 1960**

Politics are usually the executive expression of human immaturity.

**Vera Brittain, *The Rebel Passion*, 1964**

A citizen is influenced by principle in direct proportion to his distance from the political situation.

**Milton Rakove, in *The Virginia Quarterly Review*, 1965**

Political skill . . . the ability to foretell what is going to happen tomorrow, next week, next month and next year. And to have the ability afterwards to explain why it didn't happen.

**Sir Winston Churchill, quoted in 1965**

Someone has described a technicality as a point of principle which we have forgotten.

**Sir Elwyn Jones, 1966**

Everything starts as a mystique and ends as politics.

**Parisian graffito, 1968**

Being in politics is like being a football coach. You have to be smart enough to understand the game and dumb enough to think it's important.

**Senator Eugene McCarthy, 1968**

Experience suggests that the first rule of politics is never to say never. The ingenious human capacity for manoeuvre and compromise may make acceptable tomorrow what seems outrageous or impossible today.

**William V. Shannon, 1968**

Politics demands a certain rhetoric. It does not demand moral action to fit the rhetoric. Instead politics demands political action.

**Julius Lester, *Look Out Whitey!*, 1968**

All politics are based on the indifference of the majority.

**James Reston, 1968**

Co-opt is baby-talk for corrupt.
  **John Leonard, in the *New York Times Book Review*, 1969**

Politics is not the art of the possible. It consists in choosing between the disastrous and the unpalatable.
  **John Kenneth Galbraith, 1969**

The classic prescription for dealing with injustice: give everybody an equal start, above all education, and meanwhile keep the niggers off your porch.
  **Christopher Lasch**

The dirty work at political conventions is almost always done in the grim hours between midnight and dawn. Hangmen and politicians work best when the human spirit is at its lowest ebb.
  **Russell Baker, *The Sayings of Poor Russell*, 1972**

A group of politicians deciding to dump a President because his morals are bad is like the Mafia getting together to bump off the Godfather for not going to church on Sunday.
  **Russell Baker, in *The New York Times*, 1974**

In politics, a straight line is the shortest distance to disaster.
  **John P. Roche, in the *Albany Times-Union*, 1976**

Politics without ideology, and with a strong tendency towards autobiography, equals Liberalism.
  **Stephen Spender, *The Thirties and After*, 1978**

I used to say that politics was the second oldest profession, and I have come to know that it bears a gross similarity to the first.
  **Ronald Reagan, 1979**

The first rule of politics: Never Believe Anything Until It's Been Officially Denied.
  **Antony Jay and Jonathan Lynn, *Yes, Prime Minister*, 1986**

'The truth' in politics means any statement that cannot be proved false.
  **Antony Jay and Jonathan Lynn, *Yes, Prime Minister*, 1986**

Socialism is about giving people what socialists think is good for them.
  **Brian Walden, in the *Sydney Morning Herald*, 1986**

Politics are a lousy way for a free man to get things done. Politics are, like God's infinite mercy, a last resort.

**P.J. O'Rourke, *Parliament of Whores*, 1991**

There's a certain joy in giving away other people's money. That is what drives many people to politics.

**Auberon Waugh, in the *Independent*, 1993**

*See also* GOVERNMENT, PARTIES, POLITICIANS

# POVERTY & THE POOR

I owe much; I have nothing; the rest I leave to the poor.

**François Rabelais, last words, 1533**

There's no scandal like rags, nor any crime so shameful as poverty.

**George Farquhar, *The Beaux Strategem*, 1707**

To be idle and to be poor have always been reproaches, and therefore every man endeavours with his utmost care to hide his poverty from others and his idleness from himself.

**Samuel Johnson, *The Idler*, 1758–60**

Poverty, like many other miseries of life, is often little more than an imaginary calamity. Men often call themselves poor, not because they want necessaries, but because they have not more than they want.

**Samuel Johnson, *Works* vol. ix, 1787**

Poverty is an anomaly to rich people. It is very difficult to make out why people who want dinner do not ring the bell.

**Walter Bagehot, *Literary Studies*, 1879–95**

It is easy enough to say poverty is no crime. If it were, men wouldn't be ashamed of it.

**Jerome K. Jerome, *Idle Thoughts of an Idle Fellow*, 1886**

I don't know how the poor live. My only regret is that they live at all.

**George Moore, *Confessions of a Young Man*, 1888**

The very poor are unthinkable and only to be approached by the statistician and the poet.

**E.M. Forster, *Howards End*, 1910**

The rich bachelor who dines out every evening is what is called a society man; the same poor is a sponger.

**Charles Nairey, quoted in *A Cynic's Breviary* by J.R. Solly, 1925**

It is only the poor who pay cash, and that not from virtue, but because they are refused credit.

**Anatole France, quoted in *A Cynic's Breviary* by J.R. Solly, 1925**

The poor and ignorant will continue to lie and steal as long as the rich and educated show them how.

**Elbert Hubbard, *Notebook*, 1927**

Poverty must have its satisfactions, else there would not be so many poor people.

**Don Herold**

The poor don't know that their function in life is to exercise our generosity.

**Jean-Paul Sartre, *The Words*, 1964**

The poor insist on being buried. It's usually the only way they ensure getting a garden of their own.

**Derek Marlowe, *A Dandy In Aspic*, 1966**

The best way to help the poor is not to become one of them.

**Laing Hancock, in *The Bulletin* magazine, 1977**

*See also* CHARITY, MONEY, THE RICH

# POWER

Men ought either to be indulged or utterly destroyed, for if you merely offend them they take vengeance, but if you injure them greatly they are unable to retaliate, so that the injury done to a man ought to be such that vengeance cannot be feared.

**Niccolò Machiavelli, *The Prince*, 1513**

Treason doth never prosper: what's the reason? For if it prosper, none dare call it treason.

**Sir John Harington, *Epigrams*, 1618**

Fortune often makes up for the eminence of office by the inferiority of the office-holder.

**Baltasar Gracian, *The Art of Worldly Wisdom*, 1647**

So that in the first place I put for a general inclination of all mankind a perpetual and restless desire of power after power, that ceases only in death.

**Thomas Hobbes, *Leviathan*, 1651**

The opinion of the strongest is always the best.

**Jean de La Fontaine, *Fables*, 1668–94**

Fear is what is needed in a despotism. Virtue is not at all necessary, and honour would be dangerous.

**Charles de Secondat, Baron de Montesquieu, *The Spirit of the Laws*, 1748**

There are few minds to which tyranny is not delightful.

**Samuel Johnson**

It is dangerous to be right in matters on which the established authorities are wrong.

**Voltaire, quoted in *A Cynic's Breviary* by J.R. Solly, 1925**

I am more and more convinced that man is a dangerous creature and that power, whether vested in many or a few, is ever grasping, and like the grave, cries 'Give, give'.

**Abigail Adams, 1775**

If you would be powerful, pretend to be powerful.

**Horne Tooke**

My opinion is that power should be distrusted, in whatever hands it is based.

**Sir William Jones, 1782**

Necessity is the plea for every infringement of human freedom. It is the argument of tyrants; it is the creed of slaves.

**William Pitt the Younger, 1783**

Monarchy is only the string which ties the robbers' bundle.

**Percy Bysshe Shelley, *A Philosophical View of Reform*, 1820**

Power, like the diamond, dazzles the beholder, and also the wearer; it dignifies meanness, it magnifies littleness, to what is contemptible it gives authority, to what is low exaltation.

**Charles Caleb Colton, *Lacon*, 1820**

The imbecility of men is always inviting the impudence of power.

**Ralph Waldo Emerson, *Representative Men*, 1850**

That which is called firmness in a king is called obstinacy in a donkey.

**Thomas Erskine**

Power tends to corrupt and absolute power corrupts absolutely. Great men are almost always bad men, even when they exercise influence and not authority. There is no worse heresy than that the office sanctifies the holder of it.

**Sir J.E.E. Dalberg, First Baron Acton, letter to Bishop Mandell Creighton, 1887**

There are men who desire power simply for the sake of the happiness it will bring; these belong chiefly to political parties.

**Friedrich Wilhelm Nietzsche, *The Will To Power*, 1900**

What is the ballot? It is neither more nor less than a paper representative of the bayonet, the billy and the bullet. It is a labour-saving device for ascertaining on which side force lies and bowing to the inevitable. The voice of the majority saves bloodshed, but it is no less the arbitrament of force than is the decree of the most absolute of despots backed by the most powerful of armies.

**Benjamin R. Tucker, *Instead of a Book*, 1893**

Knowledge is power – if you know it about the right person.

**Addison Mizner and Oliver Herford, *The Entirely New Cynic's Calendar*, 1905**

Compulsion, n. The eloquence of power.

**Ambrose Bierce, *The Devil's Dictionary*, 1911**

Next to enjoying ourselves, the next greatest pleasure consists in preventing others from enjoying themselves, or, more generally, the acquisition of power.

**Bertrand Russell, *Sceptical Essays*, 1928**

Brutality is respected. The people need wholesome fear. They want to fear something. They want someone to frighten them and make them shudderingly submissive . . . Why babble about brutality and get indignant about tortures. The masses want them. They need something that will give them a thrill of horror.

**Ernst Röhm**

If people say that here and there someone has been taken away and maltreated, I can only reply: You can't make an omelette without breaking eggs.

**Hermann Göring, 1933**

Mr Salter's side of the conversation was limited to expressions of assent. When Lord Copper was right he said 'Definitely, Lord Copper'; when he was wrong, 'Up to a point.' 'Let me see, what's the name of the place I mean? Capital of Japan? Yokohama, isn't it?' 'Up to a point, Lord Copper.' 'And Hong Kong definitely belongs to us, doesn't it?' 'Definitely, Lord Copper.'

**Evelyn Waugh, *Scoop*, 1933**

The exercise of power is agreeable, especially when it is an obscure individual who exercises power over a prominent one.

**Bertrand Russell, in the *American Mercury*, 1940**

The future is the only kind of property that the masters willingly concede to slaves.

**Albert Camus, *The Rebel*, 1951**

Not only do people accept violence if it is perpetuated by legitimate authority, they also regard violence against certain kinds of people as inherently legitimate, no matter who commits it.

**Edgar Z. Friedenberg, 1966**

Command is getting people to go the way you want them to go – enthusiastically.

**General William Westmoreland**

Nothing is impossible for the man who doesn't have to do it himself.

**A.H. Weiler, in the *New York Times*, 1968**

People who have the power to make things happen don't do the things that people do, so they don't know what needs to happen.

**Russell Baker, *The Sayings of Poor Russell*, 1972**

Women are always attracted to power. I do not think there could ever be a conqueror so bloody that most women would not willingly lie with him in the hope of bearing a son who would be every bit as ferocious as the father.

**Gore Vidal, *Creation*, 1981**

All power is delightful, and absolute power is absolutely delightful.

**Kenneth Tynan, quoted in *the New York Review of Books*, 1982**

*See also* EGOTISM, LEADERS, POLITICIANS, POLITICS

# PRAISE

He who refuses praise only wants to be praised again.

**François, Duc de La Rochefoucauld, *Maxims*, 1665**

We do not like to praise and we never praise without a motive. Praise is flattery, artful, hidden, delicate, which gratifies differently him who praises and him who is praised. The one takes it as the reward of merit, the other bestows it to show his impartiality and discernment.

**François, Duc de La Rochefoucauld, *Maxims*, 1665**

The praise we give newcomers into the world arises from the envy we bear to those who are established.

**François, Duc de La Rochefoucauld, *Maxims*, 1665**

Praise is like ambergris: a little whiff of it, and by snatches, is very agreeable; but when a man holds a whole lump of it to our nose, it is a stink, and strikes you down.

**Alexander Pope**

You must never seem to affect the character in which you have a mind to shine. Modesty is the only sure bait when you angle for praise.

**Lord Chesterfield, *Letters to his Son*, 1774**

We praise or blame according to whether the one or the other offers a greater opportunity for our power of judgement to shine out.

**Friedrich Wilhelm Nietzsche, *Human, All Too Human*, 1878**

Nothing is harder to resist than a bit of flattery.

**Arnold Lobel, *Fables*, 1980**

*See also* TALK

# PROGRESS

Progress is written in the lives of infidels.

**Robert G. Ingersoll, speech, 1881**

What we call 'progress' is the exchange of one nuisance for another nuisance.

**Havelock Ellis**

It is the same with men as with horses: those which do the most prancing are generally the ones which make the least progress.

**Baron de Stassart, quoted in *Reflections on the Art of Life* by J.R. Solly, 1902**

All progress is based upon a universal innate desire of every organism to live beyond its income.

**Samuel Butler, *Notebooks*, 1912**

Anything that is worth doing has been done frequently. Things hitherto undone should be given, I suspect, a wide berth.

**Max Beerbohm, *Mainly on the Air*, 1957**

Progress was all right; it just went on too long.

**James Thurber**

Ours is the age of substitutes: instead of language we have jargon; instead of principles, slogans; and, instead of genuine ideas, bright ideas.

**Eric Bentley, *The Dramatic Event*, 1954**

Is it progress if a cannibal uses a fork?

**Stanislaw J. Lec, *Unkempt Thoughts*, 1962**

*See also* SCIENCE

# PROPAGANDA

Propaganda is that branch of lying which often deceives your friends without ever deceiving your enemies.

**Walter Lippmann, quoted in *The Laugh's On Me* by B. Cerf, 1911**

I shall give a propagandist reason for starting the war, no matter whether it is plausible or not. The victor will not be asked afterwards whether he told the truth or not. When starting and waging war it is not right that matters, but victory.

**Adolf Hitler**

What I'm out for's a good time. All the rest is propaganda.

**Alan Sillitoe, screenplay for *Saturday Night and Sunday Morning*, 1960**

We must remember that in time of war what is said on the enemy's side of the front is always propaganda and what is said on our side of the front is truth and righteousness, the cause of humanity and a crusade for peace. Is it necessary for us at the height of our power to stoop to such self-deceiving nonsense?

**Walter Lippmann, quoted 1966**

Propaganda is a monologue which seeks not a response but an echo.

**W.H. Auden, address to International PEN, 1967**

Propaganda is the art of persuading others of what one does not believe oneself.

**Abba Eban**

What's public is propaganda, what's secret is serious.

**Charles Bohlen, quoted in the *New York Post*, 1969**

Propaganda is that branch of the art of lying which consists in nearly deceiving your friends without quite deceiving your enemies.

**F.M. Cornford, quoted in the *New Statesman* magazine, 1978**

One ought to acknowledge the significance for mankind of the simultaneous invention of gunpowder and printer's ink.

**Karl Kraus, *Half Truths and One and a Half Truths*, 1986**

*See also* LYING

# PSYCHOANALYSIS

Psychoanalysis is the disease of emancipated Jews; the religious ones are satisfied with diabetes.

**Karl Kraus**

Psychoanalysis is that mental illness for which it regards itself as therapy.

**Karl Kraus,** *Half Truths and One and a Half Truths,* **1986**

Psychotherapy – the theory that the patient will probably get well anyhow, and is certainly a damned ijjit.

**H.L. Mencken,** *Sententiae,* **1916**

Psychiatry enables us to correct our faults by confessing our parents' shortcomings.

**Laurence J. Peter,** *Peter's Principles,* **1977**

Group therapy – the theory that a cure will come if a group of similarly afflicted people are rude enough to each other.

**Walter Merricks, on BBC-2 TV, 1979**

# QUOTATIONS

Pointed axioms and acute replies fly loose about the world, and are assigned successively to those whom it may be the fashion to celebrate.

**Samuel Johnson,** *Works* **vol. vii, 1787**

It is with epigrams as with other inventions: the best are those which annoy us because we did not think of them ourselves.

**Georg Christoph Lichtenberg,** *Reflections,* **1799**

France was long a despotism tempered by epigrams.

**Thomas Carlyle,** *The French Revolution,* **1837**

Epigram: a platitude with vine-leaves in its hair.

**H.L. Mencken,** *A Book of Burlesques,* **1916**

Bon mots are perhaps best described as the words other people wish they had said.

**Daily Herald, 1964**

The nicest thing about quotes is that they give us a nodding acquaintance with the originator which is often socially impressive.

**Kenneth Williams,** *Acid Drops,* **1980**

*See also* MAXIMS

# RACE

A racially integrated community is a chronological term, timed from the entrance of the first black family to the exit of the last white family.

**Saul Alinsky**

Black people have never rioted. A riot is what white people think blacks are involved in when they burn stores.

**Julius Lester**

# RELIGION

Since the masses of the people are inconstant, full of unruly desires, passionate and reckless of consequence, they must be filled with fears to keep them in order. The ancients did well, therefore, to invent gods, and the belief in punishment after death.

**Polybius, *Histories*, c. 125BC**

It is for the good of states that men should be deluded by religion.

**Marcus Terentius Varro, *Antiquitates rerum humanarum et divinarum*, c.40BC**

It is when we are in misery that we revere the gods; the prosperous seldom approach the altar.

**Silius Italicus, *Punica*, c.AD75**

Fear of power invisible, feigned by the mind or imagined from tales publicly allowed, [is] religion; not allowed, superstition.

**Thomas Hobbes, *Leviathan*, 1651**

In matters of religion it is very easy to deceive a man, and very hard to undeceive him.

**Pierre Bayle, *Dictionary*, 1697**

When men grow virtuous in their old age, they only make a sacrifice to God of the devil's leavings.

**Jonathan Swift**

A man is quickly convinced of the truth of religion, who finds it is not against his interest that it should be true.

**Joseph Addison, in the *Spectator*, 1712**

Religion supposed Heaven and Hell, the word of God, and sacraments, and twenty other circumstances which, taken seriously, are a wonderful check to wit and humour.

**Jonathan Swift, letter of advice to a young poet, 1720**

Theologians are all alike, of whatever religion or country they may be; their aim is always to wield despotic authority over men's consciences; they therefore persecute all of us who have the temerity to tell the truth.

**Frederick the Great, letter to Voltaire, 1736**

Religion is the idol of the mob: it adores everything it does not understand.

**Frederick the Great, letter to Voltaire, 1737**

Many a long dispute between divines may thus be abridged: It is so. It is not so. It is so. It is not so.

**Benjamin Franklin, *Poor Richard's Almanack*, 1733–58**

The Christian religion not only was at first attended by miracles, but even at this day cannot be believed by any reasonable person without one.

**David Hume, *On Miracles*, 1748**

The truths of religion are never so well understood as by those who have lost the power of reasoning.

**Voltaire, *Philosophical Dictionary*, 1764**

Whenever an important event, a revolution, or a calamity turns to the profit of the church, such is always signalised as the Finger of God.

**Voltaire, *Philosophical Dictionary*, 1764**

All religions are ancient monuments to superstitions, ignorance, ferocity; and modern religions are only ancient follies rejuvenated.

**Baron d'Holbach, 1772**

Prisons are built with stones of law, brothels with bricks of religion.

**William Blake, *The Marriage of Heaven and Hell*, 1790–3**

What is it the New Testament teaches us? To believe that the Almighty committed debauchery with a woman engaged to be married; and the belief of this debauchery is called faith.

**Thomas Paine, *The Age of Reason*, 1793–5**

The Bible: a history of wickedness that has served to corrupt and brutalise mankind.

**Thomas Paine, *The Age of Reason*, 1793–5**

The study of theology, as it stands in Christian churches, is the study of nothing; it is founded on nothing; it rests on nothing; it proceeds by no authorities; it has no data; it can demonstrate nothing and admits of no conclusion.

**Thomas Paine, *The Age of Reason*, 1793–5**

All religions are founded on the fear of the many and the cleverness of the few.

**Stendhal**

Religion is excellent stuff for keeping common people quiet.

**Napoleon Bonaparte**

A book is put into our hands when children, called the Bible, the purport of whose history is briefly this: That God made the earth in six days and there planted a delightful garden, in which He placed the first pair of human beings. In the midst of the garden He planted a tree, whose fruit, although within their reach, they were forbidden to touch. That the Devil, in the shape of a snake, persuaded them to eat of this fruit; in consequence of which God condemned both of them and their posterity yet unborn to satisfy His justice by their eternal misery. That, 4000 years after these events the human race in the meantime having gone unredeemed to perdition, God engendered with the betrothed wife of a carpenter in Judaea (whose virginity was nevertheless uninjured), and begat a son, whose name was Jesus Christ; and who was crucified and died in order that no more men might be devoted to hell-fire . . . The book states, in addition, that the soul of whoever disbelieves this sacrifice will be burned with everlasting fire.

**Percy Bysshe Shelley, *Queen Mab* (notes), 1813**

If Jesus Christ were to come today, people would not even crucify him. They would ask him to dinner, and hear what he had to say, and make fun of him.

**Thomas Carlyle**

Sir Richard Steele has observed, that there is this difference between the Church of Rome and the Church of England: the one professes to be infallible, the other to be never in the wrong.

**Charles Caleb Colton, *Lacon*, 1820**

Men will wrangle for religion, write for it, fight for it, die for it,
anything but – live for it.
  **Charles Caleb Colton, _Lacon_, 1820**

There is one passage in the Scriptures to which all the potentates of
Europe seem to have given their unanimous assent and approbation . . .
'There went out a decree in the days of Caesar Augustus, that all the
world should be taxed.'
  **Charles Caleb Colton, _Lacon_, 1820**

There are only two things in which the false professors of all religions
have agreed: to persecute all other sects and to plunder their own.
  **Charles Caleb Colton, _Lacon_, 1820**

Look through the whole histories of countries professing the Romish
religion and you will uniformly find the leaven of this besetting and
accursed principle of action – that the end will sanction any means.
  **Samuel Taylor Coleridge, _Table-Talk_, 1836**

Religion is the opium of the people.
  **Karl Marx, _A Criticism of the Hegelian Philosophy of Law_, 1844**

Monotheistic religions alone furnish the spectacle of religious wars,
religious persecutions, heretical tribunals, that breaking of idols and
destruction of images of the gods, that razing of Indian temples and
Egyptian colossi, which had looked on the sun 3,000 years: just because
a jealous god had said, 'Thou shalt make no graven image.'
  **Arthur Schopenhauer, _Religion: a Dialogue_, 1851**

Religion is the masterpiece of the art of animal training, for it trains
people as to how they shall think.
  **Arthur Schopenhauer, _Parerga und Paralipomena_, 1851**

Every established fact which is too bad to admit of any other defence is
always presented to us as an injunction of religion.
  **John Stuart Mill, _The Subjection of Women_, 1869**

The religion of one age is the literary entertainment of the next.
  **Ralph Waldo Emerson**

All religions, with their gods, demigods, prophets, messiahs and saints,
are the product of the fancy and credulity of men who have not yet

reached the full development and complete possession of their intellectual powers.

**Mikhail Bakunin, *Dieu et l'état*, 1871**

Where it is a duty to worship the sun it is pretty sure to be a crime to examine the laws of heat.

**John, Viscount Morley, *Voltaire*, 1872**

Strange but true: those who have loved God most have loved men least.

**Robert G. Ingersoll, speech, 1881**

The inspiration of the Bible depends upon the ignorance of the gentleman who reads it.

**Robert G. Ingersoll, speech, 1881**

No man with a sense of humour ever founded a religion.

**Robert G. Ingersoll**

Whatever a theologian regards as true must be false: there you have almost a criterion of truth.

**Friedrich Wilhelm Nietzsche, *The Antichrist*, 1888**

I call Christianity the one great curse, the one enormous and innermost perversion, the one great instinct for revenge, for which no means are too venomous, too underhand, too underground and too petty – I call it the one immortal blemish of mankind.

**Friedrich Wilhelm Nietzsche, *The Antichrist*, 1888**

The whole religious complexion of the modern world is due to the absence from Jerusalem of a lunatic asylum.

**Havelock Ellis**

Truth, in matters of religion, is simply the opinion that has survived.

**Oscar Wilde, *The Critic as Artist*, 1891**

Religion is the fashionable substitute for belief.

**Oscar Wilde, *The Picture of Dorian Gray*, 1891**

The preponderance of pain over pleasure is the cause of our fictitious morality and religion.

**Friedrich Wilhelm Nietzsche**

Religion is a sum of scruples which impede the free exercise of our faculties.

**Salomon Reinach, *Cultes, mythes et religions*, 1904**

Religion is an illusion . . . it derives its strength from the fact that it falls in with our intellectual desires.

**Sigmund Freud**

The most serious doubt that has been thrown on the authenticity of the biblical miracles is the fact that most of the witnesses in regard to them were fishermen.

**Arthur Binstead, *Pitcher's Proverbs*, 1909**

The man who has no mind of his own lends it to the priests.

**George Meredith, in the *Fortnightly Review*, 1909**

Sudden conversion . . . is particularly attractive to the half-baked mind.

**E.M. Forster, *Howards End*, 1910**

Saint, n. A dead sinner revised and edited.

**Ambrose Bierce, *The Devil's Dictionary*, 1911**

Scriptures, n. The sacred books of our holy religion, as distinguished from the false and profane writings on which all other faiths are based.

**Ambrose Bierce, *The Devil's Dictionary*, 1911**

Infidel, n. In New York, one who does not believe in the Christian religion; in Constantinople, one who does.

**Ambrose Bierce, *The Devil's Dictionary*, 1911**

A Christian is one who follows the teachings of Christ insofar as they are not inconsistent with a life of sin.

**Ambrose Bierce, *The Devil's Dictionary*, 1911**

Heathen, n. A benighted creature who has the folly to worship something he can see and feel.

**Ambrose Bierce, *The Devil's Dictionary*, 1911**

Prayers are to men as dolls are to children. They are not without use and comfort, but it is not easy to take them seriously.

**Samuel Butler, *Notebooks*, 1912**

Theology – an effort to explain the unknowable by putting it into the terms of the not worth knowing.

**H.L. Mencken,** *Sententiae*, **1916**

Say what you like about the Ten Commandments, you must always come back to the pleasant fact that there are only ten of them.

**H.L. Mencken,** *Sententiae*, **1916**

Formal religion was organised for slaves; it offered them consolation which earth did not provide.

**Elbert Hubbard, 1923**

We ought to have as great a regard for religion as we can, so as to keep it out of as many things as possible.

**Sean O'Casey,** *The Plough and the Stars*, **1926**

Many people believe they attracted by God, or by Nature, when they are only repelled by man.

**William R. Inge,** *More Lay Thoughts of a Dean*, **1931**

By the time a boy has been two years in a church school he is immunised against religion.

**Colin Gordon**

Christian ethics are seldom found save in the philosophy of some unbeliever.

**Heywood Broun**

Organised Christianity has probably done more to retard the ideals that were its founders than any other agency in the world.

**Richard Le Gallienne**

As with the Christian religion, the worst advertisement for Socialism is its adherents.

**George Orwell,** *The Road to Wigan Pier*, **1937**

A great deal of what passes for current Christianity consists in denouncing other people's vices and faults.

**Henry Williams**

The act of worship, as carried on by Christians, seems to me debasing, rather than ennobling. It involves grovelling before a Being who, if he really exists, deserves to be denounced instead of respected.

**H.L. Mencken**

People who feel themselves to be exiles in this world are mightily inclined to believe themselves citizens of another.

**George Santayana**

The only reason the Protestants and Catholics have given up the idea of universal domination is because they've realised they can't get away with it.

**W.H. Auden, *The Table-Talk of W. H. Auden*, ed. Alan Ansen, 1990**

Maybe this world is just another planet's hell.

**Aldous Huxley**

The Bible should be taught so early and so thoroughly that it sinks straight to the bottom of the mind where everything that comes along can settle on it.

**Northrop Frye**

So far as I can remember, there is not one word in the Gospels in praise of intelligence.

**Bertrand Russell**

Saints should always be judged guilty until they are proved innocent.

**George Orwell, *Reflections on Gandhi*, 1949**

We must respect the other fellow's religion, but only in the sense and to the extent that we respect his theory that his wife is beautiful and his children smart.

**H.L. Mencken, *Minority Report*, 1956**

The chief contribution of Protestantism to human thought is its massive proof that God is a bore.

**H.L. Mencken, *Minority Report*, 1956**

The habit of religion is oppressive, an easy way out of thought.

**Peter Ustinov, in *Everybody's* magazine, 1957**

Religion is the venereal disease of mankind.

**Henry de Montherlant**

All Gods were immortal.

**Stanislaw J. Lec, *Unkempt Thoughts*, 1962**

It is usually when men are at their most religious that they behave with the least sense and the greatest cruelty.

**Ilka Chase**

Religion is . . . parasitic in the interstices of our knowledge which have not yet been filled.

**J.B.S. Haldane,** *Science and Life*, **1968**

That's all religion is – some principle you believe in . . . man has accomplished far more miracles that the God he invented. What a tragedy it is to invent a God and then suffer to keep him King.

**Rod Steiger, in** *Playboy* **magazine, 1969**

Mythology is what grown-ups believe, folklore is what they tell children and religion is both.

**Cedric Whitman, 1969**

A myth is a religion in which no one any longer believes.

**James K. Feibleman,** *Understanding Philosophy*, **1973**

Why do born-again people so often make you wish they'd never been born the first time.

**Katherine Whitehorn, in the** *Observer*, **1979**

A cult is a religion with no political power.

**Tom Wolfe,** *In Our Time*, **1980**

What's a cult? It just means not enough people to make a minority.

**Robert Altman, in the** *Observer*, **1981**

Heresy is only another word for freedom of thought.

**Graham Greene, 1981**

*See also* BELIEF, THE CLERGY, FAITH, GOD, HYPOCRISY, IDEALS, IDEAS, MORALS, TRUE BELIEVERS, TRUTH

# REVOLUTION

By a revolution in the state, the fawning sycophant of yesterday is converted into the austere critic of the present hour.

**Edmund Burke,** *Reflections on the Revolution in France*, **1790**

Every successful revolt is termed a revolution, and every unsuccessful one a rebellion.

**Joseph Priestley, letter, 1791**

In revolutions power always remains in the hands of nobodies.

**Georges Danton, on receiving the death sentence, 1794**

It is better to abolish serfdom from above than to wait for it to abolish itself from below.

**Alexander II, 1856**

The New Jerusalem, when it comes, will probably be found so far to resemble the old as to stone its prophets freely.

**Samuel Butler, *Notebooks*, 1912**

Revolutions have never lightened the burden of tyranny, they have only shifted it to another shoulder.

**George Bernard Shaw, *Man and Superman*, 1903**

Rebel, n. The proponent of a new misrule who has failed to establish it.

**Ambrose Bierce, *The Devil's Dictionary*, 1911**

Revolution, n. In politics, an abrupt change in the form of misgovernment.

**Ambrose Bierce, *The Devil's Dictionary*, 1911**

Insurrection, n. An unsuccessful revolution. Disaffection's failure to substitute misrule for bad government.

**Ambrose Bierce, *The Devil's Dictionary*, 1911**

The revolutionary spirit is mightily convenient in this: that it frees one from all scruples as regards ideas.

**Joseph Conrad, *A Personal Record*, 1912**

A revolution only lasts fifteen years – a period which coincides with the effectiveness of a generation.

**José Ortega y Gasset, 1930**

Few revolutionists would be such if they were heirs to a baronetcy.

**George Santayana**

Every revolution evaporates and leaves behind only the slime of a new bureaucracy.

**Franz Kafka, *The Great Wall of China: Aphorisms 1917–19*, 1931**

The successful revolutionary is a statesman, the unsuccessful one is a criminal.

**Erich Fromm, *Escape from Freedom*, 1941**

Radicalism is the opium of the middle class.
  **Christina Stead,** *Letty Fox, Her Luck***, 1946**

The slave begins by demanding justice and ends by wanting to wear a crown. He must dominate in his turn.
  **Albert Camus,** *The Rebel***, 1951**

Every revolutionary ends up either by becoming an oppressor or a heretic.
  **Albert Camus,** *The Rebel***, 1951**

A revolution requires of its leaders a record of unbroken infallibility. If they do not possess it they are expected to invent it.
  **Murray Kempton,** *Part of Our Time***, 1955**

The revolution as myth is the definitive revolution.
  **Albert Camus,** *Notebooks***, 1942–51**

It is an illusion to think that you can have a revolution without prisons.
  **Muhammad Ahmed Ben Bella, 1963**

A revolution is interesting insofar as it avoids like the plague the plague it promised to heal.
  **Daniel Berrigan, in the** *New York Review of Books***, 1971**

Every successful revolution puts on in time the robes of the tyrant it has deposed.
  **Barbara Tuchman**

There is no surer way of preserving the worst aspects of the bourgeois style than liquidating the bourgeoisie. Whatever else Stalin may or may not have done, he assuredly made Russia safe for the Forsyte Saga.
  **Malcolm Muggeridge,** *Chronicles of Wasted Time* **vol. i, 1978**

The general law of development for political institutions conceived in revolutionary idealism, which is that they begin as an expression of conscience and become in due course agencies for the issuance of licences and the distribution of patronage.
  **Murray Kempton, in** *Newsday* **magazine, 1981**

*See also* DEMOCRACY, FREEDOM

# THE RICH

The shortest and best way to make your fortune is to let people see clearly that it is in their interests to promote yours.
**Jean de La Bruyère, *The Characters*, 1688**

We may see the small value God has for riches by the people he gives them to.
**Alexander Pope, *Miscellanies in Prose and Verse*, 1727**

There are some men who gain from their wealth only the fear of losing it.
**Antoine Rivaroli, Comte de Rivarol, *L'esprit de Rivarol*, 1808**

The greatest luxury of riches is, that they enable you to escape so much good advice.
**Sir Arthur Helps**

God shows his contempt for wealth by the kind of person he selects to receive it.
**Austin O'Malley**

A rich man's joke is always funny.
**Thomas Brown**

Rich bachelors should be heavily taxed. It is not fair that some men should be happier than others.
**Oscar Wilde**

The faults of the burglar are the qualities of the financier.
**George Bernard Shaw, *Major Barbara*, 1907**

That's it, baby! When you got it, flaunt it! Flaunt it!
**Mel Brooks, screenplay for *The Producers*, 1968**

The rich are different from you and me because they have more credit.
**John Leonard**

The parvenu is always someone else.
**Anka Muhlstein, *The Rise of the French Rothschilds*, 1983**

*See also* BUSINESS, MONEY, POVERTY & THE POOR

# SCIENCE

Professors in every branch of the sciences prefer their own theories to truth: the reason is that their theories are private property, but the truth is common stock.

**Charles Caleb Colton,** *Lacon,* **1820**

Science is the record of dead religions.

**Oscar Wilde,** *Phrases and Philosophies for the Use of the Young,* **1894**

Science is the religion of the suburbs.

**W.B. Yeats**

The tendency of modern science is to reduce proof to absurdity by continually reducing absurdity to proof.

**Samuel Butler,** *Notebooks,* **1912**

Science in the modern world had many uses; its chief use, however, is to provide long words to cover the errors of the rich.

**G.K. Chesterton**

A science is said to be useful if its development tends to accentuate the existing inequalities in the distribution of wealth, or more directly promotes the destruction of human life.

**Godfrey Hardy,** *A Mathematician's Apology,* **1941**

We must be aware of needless innovations, especially when guided by logic.

**Sir Winston Churchill, 1942**

One has to look out for engineers – they begin with sewing machines and end up with the atomic bomb.

**Marcel Pagnol,** *Critique des critiques,* **1949**

A new scientific truth does not triumph by convincing its opponents and making them see the light, but rather because its opponents eventually die, and a new generation grows up that is familiar with it.

**Max Planck,** *Scientific Autobiography and Other Papers,* **1950**

Science is a cemetery of dead ideas.

**Miguel de Unamuno**

No scientific theory achieves public acceptance until it has been thoroughly discredited.

**Douglas Yates**

Successful research impedes further successful research.

**Keith J. Pendred, in *The Bulletin of the Atomic Scientists*, 1963**

Creativity in science could be described as the act of putting two and two together to make five.

**Arthur Koestler, *Creation*, 1964**

A science is any discipline in which the fool of this generation can go beyond the point reached by the genius of the last generation.

**Max Gluckmann, *Politics, Law and Ritual*, 1965**

The real accomplishment of modern science and technology consists in taking ordinary men, informing them narrowly and deeply and then, through appropriate action, arranging to have their knowledge combined with that of other specialised but equally ordinary men. This dispenses with the need for genius. The resulting performance, though less inspiring, is far more predictable.

**John Kenneth Galbraith, *The New Industrial State*, 1967**

There are three roads to ruin – women, gambling and technicians. The most pleasant is with women, the quickest is with gambling, but the surest is with technicians.

**Georges Pompidou, in the *Sunday Telegraph*, 1968**

Inanimate objects are classified scientifically into three major categories – those that don't work, those that break down and those that get lost.

**Russell Baker, in the *New York Times*, 1968**

When a distinguished but elderly scientist states that something is possible, he is almost certainly right. When he states that something is impossible, he is very probably wrong.

**Arthur C. Clarke, *Profile of the Future*, 1973**

A first-rate theory predicts, a second-rate theory forbids and a third-rate theory explains after the event.

**Alexander Kitaigorodski, 1975**

The progress of science is strewn, like an ancient desert trail, with the bleached skeletons of discarded theories which once seemed to possess eternal life.

**Arthur Koestler, address to the PEN Club, 1976**

When the lay public rallies round to an idea that is denounced by distinguished but elderly scientists and supports that idea with great fervour and emotion, the distinguished but elderly scientists are then, after all, right.

**Isaac Asimov, in *Fantasy and Science Fiction* magazine, 1977**

Carson's Consolation: no experiment is ever a complete failure. It can always be used as a bad example.

**Paul Dickson, *The Official Rules*, 1978**

First Law: if an experiment works, something has gone wrong. Fourth Law: once a job is fouled up, anything done to improve it only makes it worse.

**Finagle's Laws, quoted in *Murphy's Law* by A. Bloch, 1979**

Enough research will tend to support your theory.

**Murphy's Law of Research, quoted in *Murphy's Law* by A. Bloch, 1979**

If a scientist uncovers a publishable fact, it will become central to his theory.

**Mann's Law, quoted in *Murphy's Law Book Two* by A. Bloch, 1980**

Modern science is generally practised by those who lack the flair for conversation.

**Fran Lebowitz, *Metropolitan Life*, 1981**

*See also* PROGRESS

# SENTIMENTALITY

A sentimentalist is simply one who desires to have the luxury of an emotion without paying for it.

**Oscar Wilde**

Sentimentality is a superstructure covering brutality.

**C.G. Jung, *Reflections*, 1953**

# SEX

Marriage is the price men pay for sex, sex is the price women pay for marriage.
   **Anonymous**

Filth and old age, I'm sure you will agree
Are powerful wardens upon chastity.
   **Geoffrey Chaucer, *The Canterbury Tales*, 1387**

She is chaste who was never asked the question.
   **William Congreve**

The pleasure is momentary, the position ridiculous and the expense damnable.
   **Lord Chesterfield, *Letters to his Son*, 1774**

What they call 'heart' is located far lower than the fourth waistcoat button.
   **Georg Christoph Lichtenberg, *Aphorisms*, 1764–99**

There are few things that we so unwillingly give up, even in an advanced age, as the supposition that we have still the power of ingratiating ourselves with the fair sex.
   **Samuel Johnson, *Johnsonian Miscellanies*, ed. G.B. Hill, 1897**

Were it not for imagination, Sir, a man would be as happy in the arms of a chambermaid as of a Duchess.
   **Samuel Johnson, quoted in *The Life of Samuel Johnson* by J. Boswell, 1791**

Advice to sexually bored husbands . . . Think of your mistress.
   **Honoré de Balzac, *The Physiology of Marriage*, 1829**

The duration of passion is proportionate with the original resistance of the woman.
   **Honoré de Balzac**

The garter has hanged more men than the halter.
   **Reflections of a Bachelor, 19th century**

Of all the sexual aberrations, perhaps the most peculiar is chastity.
**Rémy de Gourmont**

The advantage of being celibate is that when one sees a pretty girl one does not need to grieve over having an ugly one back home.
**Paul Léautaud, *Propos d'un jour*, 1900**

I have a technical objection to making sexual infatuation a tragic theme. Experience proves that it is only effective in the comic spirit.
**George Bernard Shaw, *Three Plays for Puritans*, 1901**

Virginity is the ideal of those who want to deflower.
**Karl Kraus, *Half Truths and One and a Half Truths*, 1986**

There comes a moment in the day, when you have written your pages in the morning, attended to your correspondence in the afternoon, and have nothing further to do. Then comes that hour when you are bored; that's the time for sex.
**H.G. Wells**

A man marries to have a home, but also because he doesn't want to be bothered with sex and all that sort of thing.
**W. Somerset Maugham, *The Circle*, 1921**

Give a man a free hand and he'll run it all over you.
**Mae West, *Klondike Annie*, 1936**

Sex: the thing that takes up the least amount of time and causes the most amount of trouble.
**John Barrymore**

Anon: Goodness, what beautiful diamonds!
Mae West: Goodness had nothing to do with it, dearie.
**Vincent Lawrence and Mae West, screenplay for *Night After Night*, 1932**

The big difference between sex for money and sex for free is that sex for money usually costs a lot less.
**Brendan Francis**

There goes the good time that was had by all.
**Bette Davis, remarking on a passing starlet**

That gentlemen prefer blondes is due to the fact that, apparently, pale hair, delicate skin and an infantile expression represent the very apex of a frailty which every man longs to violate.

**Alexander King, *Rich Man, Poor Man, Freud and Fruit*, 1945**

Older women are best because they always think they may be doing it for the last time.

**Ian Fleming**

A fox is a wolf who sends flowers.

**Ruth Weston, 1955**

Find 'em, feel 'em, fuck 'em and forget 'em.

**The Four-F Club, motto of 1950s teenage males**

Show me a genuine case of platonic friendship and I shall show you two old or homely faces.

**Austin O'Malley**

Sex is. There is nothing more to be done about it. Sex builds no roads, writes no novels, and sex certainly gives no meaning to anything in life but itself.

**Gore Vidal, *Norman Mailer's Self-Advertisements*, 1960**

Relations between the sexes are so complicated that the only way you can tell if two members of the set are 'going together' is if they are married. Then, almost certainly, they are not.

**Cleveland Amory, *Who Killed Society?*, 1960**

Money, it turned out, was exactly like sex. You thought of nothing else if you didn't have it, and thought of other things if you did.

**James Baldwin, *Nobody Knows My Name*, 1961**

Literature is mostly about sex and not much about having children, and life is the other way round.

**David Lodge, *The British Museum is Falling Down*, 1965**

The man and woman make love, attain climax, fall separate. Then she whispers 'I'll tell you who I was thinking of if you tell me who you were thinking of.' Like most sex jokes the origins of the pleasant exchange are obscure. But whatever the source, it seldom fails to evoke a certain awful recognition.

**Gore Vidal, in the *New York Review of Books*, 1966**

I'll be comfortable on the couch. Famous last words.

**Lenny Bruce, quoted in *The Essential Lenny Bruce*, ed. J. Cohen, 1967**

Love is a way with some meaning; sex is meaning enough.

**Charles Bukowski, *Notes of a Dirty Old Man*, 1969**

Each man that loves a woman must be prepared for this
For a sexual love is human and betrayal by a kiss
Is a commonplace and not just in the holy book
And it all begins when your eyes take that first long look.

**Gavin Ewart**

Is sex dirty? Only if it's done right.

**Woody Allen, *All You Ever Wanted To Know About Sex*, 1972**

I can understand companionship. I can understand bought sex in the afternoon. I cannot understand the love affair.

**Gore Vidal, in the *Sunday Times*, 1973**

Aren't women prudes if they don't and prostitutes if they do.

**Kate Millett, speech, 1975**

Love is the answer, but while you are waiting for the answer, sex raises some pretty good questions.

**Woody Allen, in the *New York Herald Tribune*, 1975**

Don't knock masturbation – it's sex with someone I love.

**Woody Allen**

Someone once remarked that in adolescence pornography is a substitute for sex, whereas in adulthood sex is a substitute for pornography.

**Edmund White, in *New Times* magazine, 1979**

The big mistake that men make is that when they turn thirteen or fourteen and all of a sudden they've reached puberty, they believe that they like women. Actually, you're just horny. It doesn't mean you like women any more at twenty-one than you did at ten.

**Jules Feiffer, quoted in *Loose Talk*, ed. L. Botts, 1980**

What is a promiscuous person – it's usually someone who is getting more sex than you are.

**Victor Lownes, quoted in *In and Out: Debrett 1980–81* by N. Mackwood, 1980**

The difference between rape and seduction is only one of technique.
**Magnus Magnusson,** *Popular Archaeology*, **1981**

For certain people, after fifty, litigation takes the place of sex.
**Gore Vidal, in the** *Evening Standard*, **1981**

From thirty-five to forty-five men go from relative youth to middle age. The transit is often rocky. As a man's life settles into a rut, in mindless rut the man is apt to go.
**Gore Vidal,** *Pink Triangle and Yellow Star*, **1982**

There is no unhappier creature on earth than a fetishist who yearns for a woman's shoe and has to embrace the whole woman.
**Karl Kraus,** *Aphorisms and More Aphorism*, **1909**

When the prick stands, the brains get buried in the ground.
**Yiddish proverb**

*See also* AFFAIRS, LOVE, LOVERS

# SIN

That which we call sin in others, is experiment for us.
**Ralph Waldo Emerson**

The advantage of the emotions is that they lead us astray.
**Oscar Wilde,** *The Picture of Dorian Gray*, **1891**

Envy is the most stupid of vices, for there is no single advantage to be gained from it.
**Honoré de Balzac, quoted in** *Reflections on the Art of Life*
**by J.R. Solly, 1902**

Scandal is merely the compassionate allowance which the gay make to the humdrum.
**Saki (H.H. Munro),** *Reginald at the Carlton*, **1904**

Only the sinner has the right to preach.
**Christopher Morley**

The urge to gamble is so universal and its practice so pleasurable that I assume it must be evil.

**Heywood Broun**

When choosing between two evils, I always like to take the one I've never tried before.

**Mae West,** *Klondike Annie,* **1936**

Keep a diary and one day it'll keep you.

**Mae West,** *Everyday's A Holiday,* **1937**

Men who make no pretensions to being good on one day out of seven are called sinners.

**Mary Wilson Little**

We don't call it sin today, we call it self-expression.

**Baroness Stocks**

Many are saved from sin by being so inept at it.

**Mignon McLaughlin,** *The Neurotic's Notebook,* **1963**

The major sin is the sin of being born.

**Samuel Beckett, in the** *New York Herald Tribune,* **1964**

*See also* HYPOCRISY, MORALS, RELIGION, VIRTUE

# SPORT

Angling – I can only compare it to a stick and a string with a worm at one end and a fool at the other.

**Samuel Johnson, 1784**

Golf is a good walk spoiled.

**Mark Twain**

When a man wantonly destroys one of the works of man, we call him a vandal; when he wantonly destroys one of the works of God we call him a sportsman.

**Joseph Wood Krutch, on hunting**

A sportsman is a man who, every now and then, simply has to go out and kill something.

**Stephen Leacock, 1920**

Serious sport has nothing to do with fair play. It is bound up with hatred, jealousy, boastfulness, disregard of all rules and sadistic pleasure in witnessing violence: in other words it is war minus the shooting.

**George Orwell, *The Sporting Spirit*, 1945**

[Boxing] . . . is the only sport in the world where two guys get paid for doing something they'd be arrested for if they got drunk and did it for nothing.

**Carl Foreman, screenplay for *Champion*, 1949**

Show me a good loser in professional sports and I'll show you an idiot. Show me a good sportsman and I'll show you a player I'm looking to trade.

**Leo Durocher, 1950**

Everyone likes hats when someone else is paying for them.

**Willie Ginsberg, testifying on corruption in sport, 1956**

Rugby is a beastly game played by gentlemen, soccer is a gentleman's game played by beasts and [US] football is a beastly game played by beasts.

**Henry Blaha, 1972**

Football is a game designed to keep coalminers off the streets.

**Jimmy Breslin, 1973**

On the cult of victory at all costs: Last guys don't finish nice.

**Stanley Kelley, quoted in *The Official Rules* by P. Dickson, 1978**

Jogging is for people who aren't intelligent enough to watch Breakfast TV.

**Victoria Wood**

# THE STATE

In taking possession of a state the conqueror should well reflect as to the harsh measures that may be necessary and then execute them at a single blow . . . cruelties should be committed all at once.

**Niccolò Machiavelli, *The Prince*, 1513**

Nothing doth hurt more in a state than that cunning men pass for wise.

**Francis Bacon, *Essays*, 1625**

Secrecy is the first essential in affairs of state.
  **Cardinal Richelieu, *Testament politique*, 1641**

What has always made the state a hell on earth has been precisely that man has tried to make it his heaven.
  **Johann Friedrich Hölderlin**

The smallest and most inoffensive state is still criminal in its dreams.
  **Michael Bakunin**

Powerful states can maintain themselves only by crime. Little states are virtuous only because they are weak.
  **Mikhail Bakunin, *Proposition motivée*, 1868**

The State is an instrument in the hands of the ruling class for suppressing the resistance of its class enemies.
  **Joseph Stalin**

It is no part of the State's duty to facilitate the spiritual redemption of rich men by impoverishing them in this life.
  **John Grigg, 1964**

*See also* DEMOCRACY, POLITICIANS, POWER

# STATESMEN

Consistency is the hobgoblin of little minds, adored by little statesmen and philosophers and divines.
  **Ralph Waldo Emerson, *Self-Reliance*, 1841**

A statesman is a successful politician who is dead.
  **Thomas B. Reed**

In statesmanship get the formalities right, never mind about the moralities.
  **Mark Twain**

It is amazing how wise statesmen can be when it is ten years too late.
  **David Lloyd George, 1932**

When you're out of office, then you can be a statesman.
  **John Connally, 1971**

One man's opportunism is another man's statesmanship.
  **Milton Friedman, in *Playboy* magazine, 1973**

Statesmen: the word politicians use to describe themselves.
  **Antony Jay and Jonathan Lynn, *Yes, Prime Minister*, 1986**

*See also* LEADERS, POLITICIANS, POWER

# SUCCESS

What matters is not that I should succeed, but that you should fail.
  **Anonymous, attrib. to Gore Vidal inter alios**

He that has nothing but merit to support him is in a fair way to starve.
  **Anonymous, in *Characters and Observations*, c.1725**

To succeed in the world we must look foolish but be wise.
  **Charles de Secondat, Baron de Montesquieu, *Mes pensées*, 1722–55**

Mediocrity is a hand-rail.
  **Charles de Secondat, Baron de Montesquieu, *Mes pensées*, 1722–55**

When we examine what glory is we discover that it is nearly nothing.
To be judged by the ignorant and esteemed by imbeciles, to hear one's
name spoken by a rabble who approve, reject, love or hate without
reason – that is nothing to be proud of.
  **Frederick the Great, letter to Voltaire, 1773**

Be commonplace and creeping and you'll be a success.
  **Pierre Augustin Caron de Beaumarchais, *The Barber of Seville*,
  1775**

One never climbs so high as when he knows not where he is going.
  **Napoleon Bonaparte, *Maxims*, 1804–15**

If you want to get on in this world make many promises, but don't
keep them.
  **Napoleon Bonaparte, *Maxims*, 1804–15**

No one is so completely disenchanted with the world, or knows it so
thoroughly, or is so utterly disgusted with it, that when it begins to
smile upon him he does not become partially reconciled to it.
  **Giacomo Leopardi, *Pensieri*, 1834–7**

Granting our wish is one of Fate's saddest jokes.
   **James Russell Lowell**

Success is the necessary misfortune of life, but it is only to the very unfortunate that it comes early.
   **Anthony Trollope**, *Orley Farm*, **1862**

When the gods wish to punish us they answer our prayers.
   **Oscar Wilde**, *An Ideal Husband*, **1895**

How many 'coming men' has one known! Where on earth do they all go to?
   **Sir Arthur Pinero**

The secret of success in life is known only to those who have not succeeded.
   **John Churton Collins**, in *The English Review*, **1914**

We must believe in luck. For how else can we explain the success of those we don't like.
   **Jean Cocteau**

If at first you don't succeed, try again. Then quit: no use being a damn fool about it.
   **W.C. Fields**

There is no such thing as a great man or woman. People believe in them, just as they used to believe in unicorns and dragons. The greatest man or woman is 99 per cent like yourself.
   **George Bernard Shaw**, interview, **1932**

To succeed pre-eminently in public life it is necessary to conform either to the popular image of a bookie or a clergyman.
   **Malcolm Muggeridge**, **1934**

Those whom the gods wish to destroy, they first call promising.
   **Cyril Connolly**, *Enemies of Promise*, **1938**

Success is relative: It is what we can make of the mess we have made of things.
   **T.S. Eliot**, *The Family Reunion*, **1939**

Once a guy starts wearing silk pyjamas, it's hard to get up early.
**Eddie Arcaro, 1950**

Success listens only to applause. To all else it is deaf.
**Elias Canetti**

If A is success in life, then A equals X plus Y plus Z. Work is X, Y is play and Z is keeping your mouth shut.
**Albert Einstein, in the *Observer*, 1950**

If you want to sell 'em fish, sell 'em big fish. That's the secret of success.
**Jack Solomons, 1950**

We all invent ourselves as we go along, and a great man's myths about himself tend to stick better than most.
**Sir Denis Brogan**

The penalty of success is to be bored by people who used to snub you.
**Nancy Astor, quoted, 1956**

Anatomise the character of a successful hostess and the knife will lay bare the fact that she owes her position to one of three things: she is liked, or she is feared, or she is important.
**Elsa Maxwell, *How To Do It*, 1957**

Many a man owes his success to his first wife and his second wife to his success.
**Jim Backus**

Some men are born mediocre, some men achieve mediocrity, and some men have mediocrity thrust upon them.
**Joseph Heller, *Catch-22*, 1961**

What is success? It is a toy balloon among children armed with pins.
**Gene Fowler, *Skyline*, 1961**

How many of our daydreams would darken into nightmares were there any danger of their coming true.
**Logan Pearsall Smith, quoted in *The Faber Book of Aphorisms*, ed. W.H. Auden and L. Kronenberger, 1964**

Having no talent is no longer enough.
**Gore Vidal**

The banalities of a great man pass for wit.
  **Alexander Chase, *Perspectives*, 1966**

Success is the result of a collective hallucination stimulated by the artist.
  **Charles Aznavour**

The trouble with the rat-race is that even if you win, you're still a rat.
  **Lily Tomlin**

Success and failure are both difficult to endure. Along with success come drugs, divorce, fornication, bullying, travel, meditation, medication, depression, neurosis and suicide. With failure comes failure.
  **Joseph Heller, in *Playboy* magazine, 1975**

Nothing succeeds like address.
  **Fran Lebowitz, *Metropolitan Life*, 1978**

Nothing succeeds like the appearance of success.
  **Christopher Lasch, *The Culture of Narcissism*, 1979**

A successful man is one who makes more money than his wife can spend. A successful woman is one who can find such a man.
  **Lana Turner, 1980**

The secret of success is sincerity. Once you can fake that you've got it made.
  **Glyme's Formula, quoted in *Murphy's Law Book Two*
  by A. Bloch, 1980**

*See also* AMBITION, APPLAUSE, EGOTISM, FAME

# TALK

The vanity of being known to be trusted with a secret is generally one of the chief motives to disclose it.
  **Samuel Johnson, *The Rambler*, 1749–52**

The true use of speech is not so much to express our wants as to conceal them.
  **Oliver Goldsmith, *The Citizen of the World*, 1762**

Speech was given to man to conceal his thoughts.

**Charles-Maurice de Talleyrand, quoted in *Reflections on the Art of Life* by J.R. Solly, 1902**

Swans sing before they die; 'twere no bad thing should certain persons die before they sing.

**Samuel Taylor Coleridge**

A sharp tongue is the only edged instrument that grows keener with constant use.

**Washington Irving, *The Sketch Book*, 1820**

None are so fond of secrets as those who do not mean to keep them; such persons covet secrets as a spendthrift covets money: for the purpose of circulation.

**Charles Caleb Colton, *Lacon*, 1820**

A majority is always the best repartee.

**Benjamin Disraeli, *Tancred*, 1847**

Language, human language, after all is but little better than the croak and cackle of fowls, and other utterances of brute nature – sometimes not as adequate.

**Nathaniel Hawthorne, *American Notebook*, 1850**

The conversation of men is a mixture of regrets and apprehensions.

**Ralph Waldo Emerson**

I never deny, I never contradict. I sometimes forget.

**Benjamin Disraeli, on dealing with Queen Victoria**

Blessed are they that have nothing to say, and who cannot be persuaded to say it.

**James Russell Lowell**

There is only one thing in the world worse than being talked about and that is not being talked about.

**Oscar Wilde, *The Picture of Dorian Gray*, 1891**

Arguments are to be avoided; they are always vulgar and often convincing.

**Oscar Wilde, *The Picture of Dorian Gray*, 1891**

People who want to say merely what is sensible should say it to themselves before they come down to breakfast in the morning, never after.

**Oscar Wilde**

Darling: the popular form of address used in speaking to a member of the opposite sex whose name you cannot at the moment remember.

**Oliver Herford**

Three things matter in a speech: who says it, how he says it and what he says – and of the three, the last matters least.

**John, Viscount Morley**

Confidant, confidante, n. One entrusted by A with the secrets of B, confided to himself by C.

**Ambrose Bierce, *The Devil's Dictionary*, 1911**

Never say anything remarkable. It is sure to be wrong.

**Mark Rutherford, *Last Pages from a Journal*, 1915**

Repartee is what you wish you'd said.

**Heywood Broun**

How awful to reflect that what people say of us is true.

**Logan Pearsall Smith, *All Trivia*, 1931**

Do you want to injure someone's reputation? Don't speak ill of him, speak too well.

**André Siegfried, *Quelques maximes*, 1943**

If you can't convince them, confuse them.

**Harry S. Truman**

The human brain starts working the moment you are born and never stops until you stand up to speak in public.

**Sir George Jessel, 1949**

What are compliments? They are things you say to people when you don't know what else to say.

**Constance Jones**

Conversation is anecdote tempered by interruption.

**Raymond Mortimer**

When there are two conflicting versions of the story, the wise course is to believe the one in which people appear at their worst.
**H. Allen Smith, *Let the Crabgrass Grow*, 1960**

If you can talk brilliantly about a problem, it can create the consoling illusion that it has been mastered.
**Stanley Kubrick**

The telephone is a good way to talk to people without having to offer them a drink.
**Fran Lebowitz, in *Interview* magazine, 1978**

The opposite of talking isn't listening. The opposite of talking is waiting.
**Fran Lebowitz, *Social Studies*, 1981**

I hate to spread rumours – but what else can one do with them.
**Amanda Lear**

*See also* BORES

# TELEVISION & RADIO

Television has proved that people will look at anything rather than at each other.
**Ann Landers**

Television – the bland leading the bland.
**Anonymous, quoted in *The Filmgoer's Book of Quotes*, ed. L. Halliwell, 1973**

No television performance takes as much preparation as an off-the-cuff talk.
**Richard M. Nixon**

A television critic is a man forced to be literate about the illiterate, witty about the witless and coherent about the incoherent.
**John Crosby, 1955**

Television is chewing gum for the eyes.
**Fred Allen**

Television is summer stock in an iron lung.
**Anonymous actor, quoted in the *Manchester Guardian*, 1959**

If TV were to do the Second Coming of Christ in full colour for an hour, there would a considerable number of stations which would decline to carry it on the grounds that a Western or a quiz show would be more profitable.
**Ed Murrow, 1964**

TV is the golden goose that lays scrambled eggs; and it is futile, and probably fatal, to beat it for not laying caviar.
**Lee Loevinger, 1966**

There is an insistent tendency among serious social scientists to think of any institution which features rhymed and singing commercials, intense and lachrymose voices urging highly improbable enjoyment, caricatures of the human oesophagus in normal or impaired operation, and which hints implausibly at opportunities for antiseptic seduction as inherently trivial. This is a great mistake. The industrial system is profoundly dependent on commercial television and could not exist in its present form without it.
**John Kenneth Galbraith, *The New Industrial State*, 1967**

Television is the first truly democratic culture – the first culture available to everybody and entirely governed by what the people want. The most terrifying thing is what the people do want.
**Clive Barnes, in the *New York Times*, 1969**

Television has lifted the manufacture of banality out of the sphere of handicraft and placed it in that of a major industry.
**Nathalie Sarraute, in the *Times Literary Supplement*, 1960**

Imitation is the sincerest form of television.
**Fred Allen, quoted in *Esquire* magazine, 1971**

Television is an invention that permits you to be be entertained in your living room by people you wouldn't have in your home.
**David Frost, on CBS-TV, 1971**

Television – a medium. So called because it is neither rare nor well done.
**Ernie Kovacs, quoted in *The Filmgoer's Book of Quotes*,
ed. L. Halliwell, 1973**

Television . . . the longest amateur night in history.
**Robert Carson, quoted in** *The Filmgoer's Book of Quotes,*
**ed. L. Halliwell, 1973**

I'm delighted with television because it used to be that films were the lowest form of art. Now we've got something to look down on.
**Billy Wilder**

Television is democracy at its ugliest.
**Paddy Chayevsky**

In California they don't throw their garbage away – they make it into television shows.
**Woody Allen,** *Annie Hall,* **1977**

Television is a whore. Any man who wants her full favours can have them in five minutes with a pistol.
**Anonymous hijacker, quoted in** *Esquire* **magazine, 1977**

If any reader of this book is in the grip of some habit of which he is deeply ashamed, I advise him not to give way to it in secret but to do it on television. No one will pass him with averted gaze on the other side of the street. People will cross the road at the risk of losing their own lives in order to say 'We saw you on the telly.'
**Quentin Crisp,** *How To Become a Virgin,* **1981**

Television is more interesting than people. If it were not, we should have people standing in the corners of our rooms.
**Alan Coren, quoted in** *The Penguin Dictionary of Modern Quotations,* **ed. J. and M. Cohen, 1981**

Radio news is bearable: this is due to the fact that while the news is being broadcast the DJ is not allowed to talk.
**Fran Lebowitz**

*See also* JOURNALISM

# TIME

Time is a great teacher, but unfortunately it kills all its pupils.
**Hector Berlioz**

Time is that in which all things pass away; it is the form under which the will to live has revealed to it that its efforts are in vain; it is the agent by which at every moment all things in our hands become as nothing and lose all value.

**Arthur Schopenhauer, *The Vanity of Existence*, 1851**

Between time and ourselves, it is a struggle as to which shall kill the other.

**Guy Delaforest, quoted in *Reflections on the Art of Life* by J.R. Solly, 1902**

There is no time like the pleasant.

**Addison Mizner and Oliver Herford, *The Entirely New Cynic's Calendar*, 1905**

Time is so much kinder to a man than to a woman that a careful bachelor often lives to flirt with the daughter of the woman he once came within an ace of marrying.

**Arthur Binstead, *Pitcher's Proverbs*, 1909**

Future, n. That period of time in which our affairs prosper, our friends are true and our happiness is assured.

**Ambrose Bierce, *The Devil's Dictionary*, 1911**

So little time, so little to do.

**Oscar Levant**

Time: that which man is always trying to kill, but which ends in killing him.

**Herbert Spencer**

Satire is tragedy plus time.

**Lenny Bruce, quoted in *The Essential Lenny Bruce*, ed. J. Cohen, 1967**

Hindsight is always 20:20.

**Billy Wilder**

*See also* AGE, EXPERIENCE

# TRAVEL

Visits always give pleasure: if not in the arrival, then on the departure.
  **Edouard Le Berquier**

Pedestrian: anyone who is knocked down by a motor-car.
  **J.B. Morton ('Beachcomber')**

If you look like your passport photo, in all probability you need the journey.
  **Earl Wilson, in the *Ladies Home Journal*, 1961**

Holidays are an expensive trial of strength. The only satisfaction comes from survival.
  **Jonathan Miller, in the *Daily Herald*, 1962**

It is imperative when flying coach that you restrain any tendency toward the vividly imaginative. For although it may momentarily appear to be the case, it is not at all likely that the cabin is entirely inhabited by crying babies smoking inexpensive domestic cigars.
  **Fran Lebowitz, *Social Studies*, 1981**

# TRUE BELIEVERS

Pure in show, an upright holy man,
Corrupt within – and called a Puritan.
  **Anonymous, *A Song of the Puritan*, c.1605**

A pious man is one who would be an atheist if the king were.
  **Jean de La Bruyère, *The Characters*, 1688**

No rogue like to the godly rogue.
  **Thomas Fuller, M.D., *The Holy and Profane State*, 1732**

Suspect, in general, those who remarkably affect any one virtue . . . for they are commonly imposters.
  **Lord Chesterfield, *Letters to his Son*, 1774**

Bear-baiting was esteemed heathenish and un-christian; the sport of it, not the inhumanity, gave offence.
  **David Hume, *The History of Great Britain*, 1754–62**

Men whose trade is rat-catching love to catch rats; the bug destroyer seizes on his bug with delight; and the suppressor is gratified by finding his vice.

**Sydney Smith, on self-appointed moralists, 1801**

We have no doubt but that the immediate effect of a voluntary combination for the suppression of vice is an involuntary combination in favour of the vices to be suppressed.

**Sydney Smith, on the newly formed Society for the Suppression of Vice, 1801**

As no roads are as rough as those that have just been mended, so no sinners are as intolerant as those that have just turned saints.

**Charles Caleb Colton, *Lacon*, 1820**

The Puritan hated bear-baiting, not because it gave pain to the bear, but because it gave pleasure to the spectators.

**Thomas Babington Macaulay, Baron Macaulay**

The Puritans nobly fled from a land of despotism to a land of freedom, where they could not only enjoy their own religion, but prevent everybody else from enjoying *his*.

**Artemus Ward (C.F. Browne), *The London Punch Letters*, 1866**

The reformer . . . unable to beget or bear, possessing neither fecundity nor virility, endowed with the contempt of men and the disdain of women, and doomed to sterility, isolation and extinction.

**J.J. Ingalls, speech, 1885**

Any preoccupation with ideas of what is right and wrong in conduct shows an arrested intellectual development.

**Oscar Wilde, *Phrases and Philosophies for the Use of the Young*, 1894**

The more things a man is ashamed of, the more respectable he is.

**George Bernard Shaw, *Man and Superman*, 1903**

No people do so much harm as those who go about doing good.

**Bishop Mandell Creighton, quoted in *Life and Letters*, 1904**

All reformers, however strict their social conscience, live in houses just as big as they can pay for.

**Logan Pearsall Smith**

Unless the reformer can invent something which substitutes attractive virtues for attractive vices, he will fail.

**Walter Lippmann, *A Preface to Politics*, 1914**

Puritanism – the haunting fear that someone, somewhere, may be happy.

**H.L. Mencken, *A Book of Burlesques*, 1920**

The infliction of cruelty with a good conscience is a delight to moralists – that is why they invented hell.

**Bertrand Russell, *Sceptical Essays*, 1928**

A reformer is a man who rides through a sewer in a glass-bottomed boat.

**James J. Walker**

The most distressing thing that can happen to a prophet is to be proved wrong. The next most distressing thing is to be proved right.

**Aldous Huxley, *Brave New World Revisited*, 1958**

Puritanism . . . helps us enjoy our misery while we are inflicting it on others.

**Marcel Ophuls, in *The Listener* magazine, 1978**

The name 'moralist' sounds like a perversion – one wouldn't be surprised at finding it suddenly in Krafft-Ebing.

**Elias Canetti, *The Human Province*, 1978**

Fear prophets . . . and those prepared to die for the truth, for as a rule they make many others die with them.

**Umberto Eco, *The Name of the Rose*, 1981**

*See also* BELIEF, FAITH, HYPOCRISY, IDEALS, IDEAS, MORALS, RELIGION, TRUTH

# TRUTH

If you want to annoy your neighbours, tell the truth about them.

**Pietro Aretino**

Truth always lags behind, limping along on the arm of time.

**Baltasar Gracian, *The Art of Worldly Wisdom*, 1647**

Truth . . . never comes into the World, but like a Bastard, to the ignominy of him that brought her forth.

**John Milton**

Truth does not do so much good in the world as its appearances do evil.

**François, Duc de La Rochefoucauld, *Maxims*, 1665**

The exact contrary of what is generally believed is often the truth.

**Jean de La Bruyère, *The Characters*, 1688**

A Man that should call everything by its right Name would hardly pass the Streets without being knocked down as a common Enemy.

**George Savile, Marquis of Halifax, *Political, Moral and Miscellaneous Thoughts and Reflexions*, c.1694**

Nothing has an uglier look to us than reason, when it is not on our side

**George Savile, Marquis of Halifax, *Political, Moral and Miscellaneous Thoughts and Reflexions*, c.1694**

Honour's a fine imaginary notion
That draws in raw and unexperienced men
To real mischiefs.

**Joseph Addison, *Cato*, 1713**

Beware of telling an improbable truth.

**Thomas Fuller, M.D., *Introductio ad Prudentiam*, 1727**

Seldom any splendid story is wholly true.

**Samuel Johnson, *Works* vol. vii, 1787**

To announce truths, to propose something useful to mankind, is an infallible receipt for being persecuted.

**Voltaire, quoted in *A Cynic's Breviary* by J.R. Solly, 1925**

Truth lights – but money warms.

**Anonymous**

A man had rather have a hundred lies told of him, than one truth which he does not wish should be told.

**Samuel Johnson, *The Life of Samuel Johnson* by J. Boswell, 1791**

In argument, truth always prevails finally, in politics falsehood always.

**Walter Savage Landor**

No man speaks the truth or lives a true life two minutes together.
  **Ralph Waldo Emerson,** *Journals,* **1909–14**

Something unpleasant is coming when men are anxious to tell the truth.
  **Benjamin Disraeli**

It is the customary fate of new truths to begin as heresies and to end as superstitions.
  **T.H. Huxley, in** *Science and Culture,* **1893–4**

When you want to fool the world, tell the truth.
  **Otto von Bismarck**

All true knowledge contradicts common sense.
  **Bishop Mandell Creighton, in** *Life and Letters,* **1904**

It is always the best policy to tell the truth, unless, of course, you are an exceptionally good liar.
  **Jerome K. Jerome**

A thing is not necessarily true because a man dies for it.
  **Oscar Wilde,** *The Portrait of Mr W.H.,* **1889**

If one tells the truth, one is sure, sooner or later, to be found out.
  **Oscar Wilde,** *Phrases and Philosophies for the Use of the Young,* **1894**

Vulgarity is simply the conduct of other people, just as falsehoods are the truths of other people.
  **Oscar Wilde,** *An Ideal Husband,* **1895**

The truth is rarely pure and never simple. Modern life would be very tedious if it were either, and modern literature a complete impossibility.
  **Oscar Wilde,** *The Importance of Being Earnest,* **1895**

Liar: one who tells an unpleasant truth.
  **Oliver Herford**

Tell the truth and shame the – family.
  **Addison Mizner and Oliver Herford,** *The Entirely New Cynic's Calendar,* **1905**

The course of true anything never does run smooth.

**Samuel Butler, *Notebooks*, 1912**

Some men love truth so much that they seem to be in continual fear lest she should catch a cold on overexposure.

**Samuel Butler, *Notebooks*, 1912**

Any fool can tell the truth, but it requires a man of some sense to know how to lie well.

**Samuel Butler, *Notebooks*, 1912**

Truth – something somehow discreditable to someone.

**H.L. Mencken, *Sententiae*, 1916**

It is unfortunate, considering enthusiasm moves the world, that so few enthusiasts can be trusted to speak the truth.

**Arthur James, Earl Balfour, letter, 1918**

To die for an idea – it is unquestionably noble. But how much nobler it would be if men died for ideas that were true.

**H.L. Mencken**

A platitude is simply a truth repeated till people get tired of hearing it.

**Stanley Baldwin, First Earl of Bewdley, 1924**

By telling the truth one saves oneself from a multitude of fatiguing cares.

**E.V. Lucas**

What is truth? We must adopt a pragmatic definition: it is what is believed to be the truth. A lie that is put across therefore becomes the truth and may, therefore, be justified. The difficulty is to keep up lying . . . it is simpler to tell the truth and if a sufficient emergency arises, to tell one big thumping lie that will then be believed.

**Ministry of Information, memo on the maintenance of British civilian morale, 1939**

The nearest approach to immortality for any truth is by its becoming a platitude.

**Paul Eldridge, *Horns of Glass*, 1943**

True, you can't take it with you, but then, that's not the place where it comes in handy.
**Brendan Francis**

Believe those who are seeking the truth; doubt those who find it.
**André Gide, *So Be It*, 1959**

Nagging is the repetition of unpalatable truths.
**Dr Edith Summerskill, in the *Observer*, 1960**

There aren't any embarrassing questions – only embarrassing answers.
**Carl Rowan, in the *New Yorker* magazine, 1963**

Truth and Myth are the same thing, . . . you have to simulate passion to feel it, . . . man is a creature of ceremony.
**Jean-Paul Sartre, *The Words*, 1964**

Truth means not having to guess what a candidate means.
**Gerald Ford, 1976**

The truth is always libellous.
**George Finey, in the *Sydney Morning Herald*, 1981**

Truth is what one is obliged to tell policemen.
**Bertrand Russell, quoted, 1984**

*See also* BELIEF, FAITH, HONESTY, IDEALS, IDEAS, MORALS, RELIGION, TRUE BELIEVERS

# THE UNITED STATES

You can always get the truth from an American statesman after he has turned seventy or given up all hope of the Presidency.
**Wendell Philips, 1860**

In America the President rules for four years and journalism governs for ever and ever.
**Oscar Wilde**

When good Americans die, they go to Paris; when bad Americans die, they go to America.
**Oscar Wilde, *A Woman of No Importance*, 1893 (based on Thomas G. Appleton's [1812–84] 'When good Americans die, they go to Paris' c.1860)**

The American nation in the sixth ward is a fine people; they love the eagle – on the back of a dollar.

**Finley Peter Dunne**

America is the only nation in history which, miraculously, has gone directly from barbarism to degeneration without the usual interval of civilisation.

**Georges Clemenceau**

Q: If you find so much that is unworthy of reverence in the United States, why do you live here? Mencken: Why do men go to zoos?

**H.L. Mencken, *Prejudices* 5th series, 1926**

America . . . where laws and customs alike are based on the dreams of spinsters.

**Bertrand Russell, *Marriage and Morals*, 1929**

All American writing gives me the impression that Americans don't care for girls at all. What the American male really wants is two things: he wants to be blown by a stranger while reading a newspaper and he wants to be fucked by his buddy when he's drunk. Everything else is society.

**W.H. Auden, *The Table-Talk of W.H. Auden*,
ed. Alan Ansen, 1990**

In America everybody is of the opinion that he has no social superiors, since all men are equal, but he does not admit that he has no social inferiors.

**Bertrand Russell, *Unpopular Essays*, 1950**

In America any boy may become President, and I suppose that's just the risk he takes.

**Adlai Stevenson, 1952**

The organisation of American society is an interlocking system of semi-monopolies notoriously venal, an electorate notoriously unenlightened, misled by a mass media notoriously phoney.

**Paul Goodman, *The Community of Scholars*, 1962**

America . . . just a nation of two hundred million used car salesmen with all the money we need to buy guns and no qualms about killing anybody else in the world who tries to make us uncomfortable.

**Hunter S. Thompson, *Fear and Loathing on the Campaign Trail*, 1972**

The hatred Americans have for their own government is pathological
... at one level it is simply thwarted greed: since our religion is
making a buck, giving a part of that buck to any government is an act
against nature.

**Gore Vidal**

No American who works for the CIA is a spy. A spy is a foreign agent
who commits treason.

**Jim Keehner, in *New Times* magazine, 1976**

If you're going to America, bring your own food.

**Fran Lebowitz, *Social Studies*, 1981**

Whatever it is that the government does, sensible Americans would
prefer that the government do it to somebody else. This is the idea
behind foreign policy.

**P.J. O'Rourke, *Parliament of Whores*, 1991**

The American political system is like fast food – mushy, insipid, made
out of disgusting parts of things and everybody wants some.

**P.J. O'Rourke, *Parliament of Whores*, 1991**

# VIRTUE

If you can't be good, be careful.

**Anonymous**

Everything is good or everything is bad, according to the votes they
gain.

**Baltasar Gracian, *The Art of Worldly Wisdom*, 1647**

Virtue, among other definitions, may thus be defined: an action against
the will.

**Anonymous, *Characters and Observations*, c.1725**

Those whom their virtue restrains from deceiving others are often
disposed by their vanity to deceive themselves.

**Samuel Johnson, *Works* vol. viii, 1787**

To many people virtue consists mainly in repenting faults, not in
avoiding them.

**Georg Christoph Lichtenberg, *Reflections*, 1799**

Fresh air and innocence are good if you don't take too much of them.
  **Oliver Wendell Holmes**

The good (I am convinced, for one)
Is but the bad one leaves undone.
  **Wilhelm Busch**

It is good to be without vice, but it is not good to be without
temptations.
  **Walter Bagehot**

No one does good to men with impunity.
  **Auguste Rodin**

Good breeding consists in concealing how much we think of ourselves
and how little we think of the other person.
  **Mark Twain**

Few things are harder to put up with than the annoyance of a good
example.
  **Mark Twain**

Every virtue has its privileges – for example, that of contributing its
own little faggot to the pyre of the condemned.
  **Friedrich Wilhelm Nietzsche, *Human, All Too Human*, 1878**

To be good, according to the vulgar standard of goodness is obviously
quite easy. It merely requires a certain amount of sordid terror, a certain
lack of imaginative thought, and a certain low passion for middle-class
respectability.
  **Oscar Wilde, *The Critic as Artist*, 1890**

Good resolutions are useless attempts to interfere with scientific laws.
Their origin is pure vanity. Their result is absolutely nil. They give us,
now and then, some of those luxurious sterile emotions that have a certain charm for the weak . . . They are simply cheques that men draw
on a bank where they have no account.
  **Oscar Wilde, *The Picture of Dorian Gray*, 1891**

Men become old, but they never become good.
  **Oscar Wilde, *Lady Windermere's Fan*, 1892**

Do not ask me to be kind; just ask me to act as though I were.
  **Jules Renard, *Journal*, 1898**

Self-denial is not a virtue: it is only the effect of prudence on rascality.
  **George Bernard Shaw, *Man and Superman*, 1903**

What is virtue but the trades unionism of the married?
  **George Bernard Shaw, *Man and Superman*, 1903**

Remorse is, after all, a thoroughly wholesome and healthy secretion. With what bitter anguish do we now recall those awful early virtues which we now know to have been only wasted opportunities.
  **Arthur Binstead, *Pitcher's Proverbs*, 1909**

On virtue: Our vocabulary is defective: we give the same name to woman's lack of temptation and man's lack of opportunity.
  **Ambrose Bierce, *Collected Works*, 1909–12**

I forget who it was that recommended men for their soul's good to do each day two things they disliked . . . it is a precept that I have followed scrupulously; for every day I have got up and I have gone to bed.
  **W. Somerset Maugham, *The Moon and Sixpence*, 1919**

A thing called Ethics, whose nature was confusing but if you had it you were a High-Class Realtor and if you hadn't you were a shyster, a piker and a fly-by-night. These virtues awakened Confidence and enabled you to handle Bigger Propositions. But they didn't imply that you were to be impractical and refuse to take twice the value of a house if a buyer was such an idiot that he didn't force you down on the asking price.
  **Sinclair Lewis, *Babbitt*, 1922**

Nobody's interested in sweetness and light.
  **Hedda Hopper**

Virtue is its own reward – but it has no sale at the box office.
  **Mae West**

Too much of a good thing is simply wonderful.
  **Mae West**

There are no good girls gone wrong – only bad girls found out.
  **Mae West, screenplay for *Belle of the Nineties*, 1934**

So far as we are human, what we do must be either evil or good: so far as we do evil or good, we are human; and it is better, in a paradoxical way, to do evil than to do nothing: at least we exist.
  **T.S. Eliot, essay on Baudelaire**

It's the good girls who keep the diaries; the bad girls never have the time.
  **Tallulah Bankhead**

No good deed goes unpunished.
  **Clare Booth Luce, quoted in *The Book of Laws* by H. Faber, 1980**

Good behaviour is the last refuge of mediocrity.
  **Henry Haskins, *Meditations in Wall Street*, 1940**

There's Mellot. Take a good look at him. A nicer sort of guy never put shoes on. Fine fellow, but he didn't come to win, that's the answer. Nice guys finish last.
  **Leo Durocher, 1946**

Many an attack of depression is nothing but the expression of regret at having to be virtuous.
  **Dr Wilhelm Stekhel**

If you can't say anything good about someone, sit right here by me.
  **Alice Roosevelt Longworth, general greeting**

Saintliness is also a temptation.
  **Jean Anouilh, *Becket*, 1959**

'For your own good' is a persuasive argument that will eventually make a man agree to his own destruction.
  **Janet Frame, *Faces in the Water*, 1961**

Virtue is not photogenic.
  **Kirk Douglas**

Most plain girls are virtuous because of the scarcity of opportunity to be otherwise.
  **Maya Angelou, *I Know Why the Caged Bird Sings*, 1969**

*See also* SIN

# VOTING

I never vote for anyone. I always vote against.

**W.C. Fields**

Voting is merely a handy device; it is not to be identified with democracy.

**G.D.H. Cole, *Essays in Social Theory*, 1950**

Voting is simply a way of determining which side is the stronger without putting it to the test of fighting.

**H.L. Mencken, *Minority Report*, 1956**

Ask a man which way he is going to vote, and he will probably tell you. Ask him, however, why, and vagueness is all.

**Bernard Levin, in the *Daily Mail*, 1964**

If the people of a democracy are allowed to do so, they will vote away the freedoms which are essential to that democracy.

**Snell Putney, *The Conquest of Society*, 1972**

The difference between a Democracy and a Dictatorship is that in a Democracy you vote first and take orders later; in a Dictatorship you don't have to waste your time voting.

**Charles Bukowski, *Erections, Ejaculations, Exhibitions and Tales of Ordinary Madness*, 1972**

If voting changed anything, they'd make it illegal.

**Graffito, London, 1979**

*See also* DEMOCRACY, GOVERNMENT, LEADERS, PARTIES, POLITICIANS, POLITICS

# WAR

The war is just which is necessary.

**Niccolò Machiavelli, *The Prince*, 1513**

War is delightful to those who have had no experience of it.

**Desiderius Erasmus**

Force and fraud are in war the two cardinal virtues.

**Thomas Hobbes, *Leviathan*, 1651**

Even war is pusillanimously carried on in this degenerate age: quarter is given; towns are taken and the people spared; even in a storm a woman can hardly hope for the benefit of a rape.

**Lord Chesterfield, *Letters to his Son*, 1774**

War is the faro table of government, and nations the dupes of the games.

**Thomas Paine, *The Rights of Man*, 1791–2**

A war, or any wild goose chase, is, as the vulgar use the phrase, a lucky turn up of patronage for the minister, whose chief merit is the art of keeping himself in place.

**Mary Wollstonecraft, *A Vindication of the Rights of Woman*, 1792**

There is more misery inflicted upon mankind by one year of war than by all the civil peculations and oppressions of a century. Yet it is a state into which the mass of mankind rush with the greatest avidity, hailing official murderers, in scarlet, gold and cock's feathers, as the greatest and most glorious of human creatures.

**Sydney Smith**

A man will fight harder for his interests than for his rights.

**Napoleon Bonaparte, *Maxims*, 1804–15**

There are no manifestoes like cannon and musketry.

**Arthur Wellesley, Duke of Wellington**

A great part of the information obtained in war is contradictory, a still greater part is false, and by far the greatest part is of doubtful character.

**Karl von Clausewitz, *On War*, 1832**

The lower people everywhere desire war. Not so unwisely; there is then a demand for lower people – to be shot!

**Thomas Carlyle, *Sartor Resartus*, 1833–4**

Such I hold to be the genuine use of gunpowder: that it makes all men alike tall.

**Thomas Carlyle**

Nothing should be left to an invaded people but their eyes for weeping.

**Otto von Bismarck, 1862**

As long as war is regarded as wicked it will always have its fascination.
When it is looked upon as vulgar, it will cease to be popular.

**Oscar Wilde, *Intentions*, 1891**

The love of fair play is a spectator's virtue, not a principal's.

**George Bernard Shaw, *Maxims for Revolutionists*, 1903**

Nothing is ever done in this world until men are prepared to kill one
another if it is not done.

**George Bernard Shaw, *Major Barbara*, 1907**

Battle, n. A method of untying with the teeth a political knot that will
not yield to the tongue.

**Ambrose Bierce, *The Devil's Dictionary*, 1911**

My dear . . . the noise! And the people!

**Ernest Thesiger (alleged), commenting on his involvement in
the battle of the Somme, 1916**

War is a series of catastrophes which result in a victory.

**Georges Clemenceau**

War hath no fury like a non-combatant.

**C.E. Montague, *Disenchantment*, 1922**

War is hell . . . when you're getting licked.

**Brigadier-General Henry J. O'Reilly, amending General
Sherman's famous dictum, 1931**

When the leaders speak of peace
The common folk know
That war is coming
When the leaders curse war
The mobilization order is already written out.

**Bertolt Brecht, *From a German War Primer*, 1938**

War is like love, it always finds a way.

**Bertolt Brecht, *Mother Courage*, 1941**

On the wall in chalk is written
'They want war'
He who wrote it has already fallen.

**Bertolt Brecht, in *Collected Poems 1913-1956*, 1976**

It is easier to fight for one's principles than to live up to them.

**Alfred Adler, quoted in *Alfred Adler* by P. Bottome, 1939**

Naturally the common people don't want war . . . but after all it is the leaders of a country who determine policy, and it is always a simple matter to drag the people along, whether it is a democracy, or a fascist dictatorship, or a parliament, or a communist dictatorship. All you have to do is tell them they are being attacked, and denounce the pacifists for lack of patriotism and exposing the country to danger. It works the same in every country.

**Hermann Göring, quoted in *The People's Almanac*, 1976**

You can't say civilisation don't advance . . . for in every war they kill you a new way.

**Will Rogers, *The Autobiography of Will Rogers*, 1949**

People who are vigorous and brutal often find war enjoyable, provided that it is a victorious war and that there is not too much interference with rape and plunder. This is a great help in persuading people that wars are righteous.

**Bertrand Russell, *Unpopular Essays*, 1950**

A prisoner of war is a man who tries to kill you and fails, and then asks you not to kill him.

**Sir Winston Churchill, 1952**

War is the unfolding of miscalculations.

**Barbara Tuchman, *The Guns of August*, 1962**

All wars are popular for the first thirty days.

**Arthur Schlesinger Jr**

I have never understood this liking for war. It panders to instincts already catered for within the scope of any respectable domestic establishment.

**Alan Bennett, *Forty Years On*, 1968**

No wars are unintentional or 'accidental'. What is often unintended is the length and bloodiness of the war. Defeat too is unintended.

**Geoffrey Blainey, *The Causes of War*, 1973**

Violence is the repartee of the illiterate.

**Alan Brien, in *Punch* magazine, 1973**

People who fight fire with fire usually end up with ashes.
   **Abigail van Buren, 1974**

War is capitalism with the gloves off.
   **Tom Stoppard, *Travesties*, 1974**

Only the winners decide what were war crimes.
   **Gary Wills, in the *New York Times*, 1975**

Usually, when a lot of men get together, it's called war.
   **Mel Brooks, in *The Listener magazine*, 1978**

Violence is the way of ensuring a hearing for moderation.
   **William C. O'Brien, quoted in the *Observer*, 1981**

There is no force more terroristic than a national state at war.
   **Richard E. Rubenstein, *Alchemists of Revolution: Terrorism in the Modern World*, 1987**

# WEAKNESS

It's going to be fun to watch and see how long the meek can keep the earth when they inherit it.
   **Kin Hubbard, *Abe Martin's Sayings*, 1915**

Let the meek inherit the earth – they have it coming to them.
   **James Thurber, in *Life* magazine, 1960**

The weak have one weapon: the errors of those who think they are strong.
   **Georges Bidault, quoted in the *Observer*, 1962**

That weakness in human nature which goes by the name of strength.
   **Peter Ustinov, in the *Listener* magazine, 1974**

*See also* POWER

# WIVES

He knows little who will tell his wife all he knows.
   **Thomas Fuller, D.D., *The Holy State and the Profane State*, 1642**

Next to no wife, a good wife is best.

**Thomas Fuller, D.D., *The Holy State and the Profane State*, 1642**

Here lies my wife: here let her lie! Now she's at rest, and so am I.

**John Dryden, epitaph intended for his wife**

It goes far towards reconciling me to being a woman when I reflect I am thus in no danger of marrying one.

**Lady Mary Wortley Montagu**

The comfortable estate of widowhood is the only hope that keeps up a wife's spirits.

**John Gay, *The Beggar's Opera*, 1728**

A dead wife under the table is the best goods in a man's house.

**Jonathan Swift, *Polite Conversation*, 1738**

The only solid and lasting peace between a man and his wife is, doubtless, a separation.

**Lord Chesterfield, *Letters to his Son*, 1774**

The man who enters his wife's dressing room is either a philosopher or a fool.

**Honoré de Balzac, *The Physiology of Marriage*, 1829**

After forty, men have married their habits, and wives are only an item in the list, and not the most important.

**George Meredith**

He gave way to the queer, savage feeling that sometimes takes by the throat a husband twenty years married, when he sees, across the table, the same face of his wedded wife, and knows that, as he has sat facing it, so must he continue to sit until the day of its death or his own.

**Rudyard Kipling, *Plain Tales from the Hills*, 1888**

A man likes his wife to be just clever enough to comprehend his cleverness, and just stupid enough to admire it.

**Israel Zangwill**

It is most dangerous for a husband to pay any attention to his wife in public. It always makes people think that he beats her when they are alone.

**Oscar Wilde, *Lady Windermere's Fan*, 1892**

A good wife is good, but the best wife is not so good as no wife at all.

**Thomas Hardy**

Constance: I'm tired of being the modern wife.
Martha: What do you mean by the modern wife?
Constance: A prostitute who doesn't deliver the goods.

**W. Somerset Maugham, *The Constant Wife*, 1926**

Never feel remorse for what you have thought about your wife. She has thought much worse things about you.

**Jean Rostand, *Le mariage*, 1927**

A man does not buy his wife a fur coat to keep her warm, but to keep her pleasant.

**Sir Seymour Hicks, in the *Observer*, 1946**

When a man steals your wife, there is no better revenge than to let him keep her.

**Sacha Guitry, *Elles et toi*, 1948**

There's nothing like a good dose of another woman to make a man appreciate his wife.

**Clare Booth Luce**

A man should not insult his wife publicly, at parties. He should insult her in the privacy of the home.

**James Thurber, *Thurber Country*, 1953**

Of course a platonic relationship is possible – but only between husband and wife.

**Ladies Home Journal**

A psychiatrist is a fellow who asks you a lot of expensive questions your wife asks you for nothing.

**Joey Adams, *Cindy and I*, 1959**

A man does not have to be a bigamist to have one wife too many.

**Farmer's Almanac, 1966**

Happy is the man with a wife to tell him what to do and a secretary to do it.

**Lord Mancroft, in the *Observer*, 1966**

The husband who doesn't tell his wife everything probably reasons that what she doesn't know won't hurt him.

**Leo J. Burke, quoted in *Peter's Quotations*, ed. Dr L. Peter, 1977**

*See also* AFFAIRS, DIVORCE, HUSBANDS, LOVE, LOVERS, MARRIAGE

# WOMEN

Don't assume that every sad-eyed woman has loved and lost – she may have got him.

**Anonymous**

Whether a pretty woman grants or witholds her favours, she always likes to be asked for them.

**Ovid, *Ars Amatoria*, c.AD8**

For women's tears are but the sweat of eyes.

**Juvenal, *Satires*, c.AD100**

Trust not a woman when she cries
For she'll pump water from her eyes
With a wet finger, and in faster showers
Than April when he rains down flowers.

**Thomas Dekker, *The Honest Whore*, 1604**

If that the earth could teem with woman's tears,
Each drop she falls would prove a crocodile.

**William Shakespeare, *Othello*, 1604**

There's nothing sooner dries than woman's tears.

**John Webster, *The White Devil*, 1612**

Most virtuous women are like hidden treasures: safe only because they are not sought after.

**François, Duc de La Rochefoucauld, *Maxims*, 1665**

The cruellest revenge of a woman is to remain faithful to a man.

**Jacques Bossuet**

Once a woman has given you her heart you can never get rid of the rest of her body.

**John Vanbrugh, *The Relapse*, 1696**

Men who cherish for women the highest respect are seldom popular with them.

**Joseph Addison**

Every day men sleep with women they do not love and do not sleep with women whom they do love.

**Denis Diderot, *Jacques le fataliste*, 1773**

What is woman? Only one of Nature's agreeable blunders.

**Hannah Cowley, *Who's The Dupe?*, 1779**

Women all want to be ladies, which is simply to have nothing to do, but listlessly to go they scarcely care where, for they cannot tell what.

**Mary Wollstonecraft, *Vindication of the Rights of Woman*, 1792**

A woman, if she should have the misfortune of knowing anything, should conceal it as well as she can.

**Jane Austen, *Pride and Prejudice*, 1813**

In her first passion woman loves her lover.
In all the others all she loves is love.

**George Gordon, Lord Byron, *Don Juan*, 1819–24**

It is only the man whose intellect is clouded by his sexual impulses that could give the name of 'the fair sex' to that undersized, narrow-shouldered, broad-hipped and short-legged race.

**Arthur Schopenhauer, *On Women***

Women will pardon any offence rather than a neglect of their charms.

**Charles Caleb Colton, *Lacon*, 1820**

The man's desire is for the woman, but the woman's desire is rarely other than for the desire of the man.

**Samuel Taylor Coleridge, *Table Talk*, 1836**

Man has his will, but woman has her way.

**Oliver Wendell Holmes, *The Autocrat of the Breakfast-Table*, 1857–8**

I'm not denyin' the women are foolish: God Almighty made 'em to match the men.

**George Eliot, *Adam Bede*, 1859**

Was there ever any domination which did not appear natural to those who possessed it.

**John Stuart Mill, *The Subjection of Women*, 1869**

Woman was God's second mistake.

**Friedrich Wilhelm Nietzsche**

The only way a woman can ever reform a man is by boring him so completely that he loses all possible interest in life.

**Oscar Wilde, *The Picture of Dorian Gray*, 1891**

Crying is the refuge of plain women, but the ruin of pretty ones.

**Oscar Wilde, *Lady Windermere's Fan*, 1892**

One can always recognise women who trust their husbands. They look so thoroughly unhappy.

**Oscar Wilde, *Lady Windermere's Fan*, 1892**

The history of women is the history of the worst tyranny the world has ever known: the tyranny of the weak over the strong. It is the only tyranny that ever lasts.

**Oscar Wilde, *A Woman of No Importance*, 1893**

And a woman is only a woman, but a good cigar is a Smoke.

**Rudyard Kipling, *The Betrothed*, 1899**

A woman will always sacrifice herself if you give her the opportunity. It is her favourite form of self-indulgence.

**W. Somerset Maugham**

A plain woman will have nothing forgiven her. Her fate is such that the parents of uncomely female infants should be compelled to put them to death at birth.

**Miles Franklin, *My Brilliant Career*, 1901**

Shame is the feeling you have when you agree with the woman who loves you that you are the man she thinks you are.

**Carl Sandburg, *Incidentals*, 1905**

Physically there is nothing to distinguish human society from the farm-yard except that children are more troublesome and costly than chickens and women are not so completely enslaved as farm stock.

**George Bernard Shaw, *Getting Married*, 1908**

Women at least have elegant dresses. But what can men use to cover their emptiness?

**Karl Kraus, *Half Truths and One and a Half Truths*, 1986**

A woman occasionally is quite a serviceable substitute for masturbation. It takes an abundance of imagination, to be sure.

**Karl Kraus**

Dream: fem. a term used by a woman discussing a hat; masc. term describing the woman used by the man who is destined to buy the hat.

**Oliver Herford and John Clay, *Cupid's Cyclopedia*, 1910**

Adam's Rib: the original bone of contention.

**Oliver Herford and John Clay, *Cupid's Cyclopedia*, 1910**

Woman: the peg on which the wit hangs his jest, the preacher his text, the cynic his grouch and the sinner his justification.

**Helen Rowland**

Artlessness, n. A certain engaging quality to which women attain by long study and severe practice.

**Ambrose Bierce, *The Devil's Dictionary*, 1911**

Ugliness, n. A gift of the gods to certain women, entailing virtue without humility.

**Ambrose Bierce, *The Devil's Dictionary*, 1911**

The woman who is really kind to dogs is always one who has failed to inspire sympathy in men.

**Max Beerbohm, *Zuleika Dobson*, 1911**

If God considered woman a fit helpmeet for man, he must have had a very poor opinion of man.

**Samuel Butler**

Brigands demand your money or your life; women require both.

**Samuel Butler**

When women kiss it always reminds one of prize fighters shaking hands.

**H.L. Mencken, *Sententiae*, 1916**

A woman can forgive a man for the harm he does her, but she can never forgive him for the sacrifices he makes on her account.

**W. Somerset Maugham, *The Moon and Sixpence*, 1919**

The allurement that women hold out to men is precisely the allurement that Cape Hatteras holds out to sailors: they are enormously dangerous and hence enormously fascinating.

**H.L. Mencken, in the *Smart Set* magazine, 1919**

What passes for woman's intuition is often nothing more than man's transparency.

**George Jean Nathan**

Women are always wonderfully the same. Shapes vary a little, that's all.

**Aldous Huxley, *Crome Yellow*, 1921**

Most women are not as young as they are painted.

**Max Beerbohm, *A Defence of Cosmetics*, 1922**

A man's women folk, whatever their outward show of respect for his merit and authority, always regard him secretly as an ass, and with something akin to pity . . . In this fact, perhaps, lies one of the best proofs of feminine intelligence or, as the common phrase makes it, feminine intuition.

**H.L. Mencken, *In Defence of Women*, 1923**

Women with 'pasts' interest men because men hope that history will repeat itself.

**Mae West**

When one knows women one pities men, but when one studies men, one excuses women.

**Achille Tournier, quoted in *A Cynic's Breviary* by J.R. Solly, 1925**

Women, as they grow older, rely more and more on cosmetics. Men, as they grow older, rely more and more upon a sense of humour.

**George Jean Nathan, in the *American Mercury*, 1925**

The only nice women are the ones who have had no opportunities.

**Frederick Lonsdale, *The Last of Mrs Cheyney*, 1925**

Women are like elephants to me: I like to look at them, but I wouldn't want to own one.

**W.C. Fields**

To win a woman in the first place one must please her, then undress her, and then somehow get her clothes back on her. Finally, so she will allow you to leave her, you've got to annoy her.

**Jean Giraudoux, *Amphitryon 38*, 1929**

No man who says 'I am as good as you' believes it. The St. Bernard never says it to the toy dog, nor the scholar to the dunce, nor the employable to the bum, nor the pretty woman to the plain. The claim to equality is made only by those who feel themselves to be in some way inferior.

**C.S. Lewis, *Screwtape Proposes a Toast*, 1961**

No woman should know more than a man. If she wants to be loved, that's to say.

**Virginia Graham**

A woman's best protection is a little money of her own.

**Clare Booth Luce**

An intelligent woman is one with whom one can be as stupid as one wants.

**Paul Valéry, *Mauvaises pensées et autres*, 1942**

Women never refer to their age until it would be wiser to ignore it.

**Anonymous, quoted in *Thesaurus of Epigrams*, ed. E. Fuller, 1943**

God created man, and finding him not sufficiently alone, gave him a companion to make him feel his solitude more.

**Paul Valéry, *Tel quel*, 1943**

There is one woman whom fate has destined for each of us. If we miss her we are saved.

**Anonymous, quoted in the *New York Times*, 1948**

Woman's virtue is man's greatest invention.

**Cornelia Otis Skinner**

What a man enjoys about a woman's clothes are his fantasies of how she would look without them.

**Brendan Francis**

Women like silent men. They think they're listening.

**Marcel Achard, in _Quote_ magazine, 1956**

Women want mediocre men, and men are working hard to become as mediocre as possible.

**Margaret Mead, in _Quote_ magazine, 1958**

There is no sincerity like a woman telling a lie.

**Norman Krasna, screenplay for _Indiscreet_, 1958**

The woman whose behaviour indicates that she will make a scene if she is told the truth asks to be deceived.

**Elizabeth Jenkins, quoted in _The Faber Book of Aphorisms_, ed. W.H. Auden and L. Kronenberger, 1964**

A woman needs a man like a fish needs a bicycle.

**Anonymous feminist slogan, 1970**

Woman is: finally screwing and your groin and buttocks and thighs ache like hell and you're all wet and maybe bloody and it wasn't like a Hollywood movie at all but Jesus at least you're not a virgin any more but is this what it's all about? And meanwhile, he's asking 'Did you come?'

**Robin Morgan, _Sisterhood is Powerful_, 1970**

The vast majority of women who pretend vaginal orgasms are faking it to 'get the job'.

**Ti-Grace Atkinson**

A woman's a woman until the day she dies, but a man's only a man as long as he can.

**Moms Mabley, in the _New York Daily News_, 1975**

Any woman who has a lot to offer the world is in trouble.

**Hazel Scott, in _Ms_ magazine, 1976**

Whatever women do they must do twice as well as men to be thought half as good. Luckily this is not difficult.

**Charlotte Whitton, _Canada Month_, 1963**

Being a woman is of special interest only to aspiring male trans-sexuals. To actual women it is merely a good excuse not to play football.

**Fran Lebowitz, *Metropolitan Life*, 1978**

The decisive economic contribution of women in the developed industrial society is rather simple . . . It is, overwhelmingly, to make possible a continuing and more or less unlimited increase in the sale and use of consumer goods.

**John Kenneth Galbraith, *Annals of an Abiding Liberal*, 1980**

The greatest problem with women is how to contrive that they should seem our equals.

**Cyril Connolly, *Journal 1928–1937*, ed. D. Pryce-Jones, 1983**

The major achievement of the Women's Movement in the 1970s was the Dutch treat.

**Nora Ephron, *Heartburn*, 1983**

Women's all right. The only place you can beat one and not get thrown in jail is at the poker table.

**'Amarillo Slim' Preston, quoted in *The Biggest Game in Town* by A. Alvarez, 1983**

*See also* HUMANITY, MEN

# WORK

It is easier to appear worthy of a position one does not hold, than of the office which one fills.

**François, Duc de La Rochefoucauld, *Maxims*, 1665**

Every profession has its secrets . . . if it hadn't it wouldn't be a profession.

**Saki (H.H. Munro), *The Story of St Vespalius*, 1911**

Labor, n. One of the processes whereby A acquires property for B.

**Ambrose Bierce, *The Devil's Dictionary*, 1911**

Is it hot in the rolling mill? Are the hours long? Is $15 a day not enough? Then escape is very easy. Simply throw up your job, spit on your hands, and write another 'Rosenkavalier'.

**H.L. Mencken, *Sententiae*, 1916**

I am a friend of the working man, and I would rather be his friend than be one.

**Clarence Darrow**

Unionism seldom, if ever, uses such power as it has to ensure better work – almost always it devotes a large part of that power to safe-guarding bad work.

**H.L. Mencken, *Prejudices* 3rd series, 1922**

Most people perform essentially meaningless work. When they retire that truth is borne in upon them.

**Brendan Francis**

The miracles that have been held up to us in praise of work are a little unfortunate. 'How doth the little busy bee improve each shining hour, and gather honey all the day from every opening flower.' Well, he does not. He spends most of the day in buzzing and aimless aerobatics, and gets about a fifth of the honey he would collect if he organised himself.

**Sir Heneage Ogilvie**

So much of what we call management consists in making it difficult for people to work.

**Peter Drucker**

The longer the title, the less important the job.

**George McGovern, 1960**

The price one pays for pursuing any profession or calling is an intimate knowledge of its ugly side.

**James Baldwin, *Nobody Knows My Name*, 1961**

The world is full of willing people. Some willing to work, the rest willing to let them.

**Robert Frost, in *Quote and Unquote*, 1970**

We are an indispensable team; you are overmanned; they are redundant.

**Anthony Sampson, in the *Observer*, 1981**

# WRITING

No man but a blockhead ever wrote except for money.

**Samuel Johnson, *The Life of Samuel Johnson* by J. Boswell, 1791**

An old tutor of a college said to one of his pupils: Read over your compositions, and whenever you meet with a passage which you think is particularly fine, strike it out.

**Samuel Johnson, *The Life of Samuel Johnson* by J. Boswell, 1791**

Gentlemen, I agree with you that Napoleon is a tyrant, a monster, the sworn foe of our nation. But gentlemen – he once shot a publisher.

**Thomas Campbell, toast to Napoleon**

People do not deserve to have good writing, they are so pleased with bad.

**Ralph Waldo Emerson, *Journals*, 1909–14**

The basis of literary friendship is mixing the poisoned bowl.

**Oscar Wilde**

Write without pay until somebody offers pay. If nobody offers within three years, the candidate may look upon this circumstance with the most implicit confidence as the sign that sawing wood is what he was intended for.

**Mark Twain**

A literary movement consists of five or six people who live in the same town and hate each other cordially.

**George Moore**

A favourite dodge to get your story read by the public is to assert that it's true, and then add that Truth is stranger than Fiction.

**O. Henry**

Modern literature: prescriptions written by patients.

**Karl Kraus, *Half Truths and One and a Half Truths*, 1986**

Posterity is what you write for after being turned down by many publishers.

**George Ade, *Hand-Made Fables*, 1920**

If you want to get rich from writing, write the sort of thing that's read by persons who move their lips when they're reading to themselves.

**Don Marquis**

Everything's great in this good old world;
(This is the stuff they can always use.)
God's in his heaven, the hill's dew-pearled;
(This will provide for baby's shoes.)
Hunger and War do not mean a thing;
Everything's rosy where'er we roam;
Hark, how the little birds gaily sing!
(This is what fetches the bacon home.)
   **Dorothy Parker, *The Far Sighted Muse*, 1925**

In the same way that a woman becomes a prostitute. First I did it to
please myself, then I did it to please my friends, and finally I did it for
money.
   **Ferenc Molnár, asked how he became a writer**

Coleridge was a drug addict. Poe was an alcoholic. Marlowe was killed
by a man whom he was treacherously trying to stab. Pope took money
to keep a woman's name out of a satire then wrote a piece so that she
could still be recognised anyhow. Chatterton killed himself. Byron was
accused of incest. Do you still want to be a writer – and if so, why?
   **Bennett Cerf, *Shake Well before Using*, 1948**

Translations (like wives) are seldom faithful if they are in the least
attractive.
   **Roy Campbell, in the *Poetry Review*, 1949**

Those who write clearly have readers; those who write obscurely have
commentators.
   **Albert Camus, *Notebooks*, 1942–51**

It is the rule, not the exception, that otherwise unemployable public
figures inevitably take to writing for publication.
   **Richard Condon**

Good swiping is an art in itself.
   **Jules Feiffer**

People who write fiction, if they had not taken it up, might have
become very successful liars.
   **Ernest Hemingway, *This Week*, 1959**

If there's one major cause for the spread of mass illiteracy, it's the fact
that everybody can read and write.
   **Peter De Vries, *The Tents of Wickedness*, 1959**

The profession of book writing makes horse racing seem like a solid, stable business.

**John Steinbeck, in *Newsweek* magazine, 1962**

A writer is congenitally unable to tell the truth and that is why we call what he writes fiction.

**William Faulkner, quoted in his obituary, 1962**

Only a minor talent can be a perfect gentleman; a major talent is always more than a bit of a cad. Hence the importance of minor writers – as teachers of good manners

**W.H. Auden, *The Dyer's Hand*, 1963**

There are no dull subjects. There are only dull writers.

**H.L. Mencken, quoted in *Esquire magazine*, 1965**

I can make it longer if you like the style
I can change it round and I want to be a paperback writer.

**John Lennon and Paul McCartney, *Paperback Writer*, 1966**

There is always one thing to remember: writers are always selling somebody out.

**Joan Didion, *Slouching Towards Bethlehem*, 1968**

There are three reasons for becoming a writer: the first is that you need the money; the second that you have something to say that you think the world should know; the third is that you can't think what to do with the long winter evenings.

**Quentin Crisp, *The Naked Civil Servant*, 1968**

Writing is turning one's worst moments into money.

**J.P. Donleavy, 1968**

A synonym is a word you use when you can't spell the word you first thought of.

**Burt Bacharach, in *Quote and Unquote*, 1970**

Writing . . . locking yourself in a room and inventing conversations, no way for a grown-up to behave. Then your book is published, the sun comes up, as usual, and the sun goes down, as usual, and the world is in no way altered, and it must be someone's fault.

**John Leonard, in *Esquire* magazine, 1975**

Hell hath no fury like a hustler with a literary agent.
  **Frank Sinatra, 1977**

Contrary to what you might imagine, a career in letters is not without its drawbacks – chief among them is the unpleasant fact that one is frequently called upon to sit down and write.
  **Fran Lebowitz, *Metropolitan Life*, 1978**

Writers don't need love, all they require is money.
  **John Osborne, in the *Observer*, 1980**

A freelance is one who gets paid by the word – per piece or perhaps.
  **Robert Benchley, quoted in *Selected Letters of James Thurber*, ed. H. Thurber and J. Weeks, 1981**

The only way for writers to meet is to share a quick pee over a common lamp-post.
  **Cyril Connolly, *Journal 1928–1937*, ed. D. Pryce-Jones, 1983**

*See also* AUTHORS, BEST-SELLERS, BOOKS

# THE YOUNG

Cultivate vices when you are young, and when you are old they will not forsake you.
  **Anonymous**

Young men think old men are fools; but old men know young men are fools.
  **George Chapman, *All Fools*, 1605**

The heart never grows better by age; I fear rather worse, always harder. A young liar will only be an old one, and a young knave will only be a greater knave as he grows up.
  **Lord Chesterfield, *Letters to his Son*, 1774**

Youth is a blunder, manhood a struggle, old age a regret.
  **Benjamin Disraeli, *Coningsby*, 1844**

The disappointment of manhood succeeds to the delusion of youth.
  **Benjamin Disraeli**

Young men want to be faithful and are not; old men want to be faithless and cannot.

**Oscar Wilde,** *The Picture of Dorian Gray,* **1891**

Young people, nowadays, imagine that money is everything, and when they grow older, they know it.

**Oscar Wilde,** *The Picture of Dorian Gray,* **1891**

To get back one's youth one has merely to repeat one's follies.

**Oscar Wilde,** *The Picture of Dorian Gray,* **1891**

The young have aspirations that never come to pass, the old have reminiscences of what never happened.

**Saki (H.H. Munro),** *Reginald at the Carlton,* **1904**

Only the young die good.

**Addison Mizner and Oliver Herford,** *The Entirely New Cynic's Calendar,* **1905**

There is a tide in the affairs of young men, which, if not skillfully dodged, effectually drowns them.

**Arthur Binstead,** *Pitcher's Proverbs,* **1909**

It is a lamentable but incontrovertible solecism that many young men who are highly moral . . . are inwardly never happier than when suspected of disreputable tendencies.

**Arthur Binstead,** *Pitcher's Proverbs,* **1909**

Blush: a weakness of youth and an accomplishment of experience.

**Oliver Herford and John Clay,** *Cupid's Cyclopedia,* **1910**

All that the young can do for the old [is] to shock them and keep them up to date.

**George Bernard Shaw,** *Fannie's First Play,* **1911**

From the earliest times the old have rubbed it into the young that they are wiser than they, and before the young had discovered what nonsense this was they were old too, and it profited them to carry on the imposture.

**W. Somerset Maugham,** *Cakes and Ale,* **1930**

What is more enchanting than the voices of young people when you can't hear what they say.

**Logan Pearsall Smith,** *All Trivia,* **1933**

The good die young – because they see it's no use living if you've got to be good.

**John Barrymore**

Adolescence: a stage between infancy and adultery.

**Anonymous, quoted in *H.L. Mencken's Dictionary of Quotations*, 1942**

But then, that's what young men are there for.

**Adolf Hitler, commenting on exceptionally heavy casualty lists**

A youth with his first cigar makes himself sick; a youth with his first girl makes others sick.

**Mary Wilson Little**

Every young man should have a hobby: learning how to handle money is the best one.

**Jack Hurley, 1961**

The young always have the same problem – how to rebel and conform at the same time. They have now solved this by defying their parents and copying one another.

**Quentin Crisp, *The Naked Civil Servant*, 1968**

All adolescents should be given a thoroughly beastly time of it, in order to give them something to look forward to when they grow up.

**Richard Gordon, *Doctor in the Swim*, 1962**

Youth is a disease from which we all recover.

**Dorothy Fuldheim, *A Thousand Friends*, 1974**

It has been said that there is no fool like an old fool, except a young fool. But the young fool has first to grow up to be an old fool to realise what a damn fool he was when he was a young fool.

**Harold Macmillan, Earl of Stockton**

Youth is a period of missed opportunities.

**Cyril Connolly, *Journal 1928–1937*, ed. D. Pryce-Jones, 1983**

*See also* AGE

# INDEX